TIME

FOR KIDS

ALMANAC

2013

TIME FOR KIDS

ALMANAC 2013

Produced by

DOWNTOWN BOOKWORKS INC.

EDITORIAL DIRECTOR: Sarah Parvis
EDITORIAL ASSISTANT: Sara DiSalvo
PROJECT EDITOR: Lori Stein
SENIOR CONTRIBUTOR: Beth Adelman
SERIES CONTRIBUTORS: Kerry Acker, Marge Kennedy, Katarina Lazo, Jeanette Leardi
SI KIDS PHOTO RESEARCH: Mackenzie McCluer
SPECIAL THANKS: Julie Merberg, Lorin Driggs, Krissy Roleke, Kathy Brock, Marguerite Schropp Lucarelli, J.T. O'Connor, Devin O'Connor, Kyra Sadovi, Francesca Sadovi, Aidan Sadovi, Michelle Stein, Peg Cook, Bonnie Lane Webber, Patty Brown, Stephen Callahan, Morris Katz, Nathanael Katz, Kal Katz, Janice and Jeff Wilcoxson

Designed by
Brian Michael Thomas/Our Hero Productions

TIME For Kids
PUBLISHER: Bob Der
MANAGING EDITOR, TIME For Kids MAGAZINE:
Nellie Gonzalez Cutler
EDITOR, TIME LEARNING VENTURES:
Jonathan Rosenbloom

Time HOME ENTERTAINMENT

PUBLISHER: Richard Fraiman
VICE PRESIDENT, BUSINESS DEVELOPMENT & STRATEGY: Steven Sandonato
EXECUTIVE DIRECTOR, MARKETING SERVICES: Carol Pittard
EXECUTIVE DIRECTOR, RETAIL & SPECIAL SALES: Tom Mifsud
EXECUTIVE PUBLISHING DIRECTOR, BRAND MARKETING: Joy Butts
DIRECTOR, BOOKAZINE DEVELOPMENT & MARKETING: Laura Adam
ASSISTANT GENERAL COUNSEL: Helen Wan
ASSISTANT DIRECTOR, SPECIAL SALES: Ilene Schreider
SENIOR BOOK PRODUCTION MANAGER: Susan Chodakiewicz
DESIGN & PREPRESS MANAGER: Anne-Michelle Gallero
MARKETING MANAGER: Jonathan White
ASSOCIATE PREPRESS MANAGER: Alex Voznesenskiy
EDITORIAL DIRECTOR: Stephen Koepp

SPECIAL THANKS: Christine Austin, Jeremy Biloon, Jim Childs, Rose Cirrincione, Lauren Hall Clark, Jacqueline Fitzgerald, Christine Font, Jenna Goldberg, Hillary Hirsch, Suzanne Janso, Raphael Joa, Amy Mangus, Robert Marasco, Kimberly Marshall, Amy Migliaccio, Nina Mistry, Roshni Patel, Dave Rozzelle, Adriana Tierno, Michela Wilde, Vanessa Wu

For information on TIME For Kids magazine for the classroom or home, go to **TIMEFORKIDS.COM** or call 1-800-777-8600.

For subscriptions to SI Kids, go to **SIKIDS.COM** or call 1-800-889-6007.

Published by **TIME For Kids** Books,
an imprint of Time Home Entertainment Inc.
135 West 50th Street
New York, New York 10020

ISBN 13: 978-1-60320-921-2
ISBN 10: 1-60320-921-2

TIME For Kids is a trademark of Time Inc.

We welcome your comments and suggestions about TIME For Kids Books. Please write to us at:

TIME For Kids BOOKS
ATTENTION: BOOK EDITORS
P.O. BOX 11016
DES MOINES, IA 50336-1016

If you would like to order any of our TIME For Kids or SI Kids hardcover Collector's Edition books, please call us at 1-800-327-6388 (Monday through Friday, 7:00 a.m.–8:00 p.m. or Saturday, 7:00 a.m.–6:00 p.m. Central Time).

1 QGT 12

CONTENTS

Contents

3

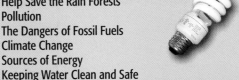

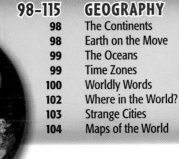

Contents

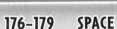

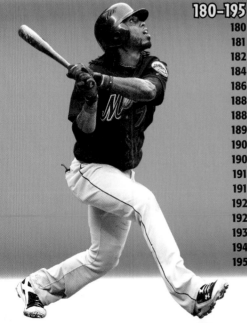

Contents

What's in the News?

NO MORE OSAMA BIN LADEN

On May 1, 2011, President Barack Obama announced that Osama bin Laden, leader of the terrorist group al-Qaeda, was killed in a firefight with U.S. forces in Abbottabad, Pakistan. The death of the world's most wanted terrorist marked the end of a 10-year search that began after the September 11, 2001, attacks on the United States by al-Qaeda.

Osama bin Laden

MONEY TROUBLE IN EUROPE

For years, the governments of Greece and Italy spent more money than they brought in. By the fall of 2011, both countries were almost bankrupt and their people were fearful of wage cuts and loss of government services.

Protesters in Athens, Greece, demonstrate against cuts in services that will make their lives more difficult.

There were many protests, some of them violent, as world leaders tried to sort out the crisis. Greece's Prime Minister George Papandreou, stepped down on November 9, 2011. Italy's Prime Minister, Silvio Berlusconi, resigned two days later.

Greece and Italy are part of the European Union (EU), a group of 27 countries that are trading partners. The EU is working to help Italy and Greece solve their financial problems. Both countries have high rates of unemployment and will continue to see major cuts in services as a result of their financial crises. The economies of other European countries, including Ireland, Spain, and Portugal, are also in trouble.

NEW LEADERS IN LIBYA AND NORTH KOREA

Muammar Gaddafi, who had ruled Libya with an iron fist for almost 42 years, was captured and killed by rebel forces on October 8, 2011. His government had been toppled several weeks before that.

Kim Jong Il was Supreme Leader of North Korea from 1994 until his death on December 17, 2011. His government was considered one of the most repressive in the world. His youngest son, Kim Jong Un, is now in charge of the country.

Kim Jong Un

AN ARAB SPRING

After years of suffering under undemocratic governments, citizens of many Middle Eastern countries demonstrated for changes. Fed up with rising rates of joblessness, government corruption, the high cost of food, and poor living conditions, protesters demanded that their leaders step down. As a result, the leaders of Tunisia, Egypt, and Libya were forced out of office. In those countries, citizens are attempting to form new, stable governments. This period of revolution, kicked off in 2011, is known as the Arab Spring. In early 2012, pro-democracy movements in some countries, such as Syria and Bahrain, were still clashing with governments.

A woman paints a mural to commemorate the important role social media played in the Egyptian revolution.

One reason that these movements succeeded was social media. Organizers were able to share information about demonstrations and other actions through Twitter, Facebook, and other online sites, often without getting into trouble with authorities. Demonstrators also posted videos, which meant that government forces could not crack down on protests without the rest of the world finding out.

guess what? When 200 protesters in Tunisia and Egypt were surveyed in March 2011, about 90% said they received information about demonstrations from social media sites.

A MODERN FAIRY TALE

Prince William, who is second in line to the British throne, married Kate Middleton in a ceremony at Westminster Abbey in London, England, on April 29, 2011. William gave Kate the engagement ring that was worn by his mother, Diana, Princess of Wales. An estimated 1 billion people worldwide watched the wedding on television.

Many women in Saudi Arabia wear a hijab, or head covering. Others wear a black cloak called an abaya, which covers everything but the head and hands.

Prince William and Kate Middleton

guess what? The cost of security for the royal wedding—estimated at more than $11 million—came from public funds.

BIG NEWS FOR WOMEN IN SAUDI ARABIA

After years of fighting for their rights, women in Saudi Arabia received some good news. In September 2011, Saudi Arabia's King Abdullah announced that Saudi women would have the right to vote beginning in 2015.

What's in the News?

WICKED WEATHER

Hurricane Irene knocked down power lines, leaving many people without electricity for days after the storm.

A record 753 tornadoes struck the United States in April 2011, causing widespread destruction, injuries, and deaths in states including Texas, Missouri, Alabama, Mississippi, and Arkansas. Then, on May 22, a powerful tornado tore through Joplin, Missouri, demolishing thousands of homes and businesses and killing more than 150 people. It was the country's worst twister in 60 years. The 2012 tornado season began early, continuing the bad-weather trend. Terrible tornadoes swept through the Midwest and South in February and March, as people in the region prepared for a season of powerful storms.

An intense heat wave struck 17 states in the central United States, from Texas to Michigan, in July 2011, and lasted for several weeks. Temperatures climbed over 110°F (43°C) in some areas. After months of severe drought, wildfires broke out in Texas and Oklahoma, destroying thousands of acres.

Hurricane Irene barreled up the East Coast at the end of August 2011. It first made landfall in the South, causing heavy flooding. New York City implemented many safety measures, including closing down bridges, tunnels, and its subway system. But by the time it reached the city, Irene had been downgraded to a tropical storm. Then it moved west, lingering over upstate New York and Vermont, causing flooding that damaged farms, roads, and towns.

OCCUPY WALL STREET

Protesters often use slogans about the 99%. This refers to the fact that 1% of the people in the country have much more wealth than the rest.

Demonstrators set up camp near Wall Street, in New York City, in September 2011. They called the protest Occupy Wall Street and aimed to raise awareness about the gap between the rich and the poor. The cause quickly spread to other cities around the country and around the world. Occupy leaders are also working to promote community activism, to increase food safety, to help people who are having trouble paying their bills keep their homes, and other specific issues. The movement is a nonviolent one. But, in some cities, the protests turned ugly as government officials tried to disperse the protesters.

DEDICATION OF A DREAM

Civil rights leader Martin Luther King Jr. fought for equal rights for all Americans. And now, a memorial to him stands on the National Mall, in Washington, D.C. Sculpted by Chinese artist Lei Yixin, the memorial shows King as the 30-foot-tall (9 m) Stone of Hope. He is pushing through two other huge slabs of granite, representing the Mountain of Despair. One side of the stone is marked with words from his famous 1963 "I Have a Dream" speech: *Out of the mountain of despair a stone of hope.*

guess what? The Martin Luther King Jr. Memorial is the only one on the National Mall dedicated to someone who was not a U.S. President. It is also the only monument to an African American on the Mall.

Martin Luther King Jr. Memorial

END OF A LONG WAR

A soldier is reunited with his family.

The U.S. combat mission in Iraq came to an end in 2010 when tens of thousands of U.S. troops left the Middle Eastern country. Nearly 40,000 troops stayed behind, however, to advise and assist Iraqi security forces. On October 21, 2011, President Barack Obama announced that the remaining troops and trainers would "be home for the holidays." He praised the efforts of the American troops who have served in Iraq. "They will cross the border with their heads held high, proud of their success," he said. U.S. troops had been in Iraq since 2003.

THE DEBT DEAL

On July 31, 2011, President Barack Obama and leaders of Congress reached an important agreement on how the U.S. government should handle its debt crisis. Currently, the government is spending and borrowing more money than it brings in through taxes. If it goes too far into debt, the U.S. government will be unable to pay its bills and will run the risk of shutting down. The last-minute deal established how much spending would have to be cut over the next 10 years.

President Obama and Vice President Biden meet with Congressmen John Boehner and Eric Cantor to discuss the U.S. debt.

What's in the News?

A PLANET WITH LIFE?

Artist's version of Kepler-22b

In December 2011, NASA confirmed that its Kepler telescope had found a planet, Kepler-22b, in the "habitable zone" of the orbit of its sun. The zone is the area that is neither too hot nor too cold, but just right for life to form on a planet.

Kepler-22b is about 2.4 times the size of Earth. Scientists haven't figured out if Kepler-22b is liquid, gaseous, or rocky. They also don't yet know if it can support life.

But finding Kepler-22b is a major step in the search for another Earth-like planet somewhere in space.

guess what? The Kepler space telescope detects a new planet by noting dips in the light as an orbiting planet passes between its star and the telescope.

IS YOUR LUNCH SAFE?

A new study found that most of the lunches kids bring to school and day care are being stored at unsafe temperatures. The average temperature of the tested foods was around 62°F (17°C). That temperature falls in the range considered to be the "danger zone"—between 40°F (5°C) and 140°F (60°C)—when harmful bacteria that cause food poisoning are more likely to grow. It's important to refrigerate kids' lunches to prevent harmful bacteria, such as salmonella and E. coli from growing.

E-readers

E-BOOKS ON THE RISE

The 2011 holiday season was a huge one for e-readers. About 10% of adults in the United States owned an e-reader in December 2011. By January 2012, that number shot up to 19%. The Pew Internet Project estimates that 44.6 million people in the United States own some kind of e-reading device. The results of the Pew survey showed that more women than men own e-readers. Another e-book study reports that e-book sales increased 17% in 2011, but that nearly three-fourths of Americans have never bought an e-book.

SOLVING A BIG BEE MYSTERY

When a bee lands on a flower, it touches a dustlike substance on the flower called pollen. When it flies around, it spreads this pollen from flower to flower. This process, called pollination, is how flowers create the seeds that grow into other flowers. Beginning in 2006, scientists recognized that something was wrong with honeybees. They were dying in large numbers. Researchers estimate that 30% of bee colonies have been lost per year since then. This is a huge problem because bees pollinate about one-third of the U.S. food supply. When all the adult bees in a colony suddenly disappear, it is called colony collapse disorder (CCD). Researchers at San Francisco State University found a new possible cause of CCD: the phorid fly. Phorid flies deposit their eggs into bees' abdomens. When the eggs hatch, the bees die. Scientists will continue to study CCD and look for ways to combat the causes they find.

A phorid fly on the back of a honeybee.

TABLETS TAKE OFF

In the first 80 days after the iPad's April 2010 release, 3 million of them were sold. In the last quarter of 2011, Apple sold more than 15 million of the latest version.

Tablets wirelessly connect to the Internet and allow users to download television shows, games, and books, on the go. In the short time since tablets have been available, more than 250,000 applications, or apps, have been created for them.

At the 2012 Toy Fair, game makers showed off new board games that incorporate the use of an iPad.

Drawing of a plesiosaur and its young

BIRTH OF A BABY DINO

For a long time, researchers wondered whether plesiosaurs—large ocean-dwelling reptiles that lived when dinosaurs existed—laid eggs like other reptiles, or gave birth to live young like whales. New fossil evidence from about 78 million years ago suggests that the whale model is the winner. The fossil includes the bones of an infant inside an adult female plesiosaur called Polycotylus. Professor R. Ewan Fordyce of the University of Otago, New Zealand, claims that the new discovery shows "that this is a fetus and not a young animal that has been eaten."

SPORTS AND ENTERTAINMENT

LOCKOUTS!

Both the National Football League (NFL) and the National Basketball Association (NBA) had labor problems recently. Management and players had some disagreements about salaries, bonus payments, health-care costs, and other policies related to the players' contracts. The NFL lockout occurred in the off-season and a deal between players and owners was reached before any games were canceled. The NBA lockout occurred during the season, and the first two weeks of the regular season were canceled.

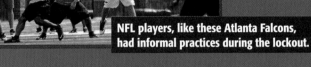

NFL players, like these Atlanta Falcons, had informal practices during the lockout.

JEREMY LIN SCORES

Jeremy Lin became a household name in 2012, setting off a media frenzy referred to as "Linsanity." The Harvard-educated player was not drafted out of college by an NBA team. After a stint with the Golden State Warriors, he joined the New York Knicks. In his first five games as a starter for the Knicks, he shocked fans by scoring 136 points (the most of any player in more than 30 years). Sports writers had fun with Lin's name, coming up with headlines like "Lincredible," "Linstant Replay," "Lin Your Face," and "May the Best Man Lin."

Jeremy Lin is the first NBA player of Chinese or Taiwanese descent.

WOMEN'S SOCCER HEATS UP

The 2011 FIFA Women's World Cup tournament was filled with excitement. In the July 2011 quarterfinals, the U.S. team played Brazil. The Brazilians were winning until American Abby Wambach tied up the game with a spectacular header in the last seconds of the game. The U.S. team then beat Brazil 5–3 with penalty kicks to move on. After defeating the French team in the semifinals, the U.S. team faced Japan. The U.S. team was heavily favored to win, but the Japanese team held steady and tied the score, forcing the game into overtime. In a tense final shoot-out, the Japanese women won their first championship.

Abby Wambach scores the U.S. team's second goal in the quarterfinal game.

SELENA SIZZLES

Selena Gomez made her mark as a television actress, starring in Disney Channel's *Wizards of Waverly Place*, for which she won a Teen Choice Award in 2011. She leads the music group Selena Gomez & the Scene, which also won Teen Choice Awards in 2011. And she starred in the film *Monte Carlo*, released in July 2011. In it, she plays not one but two characters: Grace, a small-town girl, and Cordelia, a snooty socialite who looks just like her. Gomez has a lot more fabulous projects coming up.

Adele performing on the *Today* show.

ADORATION FOR ADELE

Adele Laurie Blue Adkins—or, as she is better known, just Adele—has been a star in Britain since her first album came out in 2008, when she was 19. The album, *19*, quickly went platinum. But it was her second album, released in 2011 when she was 21—and titled *21*—that brought her superstardom. It was the best-selling album in the United States in 2011, and the single "Rolling in the Deep" was the top-selling song. Another song from the album, "Someone Like You," also topped the charts.

Selena Gomez poses for a picture with a fan.

guess what? In February 2012, Adele won six Grammy Awards, tying Beyoncé for the most Grammys won in a single night.

HUNGRY FOR *THE HUNGER GAMES*

Suzanne Collins's book, *The Hunger Games*, released in 2008, tells the story of 16-year-old Katniss Everdeen, who lives in a harsh future society in the country of Panem. It is followed by two sequels: *Catching Fire* and *Mockingjay*. As of early 2012, there were nearly 25 million copies of the three books in print in the United States, and the titles topped the e-book best seller list month after month.

In April 2011, Lionsgate, a film company, announced the cast of the movie version of the best-selling book. The starring roles went to Jennifer Lawrence, Josh Hutcherson, and Liam Hemsworth. Fans of the books flocked to the film when it opened in March 2012.

Liam Hemsworth, Jennifer Lawrence, and Josh Hutcherson

guess what? Taylor Swift and the musical group the Civil Wars wrote the haunting song "Safe & Sound" for *The Hunger Games*.

What's in the News?

Animals

FROM TIME FOR KIDS MAGAZINE

Snowy Owls Head South

By Joe Levit

Thousands of snowy owls flew south in the winter of 2011 to 2012 in a mass migration that scientists say is highly unusual. (For more on migration, see page 23.) The majestic creatures, which can grow up to two feet (61 cm) tall and have a wingspan of nearly five feet (1.5 m), call the Arctic home. But bird-watchers reported sightings across the United States, from Maine to Washington. Although it is normal for some snowy owls to head south every few winters, this particular migration was widespread.

Scientists say the rare event was likely due to an abundance of lemmings in the summer of 2011. The small Arctic rodent is the snowy owl's main source of food. Having a plentiful supply of lemmings allowed the owls to raise more young, says owl expert Denver Holt.

But competition for food up north drove the younger owls farther south than usual in search of meals. The birds also eat voles, field mice, rats, rabbits, and geese. Snowy owls are drawn to frozen lakes, which remind them of home. "If they're finding rodents there, they're staying there," says scientist Mark Robbins.

The rise in snowy owl sightings also triggered a huge amount of public interest in the birds. Holt says the extra attention will aid in conservation of the species. "It's wonderful," he says.

Snowy owl in flight

Male snowy owls are all white. The females have dark bars on their feathers.

guess what?
An adult snowy owl will eat three to five lemmings a day if possible.

WARM-BLOODED OR COLD-BLOODED?

WARM-BLOODED ANIMALS (birds, mammals) are able to keep their body temperature constant. They turn the food they eat into energy that creates heat. In hot weather, they sweat, pant, or do other things to help cool their outsides and insides.

The temperature of **COLD-BLOODED ANIMALS** (reptiles, fish, amphibians, invertebrates) is the same as that of their surroundings. Because of this, they are able to be very active in hot weather but are sluggish at low temperatures. When it is hot, chemicals in their bodies react quickly to help their muscles move, but these reactions slow down as the outside temperature drops.

KEEPING COOL IN THE DESERT

The desert is not the easiest place for animals to live. There is little water for them to drink, and they must deal with extreme temperatures. Many animals in the desert simply stay out of the sunlight. They may spend much of their time underground in burrows, only coming out at night to look for food. Some birds leave the desert during its hottest months, and some mammals, like the round-tailed ground squirrel, estivate. That means they sleep during the hottest months of the year.

Other animals have adaptations that help them deal with the heat. Camels have long legs that keep their body away from the heat of the sand. Fennec foxes and jackrabbits have large ears that lose heat. Many desert critters have paler fur or lighter skin than their relatives living in other climates. Lighter colors absorb less heat than darker ones.

STAYING SAFE IN THE COLD

Animals that live in the coldest places on Earth find ways to keep warm. Several species of penguins live in Antarctica, where gale-force winds and heavy snow can last for weeks. They developed a thick layer of blubber (a type of fat) and tightly packed overlapping feathers that protect them from the cold. Seals and polar bears have a layer of blubber that is covered by dense fur. In addition to having blubber, walruses have a system of blood circulation that shifts blood flow away from the skin to prevent the loss of heat when they are in deep, cold water.

Snowy owls stay still in very low temperatures. Flying would use up energy that they need to keep their bodies warm. Arctic foxes have brown fur in the summer but grow heavier white coats in the winter. Their white fur blends in with the snow, making it easier for them to hide from predators. These foxes can wrap their long tails around their bodies, like scarves, to keep warm. They also have an interesting blood-flow system that helps keep their body warm, but their feet cool. Ice does not stick to cold toes the way it sticks to warm ones. Unlike the desert-dwelling jackrabbit, Arctic hares have small ears, which allow less body heat to escape.

Animals

17

ANIMAL CLASSIFICATION

Scientists use many different indicators to group, or classify, animals. One way that animals can be classified involves their body structure. Animals that have backbones are called vertebrates. Animals without backbones are known as invertebrates.

VERTEBRATES

BIRDS are warm-blooded and have wings and feathers. All birds lay eggs, and most can fly (though ostriches, kiwis, and penguins cannot). Some other examples of birds are eagles, ducks, **owls,** pelicans, doves, finches, hummingbirds, cardinals, flamingos, and vultures.

AMPHIBIANS are cold-blooded and begin life in the water, breathing through gills. When they are fully grown, they breathe through lungs and can walk on land. They lay eggs. Some examples of amphibians are frogs, toads, newts, and salamanders.

REPTILES are cold-blooded and have lungs. Their skin is scaly. Most reptiles lay eggs. Reptiles include lizards, turtles, snakes, alligators, and **crocodiles.**

FISH are cold-blooded and live in water. They have scaly skin and breathe using gills. Most fish lay eggs. Carp, salmon, sturgeon, betta, trout, tuna, and eels are some examples of fish.

MAMMALS are warm-blooded and, with the exception of the platypus and the echidna, give birth to live young. Mammal mothers breast-feed their young. Most mammals have hair or fur and live on land (except for porpoises, dolphins, and whales, which live in the water). Bats, lions, giraffes, zebras, cows, elephants, guinea pigs, bears, rhinoceroses, **otters,** and humans are all mammals.

INVERTEBRATES

ECHINODERMS

(ih-*ky*-nuh-durms) live in the sea and have exoskeletons, which means that their skeletons or supporting structures are located on the outside of their bodies. Echinoderms include sea urchins, **sea stars** (starfish), brittle stars, and sand dollars.

WORMS

live in a variety of places, including underwater, in the ground, and even inside other living creatures. Examples of worms include tapeworms, flukes, pinworms, leeches, and **earthworms**.

guess what? To eat, a sea star (or starfish) pushes its stomach through its mouth to the outside of its body. It usually pries open the shell of a mussel, clam, or oyster. Its stomach slides inside and eats the other animal in its own shell!

ARTHROPODS

have bodies that are divided into different parts, or segments. They also have exoskeletons. Arthropods include crustaceans (such as lobsters, crabs, shrimps, and barnacles), arachnids (spiders, scorpions, and ticks), centipedes, millipedes, and all insects (such as fireflies, moths, ants, mosquitoes, bees, dragonflies, and **beetles**).

MOLLUSKS

(*mol*-usks) have soft bodies. To protect themselves, some have hard shells. Clams, oysters, **octopuses,** scallops, squids, slugs, and snails are all mollusks.

SPONGES

live in water and are immobile. They get their food by filtering tiny organisms that swim by.

COELENTERATES

(sih-*len*-teh-rates) have stinging tentacles around their mouths. They use their mouths not only to eat with but also to eliminate waste. Examples of coelenterates are **corals,** hydras, jellyfish, and sea anemones.

TOP 5

MOST POPULAR PETS IN THE UNITED STATES

ANIMAL	HOUSEHOLDS	POPULATION
1. Dogs	46.3 million	78.2 million
2. Cats	38.9 million	86.4 million
3. Fish	12.6 million	159.7 million
4. Birds	5.7 million	16.2 million
5. Small Pets (guinea pigs, hamsters, rabbits)	5.0 million	16.0 million

Source: American Pet Products Association

guess what? Although there are more cats and tropical fish than dogs in the United States, there are more households with dogs than with cats. That's because many people who have cats and fish have lots of them.

Labrador retriever

This is the 21st year that the Labrador retriever has been the most popular dog breed.

German shepherd

MOST POPULAR DOG BREEDS

1. Labrador retriever
2. German shepherd
3. Yorkshire terrier
4. Beagle
5. Golden retriever
6. Bulldog
7. Boxer
8. Dachshund
9. Poodle
10. Shih tzu

Source: American Kennel Club

Yorkshire terrier

Dachshund

Beagle

Shih tzu

FANTASTIC PET FISH

There are more than 100 kinds of goldfish. Goldfish are omnivorous, which means they eat both plants and animals.

Betta fish are freshwater fish that come in many colors. They are also called Japanese or Siamese fighting fish, because the males of this species will fight to the death if placed together in a tank.

Most **mollies** are black, green, silver, or gold and can have short or long fins. Some have spots. They need some plant matter in their tank to remain healthy and happy.

Tetras are tiny fish from South America that live peacefully with other fish—but bigger fish will sometimes eat them. One popular variety has a bright neon tail.

Cichlids (sick-lids) belong to a large group of freshwater fish that includes many colorful and cool species, such as the Malawi eye-biter. Most are only a few inches long, but a few are large, aggressive predators.

Swordtails are active swimmers, so they need to be in big tanks—at least 10 gallons (37 liters). They prefer salt water, but can live in freshwater. They come in many colors, and some have neon markings, spots, and patterns.

Guppies are one of the most common fish in home aquariums. They like freshwater and bear live young. Some of them are plain and gray, but others have fancy fantails and come in bright colors.

Persian

MOST POPULAR CAT BREEDS

1. Persian
2. Exotic
3. Maine coon
4. Ragdoll
5. Sphynx
6. Siamese
7. Abyssinian
8. American shorthair
9. Cornish rex
10. Oriental

Source: Cat Fanciers' Association

Exotic

Maine coon

Sphynx

Siamese

Abyssinian

THE SCOOP ON PET POOP

Going green

Hundreds of millions of pets create a huge amount of waste. And some of this waste can be useful in the garden. Rabbit droppings are free of harmful bacteria and can be used as fertilizer in gardens. You don't have to wait until it decomposes; just mix it in with garden soil. Some rabbit breeders even sell rabbit poop to gardeners. They call it "black gold." The droppings of meat-eating animals, like cats and dogs, cannot be used as fertilizer.

HELPFUL HOOVES, PAWS, AND FINS

In addition to love and companionship, animals have been trained to do important jobs for humans. These furry and feathery friends have been taught to entertain audiences, transport people and goods, carry messages, and save lives. Carrier pigeons are known for their incredible ability to find their way home. During World War I and World War II, they carried messages back and forth between soldiers. They've also been used to get medication to hard-to-reach sick people. From 1860 to 1861, the Pony Express mail service employed 400 horses to carry saddlebags of letters 2,000 miles (3,219 km) across the United States.

Today, dromedary camels, elephants, and donkeys perform many tasks. They carry heavy loads, assist in farming, and are ridden by humans. Dogs have been used to track lost or missing people, to chase pests out of tunnels, to help hunters, and as guides for blind and hearing-impaired people. Sheepdogs can be trained to herd animals and move them to safe ground during storms. Llamas can also be fierce protectors of livestock. They will stomp on wolves and foxes that try to carry off members of the herd they are protecting. The U.S. military has trained dolphins to detect and mark the locations of underwater mines, which are explosive devices that can damage or destroy ships that pass nearby.

Search dog

Military-trained dolphin

ANIMAL SOCIETY

Many wild animals form tight societies, such as hives and herds. Each member of the society knows its place and does its job. There are sometimes fights for the best position in the herd, but the group is usually loyal and protective of all its members. A pride of lions, for example, will cooperate in stalking and killing prey. Together the lions will drag a kill to a shady spot to share it. The dominant male usually gets the best parts, but everyone gets to eat. Chimpanzees are also good at sharing.

Mothers in many species, such as bears, tend their offspring with the same devotion as human moms. (Others, such as guppies, spiders, and some rodents, will often eat their young as soon as they're born.) A particularly heartwarming trait among animals is mating for life. These animals choose a mate and remain together as a pair.

ANIMALS THAT MATE FOR LIFE

Albatrosses	Gibbons
Bald eagles	Ospreys
Barn owls	Red-tailed hawks
Beavers	Swans
Black vultures	Termites
French angelfish	Turtle doves

guess what?
Albatrosses are known for their complicated courtship dance, in which the birds bob their heads and touch each other's bills.

guess what? Female elephants live together in groups, but males live alone.

SOLITARY ANIMALS

Some animals live and hunt alone. Most of them will make exceptions during mating season and when they are raising young, but these animals are not particularly sociable.

Green iguanas
Jaguars
Leopards
Rhinoceroses
Skunks
Snakes
Spiders
Tigers
Tiger sharks, great white sharks, many other types of sharks

MIGRATION: ANIMALS ON THE MOVE

If you look up at the sky at certain times of the year, you'll see huge flocks of birds flying in formation. They're part of a phenomenon called animal migration, or the journey of animals over long distances. These animals—birds, fish, insects, mammals, and others—don't use GPS or maps. They just know where they are supposed to go.

Many migrations are seasonal. Animals that live in cold climates—such as the birds we see in the sky—move to warmer areas for the winter. Monarch butterflies cannot fly in cold weather, so they head to California or Mexico in the fall. In other cases, animals move from one place to another to find food. Some animals, including salmon, move when it is time to give birth. They leave the ocean and return to freshwater streams where their young will have better chances of survival. Similarly, humpback whales travel great distances from breeding areas to feeding areas. They give birth in warm water areas near places like Hawaii or Costa Rica, and then swim toward colder areas, like Alaska or Antarctica, where there is plenty of food.

Locusts migrate when their populations get too large. They go in search of a location with more food and fewer locusts. Some migrations are temporary, with animals moving back and forth every year. Others are more permanent, and the animals stay in their new home.

One of the most fascinating journeys is the great migration made by nearly 2 million zebras, wildebeests, gazelles, and other animals as they cross the African plains each year to search for fresh grass. The sight and sound of these animals is awe-inspiring.

Black skimmers

Monarch butterflies

Wildebeests

WHO MIGRATES?

Hundreds of animals, found on every continent, migrate. Many species of the following animals migrate at least once a year.

Bats	Earthworms	Sea turtles
Birds	Elephants	Sharks
Buffalo	Frogs	Whales
Caribou	Geese	Wildebeests
Crabs	Hummingbirds	Zebras
Dolphins	Ladybugs	
Ducks	Manatees	

Bindi Irwin: Wildlife Warrior

By TFK Kid Reporter Sahil Abbi

TFK Kid Reporter Sahil Abbi spoke to Bindi Irwin about her new book series, Wildlife Adventures, and what it's like to follow in the footsteps of her late father, Steve Irwin, also known as the Crocodile Hunter. She hopes her stories motivate kids to get involved in conservation.

TFK: When did you decide that you wanted to become a conservationist?

BINDI IRWIN: I think from the day I was first hatched, pretty much. I've always wanted to be a conservationist. Many people think of conservation as protecting little woodland creatures. But ultimately conservation is about us. It's about people. Every time we lose an animal species, it's like losing a brick from the house. Pretty soon, the house just falls down. I think it's important to spread that message.

Bindi Irwin and her little brother, Bob

TFK: Why did your family found the nonprofit organization Wildlife Warriors?

BINDI: They first founded Wildlife Warriors in 2002

to help all sorts of animal projects that we have started all over the world. For instance, in Africa, we have a project with the cheetahs. What's happening with the cheetahs is that they will come in and eat some of the farmers' livestock. This upsets farmers, who then try to kill cheetahs. It's really sad. It's not good for either side. So we came up with a program in which we breed big dogs called Anatolian shepherds. These dogs protect the livestock from cheetahs. That costs about $5,000 a dog. We also put tracking devices around cheetahs' necks so that we know where they are. This way, we can alert farmers if a cheetah is getting too close to their livestock.

TFK: What inspired you to begin the Wildlife Adventures series?

BINDI: I want to share with kids the many fun adventures that we get to do. I also want to encourage kids to have their own adventures.

TFK: How does it feel to follow in the footsteps of your father? Is it overwhelming?

BINDI: I think it's wonderful. I want to carry on my dad's legacy. I think of myself as a teacher and I know my dad was a teacher too. . . . I think it's so important to empower kids, because we are the next voters. We are the next decision makers, and we are the next generation making a difference on our planet.

WHO STUDIES WHAT?

Zoologists study and classify animals. There are different types of zoologists, and each field has its own name. Here are a few. Try saying *ichthyologist* five times fast!

A **coleopterist** studies beetles.

An **entomologist** studies insects.

An **etiologist** studies animal behavior.

A **herpetologist** studies reptiles and amphibians.

An **ornithologist** studies birds.

An **ichthyologist** studies fish.

A **malacologist** studies mollusks.

A **mammalogist** studies mammals.

An entomologist inspects elderberry trees for evidence of the endangered valley elderberry longhorn beetles.

TINY CREATURES MAKE A BIG IMPACT!

When a bee is buzzing around you at a picnic or ants are tromping across your kitchen floor, it is easy to think that insects are annoying or in the way. But insects and other tiny animals play a huge role in keeping the world running smoothly. Here are a few of the special things they do.

Millipede

Pollination Insects, especially bees, carry pollen from one flower to another. Fruits, vegetables, and flowers would not grow without their help.

A honeybee visits a flower.

Decomposing debris and aerating soil Beetles and millipedes break down leaves, grass, and other organic matter into smaller pieces that decompose more easily. Earthworms wriggle through the dirt, which aerates, or lets air into, the soil. These little critters help make earth into fertile ground where new plants can grow.

Food and clothing production We get honey from honeybees and silk from silkworms.

A spider eats a beetle.

Pest control One of the best things that insects do for us is eat other insects. Ladybugs and wasps, which are called "beneficial insects," help farmers by eating pests that can destroy their crops.

Advancing science Because they live for only a short time, insects help scientists understand the cycles of life. Fruit flies were especially helpful in studying how our genes work. Carpet beetles can be used to clean skeletons. And coroners examine insect activity in human remains to estimate when a person died and help determine the cause of death.

Providing food for other species Tiny insects are at the bottom of the food chain. They are the main diet of slightly bigger critters. Those creatures are food for animals slightly larger than them, which in turn nourish even larger animals, and so on up the food chain. People in some countries eat insects. They are a great source of protein.

Fried grasshoppers

WILD ANIMAL MATCHUP

Though many animals move from place to place, some are found in the wild almost exclusively on one continent. Can you match these animals with their native place?

Answers on page 242.

BALD EAGLE

1. Africa
2. Australia
3. North America
4. South America
5. Antarctica
6. Europe
7. Asia

EMPEROR PENGUIN

PIRHANA

ZEBRA

KOALA

PANDA

ALPINE IBEX

Animals

25

What Do Kids Know About Health?

By Suzanne Zimbler

We asked more than 10,000 kids 21 questions about fitness, nutrition, and healthy habits. Their answers showed that kids know a lot about staying healthy.

YOUR HEALTH IQ

When it's time to select a snack or pick an activity, many kids would like to make a healthy choice. But to do that, they need information—knowledge is power. That's good news, because it turns out that kids have a lot of health-related knowledge.

They are smart about nutrition. More than nine out of 10 kids are aware that water is a healthier drink than soda and that a plain potato is better for you than chips. And nearly 85% know that the best way to get to a healthy weight is by exercising and eating a balanced diet.

According to the survey, three out of four kids brush their teeth at least twice a day.

HEALTHY HABITS

About 85% of kids read the nutrition facts on their food packages at least some of the time. Most kids (87%) say they would rather go outside and play than stay inside and watch a movie. Many (85%) are willing to try new fruits and vegetables too.

Health-smart kids know that staying well involves more than choosing nutritious food and being active. Dentists say it is important to brush your teeth at least twice a day.

Hand washing matters too. More than four out of five kids say they wash their hands after using the bathroom. But only seven out of 10 do so before they eat. This is one area where some kids could do better.

GOALS FOR GOOD HEALTH

While about a third of kids described their health as excellent, most kids said their health is pretty good. Kids told us which goals they want help achieving. Learning how to cook is at the top of the list. Many kids would also like to get more exercise, eat better, and learn to play new sports. How will you reach the health goals on your list?

Joining a school sports team is one great way to get more exercise.

Learning to cook is a path to good health.

Guess what? The Centers for Disease Control and Prevention (CDC) recommends washing hands for 20 seconds—about the time it takes to sing "Happy Birthday" twice. Don't forget to wash between your fingers and the backs of your hands. And keep your hands pointing down so that the germy water doesn't reach your arms.

WHY EXERCISE?

Exercising is one of the most important ways to keep your body healthy. When you exercise, you strengthen your bones, muscles, and heart. You also burn off excess fat, improve your balance, regulate your body's metabolism (the process that turns the nutrients in food into energy and heat), and improve your mood.

Today, many kids don't get enough exercise. In fact, the average kid spends about three hours each day watching television and another two and a half hours sitting down using other kinds of media, such as video games or the Internet. Does that sound like you? If it does, it's time to get up and get moving!

Playing soccer, dancing, or challenging a friend to a game of tag are all great ways to work out. To stay healthy, try to do about one hour of exercise a day. And try not to be inactive for more than two hours at a time.

MANY WAYS TO MOVE

The purpose of **aerobic exercise** is to get your body moving, which increases the flow of blood to your heart, gets your circulatory system (see page 28) working, and makes your muscles stretch. When your heart beats faster, more oxygen gets to your muscles (don't forget, your heart is a muscle)—and this makes your heart healthy. Running, hiking, biking, dancing, playing sports, and swimming are all aerobic exercises. **Anaerobic exercise** is high-intensity activity in short bursts of time. Sprints, running up hills, and lifting heavy weights are anaerobic exercises.

Resistance training aims to increase muscle tone and strength. These exercises, such as weight lifting, push-ups, and squats, all make your muscles contract, and, if you do them regularly—three or four times a week— your muscle cells will get bigger, and you will get stronger. **Flexibility exercises** help you move more smoothly and prevent stiffness and pain. You should always take a few minutes to stretch before and after other exercises.

MYSTERY PERSON

I was born in France in 1822. I discovered a way to make food safer and keep it fresh longer. I developed a vaccine for rabies.

WHO AM I? _____

Answer on page 242.

FIVE EASY WAYS TO STAY STRONG AND SAFE

Wear sunscreen. Sunburn hurts, and it can do long-term damage to your skin.

Get enough sleep. We need sleep to keep our bodies healthy, and we don't learn as well when we're tired.

Eat a good breakfast. Studies show that kids who eat a balanced breakfast do better in school.

Always wear a helmet when skateboarding, biking, or riding a scooter.

Laugh. Studies have shown that laughter invokes a response from our immune system that helps keep diseases away.

HOW DOES YOUR BODY WORK?

Your body is an amazing thing. It's made up of different systems, which consist of organs that have their own special functions. The liver, kidneys, and heart are organs. Even your skin is an organ!

The **CARDIOVASCULAR** or **CIRCULATORY SYSTEM** has one main job: to pump blood throughout the body. The system's major organ is the heart, which pumps blood through the arteries into all parts of the body. Blood contains oxygen, hormones, and nutrients that cells need to grow, work, and repair themselves.

The **SKELETAL SYSTEM** is made up of bones, joints, and cartilage, which is a flexible tissue that forms body parts like the nose and ears. The body's bones have four main functions: to support the body, to work with muscles to help it move, to protect organs from injury, and to produce blood cells.

The **DIGESTIVE SYSTEM** is responsible for taking in food and liquids and converting them into substances that are absorbable by the body. It is responsible for making sure people get the nutrients they need from what they eat. It also gets rid of solid waste.

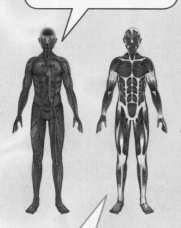 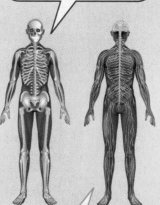 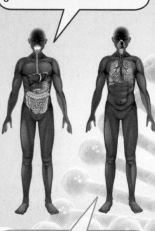

The **MUSCULAR SYSTEM** is made up of different types of muscles found throughout the body. Skeletal muscles are attached to bones and move them by contracting and releasing. Smooth muscles in the digestive system move food and water through it. Cardiac muscles in the heart pump blood through the heart to the lungs and the rest of the body.

Your **NERVOUS SYSTEM** helps the other systems in your body communicate. It's made up of the central nervous system, which includes the brain and the spinal cord, and the peripheral nervous system, which consists of neurons found all over the body. The brain sends signals down the spinal cord and through the body's nerves to all the other organs. Different parts of the brain specialize in processing thoughts, memories, feelings, dreams, speech, physical coordination, balance, hunger, and sleep.

The **RESPIRATORY SYSTEM** supplies your body with oxygen. Air enters the nose and mouth and moves down the trachea (windpipe) into large bronchial tubes that are connected to each side of the lungs. These tubes branch into many smaller tubes that end in tiny passageways called alveoli. In these teeny spaces, oxygen enters the bloodstream, and carbon dioxide is removed, sent back up the trachea, and breathed out through the nose and mouth.

Guess what?

Every step we take uses 200 muscles.

Your **IMMUNE SYSTEM** fights off bacteria, toxins, and microbes that cause disease. Lymph, a liquid produced by lymph nodes, is carried in the bloodstream to the cells to clean them of harmful bacteria and waste products. The center of bones, called the bone marrow, is where red and white blood cells are created. White blood cells produce antibodies, which kill toxins, bacteria, and viruses. The thymus, which is located in the chest, produces special cells that fight disease. The spleen filters out old red blood cells, bacteria, and other foreign bodies. The adenoids (behind the nose) and tonsils (in the throat) also trap and kill bacteria and viruses.

The **REPRODUCTIVE SYSTEM** produces sperm cells in men and egg cells in women. The reproductive system allows sperm and egg cells to combine to form an embryo, which eventually becomes a baby.

The **URINARY SYSTEM** eliminates excess fluid from the body. Two kidneys remove toxins from the water flowing in the bloodstream. Those toxins then travel through tubes called ureters to the bladder, where they remain until leaving the body as urine.

The **INTEGUMENTARY SYSTEM**—made up of skin, sweat and oil glands, nails, and hair—protects the inside of the body by forming a barrier to the outside. The skin senses touch, heat, cold, and pain and sends signals to the brain. The brain then sends signals back to the appropriate body parts so they can react correctly to those sensations. Sweat glands in your skin help the body cool itself. The skin's oil glands keep the body from drying out. Nails provide defense, and hair provides protection and warmth.

The organs of the **ENDOCRINE SYSTEM,** called glands, produce hormones, which are chemicals that travel through the bloodstream and tell organs what to do. Hormones are often called the body's messengers. The endocrine system regulates mood, growth, body development, sleep, blood pressure, and metabolism, which is the process by which the body changes food into energy.

The immune system is always fighting bacteria and viruses that can cause illness.

guess what? Today, doctors must unwrap bandages regularly to check for signs of infection. But scientists have invented a bandage that changes color when there is infection present. This could help patients heal more quickly.

IDENTIFY YOUR INSIDES

Do you know what the stuff inside you looks like? Match these body parts with their names.

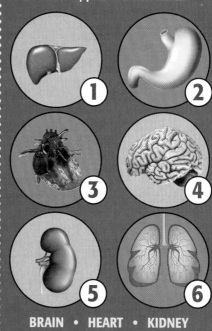

1 **2**

3 **4**

5 **6**

BRAIN • HEART • KIDNEY
LIVER • LUNGS • STOMACH

TIME FOR KIDS GAME

Answers on page 242.

Body and Health

Calendars and Holidays

2013

JANUARY

S	M	T	W	T	F	S
		1	2	3	4	5
6	7	8	9	10	11	12
13	14	15	16	17	18	19
20	21	22	23	24	25	26
27	28	29	30	31		

FEBRUARY

S	M	T	W	T	F	S
					1	2
3	4	5	6	7	8	9
10	11	12	13	14	15	16
17	18	19	20	21	22	23
24	25	26	27	28		

MARCH

S	M	T	W	T	F	S
					1	2
3	4	5	6	7	8	9
10	11	12	13	14	15	16
17	18	19	20	21	22	23
24	25	26	27	28	29	30
31						

APRIL

S	M	T	W	T	F	S
	1	2	3	4	5	6
7	8	9	10	11	12	13
14	15	16	17	18	19	20
21	22	23	24	25	26	27
28	29	30				

MAY

S	M	T	W	T	F	S
			1	2	3	4
5	6	7	8	9	10	11
12	13	14	15	16	17	18
19	20	21	22	23	24	25
26	27	28	29	30	31	

JUNE

S	M	T	W	T	F	S
						1
2	3	4	5	6	7	8
9	10	11	12	13	14	15
16	17	18	19	20	21	22
23	24	25	26	27	28	29
30						

JULY

S	M	T	W	T	F	S
	1	2	3	4	5	6
7	8	9	10	11	12	13
14	15	16	17	18	19	20
21	22	23	24	25	26	27
28	29	30	31			

AUGUST

S	M	T	W	T	F	S
				1	2	3
4	5	6	7	8	9	10
11	12	13	14	15	16	17
18	19	20	21	22	23	24
25	26	27	28	29	30	31

SEPTEMBER

S	M	T	W	T	F	S
1	2	3	4	5	6	7
8	9	10	11	12	13	14
15	16	17	18	19	20	21
22	23	24	25	26	27	28
29	30					

OCTOBER

S	M	T	W	T	F	S
		1	2	3	4	5
6	7	8	9	10	11	12
13	14	15	16	17	18	19
20	21	22	23	24	25	26
27	28	29	30	31		

NOVEMBER

S	M	T	W	T	F	S
					1	2
3	4	5	6	7	8	9
10	11	12	13	14	15	16
17	18	19	20	21	22	23
24	25	26	27	28	29	30

DECEMBER

S	M	T	W	T	F	S
1	2	3	4	5	6	7
8	9	10	11	12	13	14
15	16	17	18	19	20	21
22	23	24	25	26	27	28
29	30	31				

Guess what? A year—365 days—represents the time it takes for the Earth to orbit the sun. But the Earth actually takes 365 days, 5 hours, and 45 seconds to make its orbit. So, every four years, we have a leap year and add one day in February to even things up.

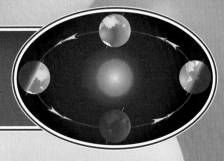

Calendars and Holidays

31

SPECIAL DATES IN 2013

January 1: New Year's Day

January 21: Martin Luther King Jr. Day

February 2: Groundhog Day

February 10: Chinese New Year

February 12: Mardi Gras

February 14: Valentine's Day

February 18: Presidents' Day

March 10: Daylight saving time begins

March 17: St. Patrick's Day

March 26–April 2: Passover*

March 31: Easter

April 1: April Fools' Day

April 22: Earth Day

May 5: Cinco de Mayo

May 12: Mother's Day

May 27: Memorial Day

June 16: Father's Day

July 4: Independence Day

September 2: Labor Day

September 5–6: Rosh Hashanah*

September 14: Yom Kippur*

October 14: Columbus Day

October 31: Halloween

November 3: Daylight saving time ends

November 11: Veterans Day

November 28: Thanksgiving

November 28–December 5: Hanukkah*

December 25: Christmas

December 26–January 1: Kwanzaa

*All Jewish holidays begin at sundown the evening before.

SUPER CELEBRATIONS

Chinese New Year It's a tradition to sweep your entire house before Chinese New Year. Some people believe that it is like sweeping away the old year's bad luck to make room for good luck.

St. Patrick's Day is a national holiday in Ireland, but the first St. Patrick's Day parade was held in Boston in 1737.

Cinco de Mayo commemorates the Mexican victory over the French at the battle of Puebla on May 5, 1862. It was an important battle in the fight for Mexican independence.

Mother's Day was created by Anna Jarvis, a Philadelphia mother who wanted it to be a day of prayer and giving thanks for mothers. She later filed a lawsuit to try to stop a Mother's Day festival in New York because she did not want the holiday to become about spending money and buying things. She lost. Today, in the United States, Mother's Day is celebrated on the second Sunday in May.

Memorial Day The first Memorial Day was celebrated on May 30, 1868. Participants placed flowers on the graves of more than 20,000 soldiers who died in the Civil War.

Independence Day The Declaration of Independence was written on July 2, 1776, and published on July 4, 1776. It was an instant holiday. John Adams wrote to his wife, Abigail, on July 3 that the following day would be celebrated with "pomp and parade, with shows, games, sports, guns, bells, bonfires, and illuminations."

Labor Day On September 5, 1882, more than 10,000 workers in New York City marched to protest 16-hour workdays and terrible working conditions. The march was organized by the Central Labor Union. A few years later, the holiday was established. And, in 1894, Congress voted to make it a national holiday.

Christmas became a U.S. national holiday on June 26, 1870.

TIME FOR KIDS GAME

A FRESH START

In 2013, the Chinese New Year begins on February 10. The Chinese celebrate with a feast. They set the table with foods and decorations that are symbols of a new beginning. Use the picture and word list to help name some of the symbols.

WORD LIST

noodles	flowers
rice	rocks
green	apples
red	oranges

1. Gold is a symbol of good fortune. This color, used to decorate, stands for happiness.

2. The Chinese eat this fruit in hope of finding wealth.

3. This kind of pasta is a symbol of long life.

4. These are put on the table for beauty and as a symbol of spring.

Answers on page 242.

Calendars and Holidays

TIME TO CELEBRATE!

Every culture, religion, and nation sets aside special days for remembrance and celebration. Some of these days commemorate important events. Some of them are spiritual and religious. Some are sweet, reminding people to spend time with friends and family. And some are just plain wacky.

Global Belly Laugh Day (January 24) Wherever you are on this day, at 1:24 p.m., throw your arms up in the air and laugh as hard as you can. Elaine Helle started this tradition in Portland, Oregon, in 2005, to recognize the gift of laughter.

Bean Throwing Day (the day before the first day of spring) On this day, in Japan, people gather and throw beans—usually roasted soybeans—and shout *"Oni wa soto,"* which means "Get out, demons," and *"Fuku wa uchi,"* which means "Come in, happiness." The ceremony is meant to chase away evil spirits. After the throwing is over, people pick up the beans and eat them. Legend says that if you eat the same number of beans as your age, you'll have a good year.

Dyngus Day (Monday after Easter) Some Christians take part in Lent, which is a period of 40 days before Easter, during which they fast, or give up something they enjoy, and reflect on their sins. Celebrated in Poland, Dyngus Day is a day of fun and silliness that follows Lent. Boys chase girls and try to drench them with water buckets or squirt guns. Girls have a chance to do the same on the following day.

Butter Lamp Festival (15th day of the first lunar month; in 2013, it will fall on April 17.) This holiday celebrates Buddha, whose teachings are the foundation of Buddhism. In some provinces of Tibet, people light thousands of candles made from vegetable oil or butter made from the milk of a yak, which is a big, shaggy animal. They also dye yak butter many colors and create sculptures with it. The sculptures are lit up, and people sing and dance around them all night long.

MONTHS TO REMEMBER

By issuing a proclamation, a President can designate a certain month for the public observation of a specific theme or group. Here are a few.

JANUARY
Mentoring Month

FEBRUARY
American Heart Month;
Black History Month

MARCH
American Red Cross Month;
Irish-American Heritage Month

APRIL
Prevent Child Abuse Month

MAY
National Physical Fitness
and Sports Month

JUNE
Great Outdoors Month;
National Oceans Month

SEPTEMBER
National Wilderness Month

SEPTEMBER 15–OCTOBER 15
National Hispanic Heritage Month

OCTOBER
Italian American Heritage
and Culture Month; National
Energy Awareness Month

NOVEMBER
Military Family Month;
National American Indian
Heritage Month

Save the Rhino Day (May 1) Rhinoceroses are near extinction, so conservationists created this day to make the world aware of the efforts to save them. Some groups hold events to raise money for animal rights organizations. Others show documentary films or read books about rhinos aloud.

Eid ul-Fitr (*eed* uhl-*fit*-tuhr) **(at the end of Ramadan; usually in late July, August, or early September)** Ramadan is the holiest month of the year for Muslims. During Ramadan, Muslims pray, perform acts of charity, and refrain from eating or drinking during the day. Eid ul-Fitr is the festival at the end of the month. It's celebrated with prayers, gifts, charity, new clothing, and big family meals that include lots of sweet dishes.

Tomatina Festival (last Wednesday in August) In 1945, a group of young men who wanted to join a parade in the Spanish town of Buñol picked some tomatoes off a farmer's stand and started throwing them. They were arrested. They came back the next year and did it again, and were arrested again. But after a few years, everyone decided that tomato throwing was fun, and now Tomatina is an annual party with music, hundreds of participants, and rules. Here are some of the rules.

- You may throw only precrushed fruit. This way, no one gets hurt.
- You may throw only tomatoes, no other objects.
- You may not tear another person's T-shirt.

Other cities, including Reno, Nevada, and Milwaukee, Wisconsin, now hold Tomatina festivals.

World Teachers' Day (October 5) UNESCO (the United Nations Educational, Scientific and Cultural Organization) set up this holiday, first celebrated in 1994, to recognize teachers and the work they do. Take this day to say thank you to all of your teachers.

Day of the Dead (November 1 and 2) For thousands of years, families in Mexico have gathered on these days to honor loved ones who have passed away. Families visit cemeteries, build small altars, and offer gifts to the dead. Sometimes, they bring pillows and blankets with them and stay all night, talking, singing, and remembering. The skull is a symbol of the holiday. There are similar holidays in Europe and Asia.

MYSTERY PERSON

I was born on February 12, 1809. Although my birthday was never a national holiday, it was celebrated in many states. Now my legacy is remembered on Presidents' Day. As the 16th President of the United States, I governed over a terrible division in the country. I once said that the most important paper I ever signed was the Emancipation Proclamation.

WHO AM I? _____

Answer on page 242.

FROM
TIME
FOR KIDS
MAGAZINE

Cyber School

By Suzanne Zimbler

For Amakhut Tyehimba, 13, getting to school is easy. All she has to do is turn on her computer. That's because Amakhut goes to cyber school.

Her teacher at Ohio Virtual Academy offers lessons using a video camera. She answers Amakhut's questions by e-mail or over the phone. With help from her mom, Amakhut does her classwork online. She even chats with her classmates throughout the school day. Of course, it's with instant messages and texts. "I do everything a regular kid would do," Amakhut told TFK.

Amakhut's school day may not sound regular to most kids. But some experts say that could change in the future. "This is one of the fastest-growing innovations in all of K–12 education," says Susan Patrick, president of the International Association for K–12 Online Learning (iNACOL).

Just five years ago, only a few states offered full-time online learning options. Today, according to iNACOL, 27 states have public cyber schools. There are more than 225,000 full-time cyber school students in the United States.

DO CYBER SCHOOLS RULE?

Cyber school supporters say that online learning lets kids move at their own pace. "If I have a problem with a lesson, I might spend two days on it," says Amakhut. Online schools are also popular among students in need of a flexible schedule. Cyber-school students can go to class at whatever time works for them.

But critics say cyber students could be missing out on important lessons in getting along with others. "What about learning to cooperate and work in groups? Cyber school kids are not getting that," says Gene Glass. He is an education expert.

When it comes to the future of online learning, critics and supporters can agree on one thing: cyber schools are not going away. Experts believe that online learning opportunities will continue to grow.

Still, that does not mean that cyber school is right for every kid. "It depends on the person," says Amakhut. "It is for me."

Michael Dieffenbach attends Wisconsin Virtual Learning school.

guess what? After a severe winter in 2011, schools in Missouri experimented with "virtual snow days" to help students make up work missed because of blizzards.

CRAZY COMPUTER FACTS

🖥 The first Web page was put online on August 6, 1991.

🖥 The first Apple computer, the Apple I, was made in 1976 and sold for less than $700. Only about 200 were made—by hand—by Steve Wozniak and Steve Jobs. They were made from parts that Jobs and Wozniak got for free from their employers.

🖥 An average cell phone today has more processing power than the computers on the *Apollo 11* **lunar module,** which landed two men on the moon.

🖥 As of 2012, there were approximately 17 billion devices connected to the Internet.

🖥 About 250 billion e-mails are sent every day. Almost 80% of them are spam.

THAT'S ONE HUGE COMPUTER!

The earliest electronic computers were a bit different from what we use today. The ENIAC computer from 1946 cost more than $400,000, was 8 feet (3 m) tall and more than 100 feet (30.5 m) long, and weighed 60,000 lbs (27,216 kg)— not exactly a laptop!

WHAT'S BUGGING YOUR COMPUTER?

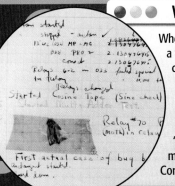

When a computer program doesn't work, we say that it has a "bug," which means there is a problem in the software code. But the first bug was actually a bug. In 1947, Grace Murray Hopper was having trouble with a computer at Harvard University. She couldn't find a problem in the code. Finally, some technicians took apart the computer and found a moth stuck inside. After it was cleaned, or "debugged," the computer worked just fine. The famous moth (pictured) is now at the Naval Surface Warfare Center Computer Museum at Dahlgren, Virginia.

SAFE SURFING

⚠ **Protect yourself from being a cyber victim by following these simple tips.** ⚠

🖥 Never give out personal information—such as your name, address, phone number, school, a photo, where you like to hang out, or whether you are home alone—to anyone who contacts you, unless your parents say it's okay.

🖥 If you ever receive a message that frightens you or makes you uncomfortable, tell your parents (or your teacher or a trusted adult).

🖥 Never share your password with anyone except your parents.

🖥 Treat everyone on the Internet the same way you want to be treated.

WHAT COMPUTERS CAN DO FOR YOU

● ● ● COMPUTER ANIMATION

Two of the most exciting things computers are used for today are animation and special effects in movies. Moviemakers used to create animated films by drawing a picture for each frame by hand—20 or 24 frames per second. Today, this work can be done by computers, and the results are amazing. *Toy Story* (1995) was the first completely computer-animated feature film. Since then, computer effects and animation have continued to wow audiences in movies like *Puss in Boots* (2011) and *The Adventures of Tintin* (2011).

Computer-generated effects aren't just for animated movies. Some special effects, like the octopus-faced Davy Jones in the Pirates of the Caribbean series, are generated by computer. Many movies have used effects and animation to create characters that aren't really there. *Jurassic Park* (1993) was one of the first movies to use CG (computer graphics) to simulate realistic-looking dinosaurs "acting" alongside actual people. And computers also bring us stunning 3-D effects, like the ones in *Transformers: Dark of the Moon* (2011).

Puss in Boots

● ● ● FIX UP YOUR PHOTOS

Computer programs like Adobe Photoshop can be used to change digital photos. Here are some of the basic things that can be done with a photo-editing program.

🖥 Making a picture lighter or darker

🖥 Cropping, or cutting, a picture down to a different size or shape

🖥 Reducing or eliminating the red-eye effect that sometimes happens when a flash is used

You can also do creative, silly, or wacky things. For example, if your aunt cannot make it to the family reunion, you can use photo-editing software to pluck her likeness from one picture and add her to a group portrait. You could even add Justin Bieber to your basketball team!

guess what? Since 2009, just about 100% of public schools have computers with Internet access available to students. On average, there is one computer for every 3.1 students.

38

MAPPING AND GPS

Rather than pulling paper maps from the glove box, more and more drivers are using the Global Positioning System (GPS). A GPS device (such as TomTom or Garmin) relies on satellites that orbit about 12,500 miles (20,200 km) above Earth. There are currently 32 of these satellites in orbit. A GPS device on the ground receives signals from four or five of them to pinpoint its exact location. Then it matches up its current location with a map to give the user precise directions. GPS units usually have built-in speakers so instructions are broadcast out loud, and drivers can keep their eyes on the road. Smartphones, iPhones, and iPads often include GPS applications as well.

CYBERMEDICINE

There are many ways that computers are used in medicine. They help hospitals keep medical records neat and organized, and allow doctors to access a huge amount of information quickly. Computers are also used to take high-resolution, magnified images of our internal organs that help doctors diagnose all sorts of diseases. And there are many scientific experiments that doctors can now perform that would have taken years to complete without computers. For example, scientists create programs that can reproduce a process over and over under varying circumstances. This might be used to show how blood flows through veins when patients are on different medications.

A pacemaker is a tiny computer that can be implanted into a person's body to keep the heart beating regularly.

GAME GUIDE

MONKEY QUEST
Welcome to a free, adventure-filled, virtual world. Visitors explore the land of Ook, a mysterious kingdom where monkeys rule.
Made by Nickelodeon
Platform: Online

HEROTOPIA
This free, online universe is modeled after the real world. But in Herotopia, every kid is a superhero! Travel the globe, fight crime, and make the world a better place.
Made by Herotainment, LLC
Platform: Online

MYSTERY CASE FILES
Get out a magnifying glass and put on your detective cap! There's a mystery brewing on Malgrave Island, and it's up to you to solve it.
Made by Nintendo
Platform: Nintendo Wii

SQUINKIES
Players take control as the Squinkies Princess, who is searching for her missing friends.
Made by Activision
Platform: Nintendo 3DS/DS

TOWER BLOXX DELUXE
Use your quick reflexes and puzzle skills to build towering skyscrapers in this group of three exciting games.
Made by Digital Chocolate
Platform: PC, Mobile

Computers and Communication

APPS FOR EVERYTHING

There are more than 500,000 applications available for mobile electronic devices, and the number is growing every day. See if any of these games and activities are for you.

Faces iMake HD
Use more than 200 objects and colors to create faces, scenes, and more.
Made by iMagine Machine LLC
Platform: iPad

Casey's Contraptions
Find Casey's toys by creating complex machines and solving puzzles.
Made by Snappy Touch
Platform: iPad

Math Bingo
When you answer math questions correctly, a bingo bug will appear on your card.
Made by ABCya.com
Platforms: iPad, iPhone

BrainPOP
Tim, the teacher, and an expressive robot help you learn something new every day about topics ranging from the solar system to civil rights.
Made by BrainPOP
Platforms: iPad, iPhone

Bookworm
This educational word-search game lets you earn points as you move letters around the screen.
Made by PopCap
Platforms: Android, iPad, iPhone

Master Pieces
Learn about art as you use your powers of observation to identify details from famous paintings.
Made by Ballast Lane Applications, LLC
Platforms: iPad, iPhone

Scribblenauts Remix
If you can think it, you can create it! Bring fantastic objects to life by spelling them out.
Made by Warner Bros.
Platforms: iPad, iPhone

Pocket Frogs
Create unique frogs and frog habitats and trade them with your friends.
Made by NimbleBit LLC
Platforms: Android, iPad, iPhone

HOW SMART IS YOUR SMARTPHONE?

Here are a few of the things that smartphones can do:

Connect to the Internet

Take photos and record video

Play music

Control devices like DVRs and TVs remotely

Stream Internet radio stations

Store important files

And, yes, make telephone calls!

ELECTRONICS WISH LIST

During the 2010 holiday season, 31% of kids wanted an iPad. By 2011, that number jumped to 44%. A research group surveyed kids in the United States ages 6 to 12 about the tech items they wanted most in late 2011 and early 2012. The iPad and the iPod Touched topped the list.

iPad	44%
iPod Touch	30%
iPhone	27%
Computer	25%
Tablet computer (other than an iPad)	25%
Nintendo 3DS	25%
Kinect for Xbox 360	23%
Nintendo DS/DSi/DS Lite	22%
Television	20%
Smartphone (other than iPhone)	19%
Sony PlayStation 3/PS3 Slim	17%
Blu-Ray player	17%
E-reader	17%
Microsoft Xbox 360	16%
Other mobile phone	12%
Nintendo Wii	11%
PlayStation Move	10%
PlayStation Portable	10%

● ● ● WEBBY AWARDS

Since 1996 (when the Internet was still quite new), the International Academy of Digital Arts and Sciences has given out yearly awards to recognize excellence on the Internet. Winners of the 15th Annual Webby Awards were announced May 3, 2011. Check them out online.

Best Home/Welcome Page
Lego.com

Best Use of Photography
Nationalgeographic.com

Charitable Organizations/Nonprofits
Historypin.com

Cultural Institutions
Anne Frank House Secret Annex Online
annefrank.org/en/subsites/home

Games
Lego Star Wars III
lucasarts.com/games/legostarwarsiii

Government
The Architect's Virtual Capitol
capitol.gov

Green
SHFT.com

Online Film and Video Animation Do You Know What Nano Means?
Wonderville.ca/asset/do-you-know-what-nano-means

Music
Pandora.com

News
NPR.org

Science
NASA Global Climate Change
climate.nasa.gov

Sports
MLB.com

Learn about wildlife and play adventure games at *nationalgeographic.com.*

See how much the Toboggan Glacier, in Alaska, has melted from 1909 to 2000, at *climate.nasa.gov.*

TIME FOR KIDS GAME

READ THE SIGNS

Use these clues to piece together the name of a popular social messaging tool.

 -NS +  -

+ - = ?

Answer on page 242.

Computers and Communication

THE UNITED NATIONS

After World War II ended in 1945, representatives from 51 nations met to set up an international organization that would try to maintain peace worldwide and promote friendly relations between countries. It would work to make the world a better place for everyone, by spreading knowledge and opportunities from the wealthier nations to the ones that were still developing. That is how the United Nations (UN) started. Today, the United Nations has 193 member countries and has a strong record of preventing wars, fighting terrorism, and slowing the development and spread of deadly weapons.

In addition to promoting international peace efforts, the UN has many other functions and goals. One branch, the World Health Organization (WHO) brings modern medicine and disease prevention to countries all over the world. UNESCO (United Nations Educational, Scientific, and Cultural Organization) conducts studies and spreads knowledge and cooperation. UNICEF (United Nations Children's Fund) looks after the needs of the youngest citizens of the world. The UN also leads in the fight to prevent diseases like malaria and diabetes and to stop climate change.

The main headquarters of the UN is in New York City. There are other offices in Geneva, Switzerland, and Nairobi, Kenya. Here are a few of the projects overseen by the UN right now.

UN peacekeepers visit a camp for displaced people in Darfur, Sudan.

» **Providing aid and protection to more than 34 million refugees and others fleeing war, famine, or persecution**

» **Bringing food to about 90 million hungry people in 80 countries every year through the World Food Programme (WFP)**

» **Vaccinating 40% of the world's children through UNICEF, which saves 2 million lives a year**

» **Supporting more than 100,000 UN peacekeepers in 16 peace operations**

guess what? The budget for the United Nations is divided among all its members—but it's not divided equally. The United States pays the most—about 22% of the total budget. This came to around $450 million, or about $1.50 per U.S. citizen.

MAIN BODIES OF THE UNITED NATIONS

The **General Assembly** refers to the main body of the UN. It is made up of all 193 members.

Made up of 15 member countries, the **UN Security Council** works to maintain peace in the world, settle disputes, and calm crises when they arise. When necessary, it sends peacekeeping forces to trouble spots.

The **Economic and Social Council** promotes well-being of all nations, especially after conflicts or natural disasters.

The **International Court of Justice** is based in The Hague, in the Netherlands. When there is a legal dispute between nations, the Court of Justice settles it based on international law.

The **Secretariat** runs the day-to-day business of the UN. The chief officer is the **Secretary-General**.

NATIONS FROM A TO Z

This sample entry for Taiwan explains the kinds of information you will find in this section.

This tells the main languages and the official languages (if any) spoken in a nation.

This is the type of currency, or money, used in the nation.

Life expectancy is the number of years a person can expect to live. It's affected by heredity, a person's health and nutrition, the health care and wealth of a nation, and a person's occupation.

This tells the percentage of people who can read and write.

This is an interesting fact about the country.

TAIWAN

LOCATION: Asia
CAPITAL: Taipei
AREA: 13,892 sq mi (35,980 sq km)
POPULATION ESTIMATE (2012): 23,113,901
GOVERNMENT: Multiparty democracy
LANGUAGES: Chinese (Mandarin), Taiwanese, Hakka dialects
MONEY: New Taiwan dollar
LIFE EXPECTANCY: 78
LITERACY RATE: 96%

 guess what? *The Formosan black bear is found only in Taiwan.*

AFGHANISTAN

LOCATION: Asia
CAPITAL: Kabul
AREA: 251,737 sq mi (652,230 sq km)
POPULATION ESTIMATE (2012): 30,419,928
GOVERNMENT: Islamic republic
LANGUAGES: Afghan Persian (Dari) and Pashto (both official)
MONEY: Afghani
LIFE EXPECTANCY: 50
LITERACY RATE: 28%

guess what? *Lapis lazuli, a bright blue stone used to decorate the tomb of Egyptian King Tut, is abundant in Afghanistan.*

ALBANIA

LOCATION: Europe
CAPITAL: Tirana
AREA: 11,100 sq mi (28,748 sq km)
POPULATION ESTIMATE (2012): 3,002,859
GOVERNMENT: Parliamentary democracy
LANGUAGES: Albanian (Tosk is the official dialect), Greek, others
MONEY: Lek
LIFE EXPECTANCY: 78
LITERACY RATE: 99%

guess what? *Albania is the only country in Europe with a Muslim majority population.*

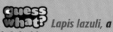

ALGERIA

LOCATION: Africa
CAPITAL: Algiers
AREA: 919,590 sq mi (2,381,741 sq km)
POPULATION ESTIMATE (2012): 35,406,303
GOVERNMENT: Republic
LANGUAGES: Arabic (official), French, Berber dialects
MONEY: Dinar
LIFE EXPECTANCY: 75
LITERACY RATE: 70%

guess what? *The Sahara desert covers four-fifths of Algeria, and it includes some of the world's biggest sand dunes.*

ANDORRA

LOCATION: Europe
CAPITAL: Andorra la Vella
AREA: 181 sq mi (468 sq km)
POPULATION ESTIMATE (2012): 85,082
GOVERNMENT: Parliamentary democracy
LANGUAGES: Catalan (official), French, Castilian, Portuguese
MONEY: Euro (formerly French franc and Spanish peseta)
LIFE EXPECTANCY: 83
LITERACY RATE: 100%

guess what? *There are no airports or train stations in Andorra.*

ANGOLA

LOCATION: Africa
CAPITAL: Luanda
AREA: 481,350 sq mi (1,246,700 sq km)
POPULATION ESTIMATE (2012): 18,056,072
GOVERNMENT: Republic
LANGUAGES: Portuguese (official), Bantu, other African languages
MONEY: Kwanza
LIFE EXPECTANCY: 55
LITERACY RATE: 67%

Guess what? *Angola's civil war lasted 27 years, ending in 2002. Dangerous land mines are still hidden throughout the countryside.*

ANTIGUA AND BARBUDA

LOCATION: Caribbean
CAPITAL: Saint John's
AREA: 171 sq mi (443 sq km)
POPULATION ESTIMATE (2012): 89,018
GOVERNMENT: Constitutional monarchy with a parliamentary system of government
LANGUAGES: English (official), local dialects
MONEY: East Caribbean dollar
LIFE EXPECTANCY: 76
LITERACY RATE: 86%

Guess what? *Crab racing is a popular local event in Antigua. Crabs are set in the center of a circle drawn with chalk. The winning crab is the first one to exit the circle.*

ARGENTINA

LOCATION: South America
CAPITAL: Buenos Aires
AREA: 1,073,518 sq mi (2,780,400 sq km)
POPULATION ESTIMATE (2012): 42,192,494
GOVERNMENT: Republic
LANGUAGES: Spanish (official), Italian, English, German, French
MONEY: Argentine peso
LIFE EXPECTANCY: 77
LITERACY RATE: 97%

Guess what? *The national sport of Argentina, pato, is played on horseback and is a combination of polo and basketball. Today, a ball is used, but traditionally, players used a live duck!*

ARMENIA

LOCATION: Asia
CAPITAL: Yerevan
AREA: 11,484 sq mi (29,743 sq km)
POPULATION ESTIMATE (2012): 2,970,495
GOVERNMENT: Republic
LANGUAGES: Armenian (official), others
MONEY: Dram
LIFE EXPECTANCY: 73
LITERACY RATE: 99%

Guess what? *Armenia became the first Christian nation in 301 A.D.*

AUSTRALIA

LOCATION: Between the Pacific Ocean and Indian Ocean
CAPITAL: Canberra
AREA: 2,988,902 sq mi (7,741,220 sq km)
POPULATION ESTIMATE (2012): 22,015,576
GOVERNMENT: Federal parliamentary democracy
LANGUAGE: English
MONEY: Australian dollar
LIFE EXPECTANCY: 82
LITERACY RATE: 99%

Guess what? *From 1838 to 1902, it was illegal to swim during the day at public beaches in Australia. The authorities considered it immoral.*

AUSTRIA

LOCATION: Europe
CAPITAL: Vienna
AREA: 32,382 sq mi (83,871 sq km)
POPULATION ESTIMATE (2012): 8,219,743
GOVERNMENT: Federal republic
LANGUAGES: German (official), Croatian (official in Burgenland), Turkish, Serbian, others
MONEY: Euro (formerly schilling)
LIFE EXPECTANCY: 80
LITERACY RATE: 98%

Guess what? *The Viennese waltz, named for Austria's capital, is danced worldwide in ballroom dance competitions.*

AZERBAIJAN

LOCATION: Asia
CAPITAL: Baku
AREA: 33,400 sq mi
(86,600 sq km)
POPULATION ESTIMATE (2012):
9,493,600
GOVERNMENT: Republic
LANGUAGES: Azerbaijani, Lezgi,
Russian, Armenian, others
MONEY: Azerbaijani manat
LIFE EXPECTANCY: 71
LITERACY RATE: 99%

guess what? *Azerbaijan is home to more than half of the world's mud volcanoes, which spew mud and gases instead of magma and water.*

BAHAMAS

LOCATION: Caribbean
CAPITAL: Nassau
AREA: 5,359 sq mi
(13,880 sq km)
POPULATION ESTIMATE (2012): 316,182
GOVERNMENT: Constitutional
parliamentary democracy
LANGUAGES: English (official),
Creole
MONEY: Bahamian dollar
LIFE EXPECTANCY: 71
LITERACY RATE: 96%

guess what? *The national bird of the Bahamas is the flamingo.*

BAHRAIN

LOCATION: Middle East
CAPITAL: Manama
AREA: 293 sq mi (760 sq km)
POPULATION ESTIMATE (2012):
1,248,348
GOVERNMENT: Constitutional
monarchy
LANGUAGES: Arabic (official),
English, Farsi, Urdu
MONEY: Bahraini dinar
LIFE EXPECTANCY: 78
LITERACY RATE: 87%

guess what? *Women in Bahrain were granted the right to vote in 2002.*

BANGLADESH

LOCATION: Asia
CAPITAL: Dhaka
AREA: 55,598 sq mi
(143,998 sq km)
POPULATION ESTIMATE (2012):
161,083,804
GOVERNMENT: Parliamentary
democracy
LANGUAGES: Bangla (official),
English
MONEY: Taka
LIFE EXPECTANCY: 70
LITERACY RATE: 48%

guess what? *Plastic bags have clogged drainage systems and been a major cause of flooding in Bangladesh. Now plastic bags are banned throughout the country.*

BARBADOS

LOCATION: Caribbean
CAPITAL: Bridgetown
AREA: 166 sq mi (430 sq km)
POPULATION ESTIMATE (2012): 287,733
GOVERNMENT: Parliamentary
democracy
LANGUAGE: English
MONEY: Barbadian dollar
LIFE EXPECTANCY: 75
LITERACY RATE: 100%

guess what? *The whistling frogs of Barbados do not have tadpoles like other frogs. Instead, they give birth to live young.*

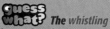

BELARUS

LOCATION: Europe
CAPITAL: Minsk
AREA: 80,154 sq mi
(207,600 sq km)
POPULATION ESTIMATE (2012):
9,542,883
GOVERNMENT: Republic in name,
but actually a dictatorship
LANGUAGES: Belarusian, Russian
MONEY: Belarusian ruble
LIFE EXPECTANCY: 71
LITERACY RATE: 100%

guess what? *Belarus is slightly smaller than the state of Kansas.*

Countries

BELGIUM

LOCATION: Europe
CAPITAL: Brussels
AREA: 11,787 sq mi (30,528 sq km)
POPULATION ESTIMATE (2012): 10,438,353
GOVERNMENT: Federal parliamentary democracy under a constitutional monarchy
LANGUAGES: Dutch, French, and German (all official)
MONEY: Euro (formerly Belgian franc)
LIFE EXPECTANCY: 80
LITERACY RATE: 99%

guess what? *In 1958, the comic strip The Smurfs was created by Belgian comic-strip artist Peyo.*

BELIZE

LOCATION: Central America
CAPITAL: Belmopan
AREA: 8,867 sq mi (22,966 sq km)
POPULATION ESTIMATE (2012): 327,719
GOVERNMENT: Parliamentary democracy
LANGUAGES: English (official), Spanish, Creole, Mayan dialects, others
MONEY: Belizean dollar
LIFE EXPECTANCY: 68
LITERACY RATE: 77%

guess what? *The Mayan ruins of Altun Ha, built from 200 to 900 A.D., are one of the most visited sites in Belize.*

BENIN

LOCATION: Africa
CAPITAL: Porto-Novo
AREA: 43,483 sq mi (112,622 sq km)
POPULATION ESTIMATE (2012): 9,598,787
GOVERNMENT: Republic
LANGUAGES: French (official), Fon, Yoruba, other African languages
MONEY: CFA franc
LIFE EXPECTANCY: 60
LITERACY RATE: 35%

guess what? *The village of Ganvie in Benin is built on stilts above Lake Nokoué.*

BHUTAN

LOCATION: Asia
CAPITAL: Thimphu
AREA: 14,824 sq mi (38,394 sq km)
POPULATION ESTIMATE (2012): 716,896
GOVERNMENT: Constitutional monarchy
LANGUAGES: Dzongkha (official), various Tibetan and Nepalese dialects
MONEY: Ngultrum
LIFE EXPECTANCY: 68
LITERACY RATE: 47%

guess what? *There are no traffic lights in Thimphu.*

BOLIVIA

LOCATION: South America
CAPITALS: La Paz (seat of government), Sucre (legislative capital)
AREA: 424,162 sq mi (1,098,581 sq km)
POPULATION ESTIMATE (2012): 10,290,003
GOVERNMENT: Republic
LANGUAGES: Spanish, Quechua, and Aymara (all official)
MONEY: Boliviano
LIFE EXPECTANCY: 68
LITERACY RATE: 87%

guess what? *Santa Cruz, Bolivia, is home to the Guembe Butterfly Sanctuary, one of the largest butterfly sanctuaries in the world.*

BOSNIA AND HERZEGOVINA

LOCATION: Europe
CAPITAL: Sarajevo
AREA: 19,767 sq mi (51,197 sq km)
POPULATION ESTIMATE (2012): 4,622,292
GOVERNMENT: Emerging federal democratic republic
LANGUAGES: Bosnian and Croatian (both official), Serbian
MONEY: Convertible mark
LIFE EXPECTANCY: 79
LITERACY RATE: 97%

guess what? *Bosnia's name comes from the Bosna River, which flows through it.*

BOTSWANA

LOCATION: Africa
CAPITAL: Gaborone
AREA: 224,607 sq mi (581,730 sq km)
POPULATION ESTIMATE (2012): 2,098,018
GOVERNMENT: Parliamentary republic
LANGUAGES: English (official), Setswana, Kalanga, Sekgalagadi
MONEY: Pula
LIFE EXPECTANCY: 56
LITERACY RATE: 81%

 Botswana is home to the largest elephant population in Africa.

BRAZIL

LOCATION: South America
CAPITAL: Brasília
AREA: 3,287,612 sq mi (8,514,877 sq km)
POPULATION ESTIMATE (2012): 205,716,890
GOVERNMENT: Federal republic
LANGUAGES: Portuguese (official), Spanish, German, Italian, Japanese, English, various Amerindian languages
MONEY: Real
LIFE EXPECTANCY: 73
LITERACY RATE: 89%

 More species of monkeys live in Brazil than anywhere else in the world.

BRUNEI

LOCATION: Asia
CAPITAL: Bandar Seri Begawan
AREA: 2,226 sq mi (5,765 sq km)
POPULATION ESTIMATE (2012): 408,786
GOVERNMENT: Constitutional sultanate
LANGUAGES: Malay (official), English, Chinese
MONEY: Bruneian dollar
LIFE EXPECTANCY: 76
LITERACY RATE: 93%

The same family has ruled Brunei for six centuries.

BULGARIA

LOCATION: Europe
CAPITAL: Sofia
AREA: 42,811 sq mi (110,879 sq km)
POPULATION ESTIMATE (2012): 7,037,935
GOVERNMENT: Parliamentary democracy
LANGUAGES: Bulgarian (official), Turkish, Roma, others
MONEY: Lev
LIFE EXPECTANCY: 74
LITERACY RATE: 98%

The Bulgarian town of Kazanluk exports rose oil, an important and rare ingredient in many perfumes.

BURKINA FASO

LOCATION: Africa
CAPITAL: Ouagadougou
AREA: 105,870 sq mi (274,200 sq km)
POPULATION ESTIMATE (2012): 17,275,115
GOVERNMENT: Parliamentary republic
LANGUAGES: French (official), native African languages
MONEY: CFA franc
LIFE EXPECTANCY: 54
LITERACY RATE: 22%

Burkina Faso's main export is gold.

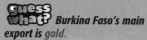

BURUNDI

LOCATION: Africa
CAPITAL: Bujumbura
AREA: 10,745 sq mi (27,830 sq km)
POPULATION ESTIMATE (2012): 10,557,259
GOVERNMENT: Republic
LANGUAGES: Kirundi and French (both official), Swahili
MONEY: Burundi franc
LIFE EXPECTANCY: 59
LITERACY RATE: 59%

One of the world's biggest crocodiles, named Gustave, haunts the waters of Burundi. He is estimated to be 20 feet (6.1 m) long and to weigh 1 ton (907.2 kg).

CAMBODIA

LOCATION: Asia
CAPITAL: Phnom Penh
AREA: 69,900 sq mi
(181,035 sq km)
POPULATION ESTIMATE (2012):
14,952,665
GOVERNMENT: Multiparty
democracy under a
constitutional monarchy
LANGUAGES: Khmer (official),
French, English
MONEY: Riel
LIFE EXPECTANCY: 63
LITERACY RATE: 74%

Guess what? *Angkor Wat, a city of magnificent temples, is often called the eighth wonder of the world. It was abandoned for many years and rediscovered by French explorers in the 1860s.*

CAMEROON

LOCATION: Africa
CAPITAL: Yaoundé
AREA: 183,567 sq mi
(475,440 sq km)
POPULATION ESTIMATE (2012):
20,129,878
GOVERNMENT: Republic
LANGUAGES: French and
English (both official),
various African languages
MONEY: CFA franc
LIFE EXPECTANCY: 55
LITERACY RATE: 68%

Guess what? *The rare bongo antelope lives in Cameroon. Bongos have been known to snack on burned wood after lightning storms.*

CANADA

LOCATION: North America
CAPITAL: Ottawa
AREA: 3,855,081 sq mi
(9,984,670 sq km)
POPULATION ESTIMATE (2012):
34,300,083
GOVERNMENT: Parliamentary
democracy, federation, and
constitutional monarchy
LANGUAGES: English and French
(both official)
MONEY: Canadian dollar
LIFE EXPECTANCY: 81
LITERACY RATE: 99%

Guess what? *A popular Canadian dish is poutine, french fries covered in cheese curds and gravy.*

CAPE VERDE

LOCATION: Africa
CAPITAL: Praia
AREA: 1,557 sq mi (4,033 sq km)
POPULATION ESTIMATE (2012): 523,568
GOVERNMENT: Republic
LANGUAGES: Portuguese, Crioulo
MONEY: Cape Verdean escudo
LIFE EXPECTANCY: 71
LITERACY RATE: 77%

Guess what? *An early version of today's popular game mancala was called ouri, or ouril. It was first played in Cape Verde.*

CENTRAL AFRICAN REPUBLIC

LOCATION: Africa
CAPITAL: Bangui
AREA: 240,534 sq mi
(622,984 sq km)
POPULATION ESTIMATE (2012):
5,057,208
GOVERNMENT: Republic
LANGUAGES: French (official),
Sangho, other African
languages
MONEY: CFA franc
LIFE EXPECTANCY: 50
LITERACY RATE: 49%

Guess what? *This country was known as Ubangi-Shari before gaining its independence from France in 1960.*

CHAD

LOCATION: Africa
CAPITAL: N'Djamena
AREA: 495,752 sq mi
(1,284,000 sq km)
POPULATION ESTIMATE (2012):
10,975,648
GOVERNMENT: Republic
LANGUAGES: French and Arabic
(both official), Sara, others
MONEY: CFA franc
LIFE EXPECTANCY: 49
LITERACY RATE: 26%

Guess what? *Chad is a landlocked country, which means it has no seacoast and no parts of it are along an ocean.*

CHILE

LOCATION: South America
CAPITAL: Santiago
AREA: 291,933 sq mi
(756,102 sq km)
POPULATION ESTIMATE (2012):
17,067,369
GOVERNMENT: Republic
LANGUAGES: Spanish (official),
Mapudungun, German, English
MONEY: Chilean peso
LIFE EXPECTANCY: 78
LITERACY RATE: 96%

Guess what?
Chile's Easter Island is home to 887 moai statues, often called the "Easter Island heads."

CHINA

LOCATION: Asia
CAPITAL: Beijing
AREA: 3,705,386 sq mi
(9,596,961 sq km)
POPULATION ESTIMATE (2012):
1,343,239,923
GOVERNMENT: Communist state
LANGUAGES: Chinese (Mandarin;
official), Yue (Cantonese), local
dialects
MONEY: Renminbi yuan
LIFE EXPECTANCY: 75
LITERACY RATE: 92%

Guess what?
Kites were invented in China 3,000 years ago and were primarily used for frightening opponents in battle.

COLOMBIA

LOCATION: South America
CAPITAL: Bogotá
AREA: 439,733 sq mi
(1,138,914 sq km)
POPULATION ESTIMATE (2012):
45,239,079
GOVERNMENT: Republic
LANGUAGE: Spanish
MONEY: Colombian peso
LIFE EXPECTANCY: 75
LITERACY RATE: 90%

Guess what?
More than 3,500 species of orchids grow in Colombia.

COMOROS

LOCATION: Africa
CAPITAL: Moroni
AREA: 863 sq mi (2,235 sq km)
POPULATION ESTIMATE (2012): 737,284
GOVERNMENT: Republic
LANGUAGES: French and Arabic
(both official), Shikomoro
MONEY: Comoran franc
LIFE EXPECTANCY: 63
LITERACY RATE: 57%

Guess what? *Shikomoro (also known as Comoran), one of the major languages spoke in Comoros, is a blend of Swahili and Arabic.*

CONGO, DEMOCRATIC REPUBLIC OF THE

LOCATION: Africa
CAPITAL: Kinshasa
AREA: 905,355 sq mi
(2,344,858 sq km)
POPULATION ESTIMATE (2012):
73,599,190
GOVERNMENT: Republic
LANGUAGES: French (official),
Lingala, Kingwana, Kikongo,
Tshiluba
MONEY: Congolese franc
LIFE EXPECTANCY: 56
LITERACY RATE: 67%

Guess what? *The equator, which is the imaginary line that circles Earth halfway between the North and South Poles, passes through the Democratic Republic of the Congo.*

CONGO, REPUBLIC OF THE

LOCATION: Africa
CAPITAL: Brazzaville
AREA: 132,046 sq mi
(342,000 sq km)
POPULATION ESTIMATE (2012):
4,366,266
GOVERNMENT: Republic
LANGUAGES: French (official),
Lingala, Monokutuba,
Kikongo, others
MONEY: CFA franc
LIFE EXPECTANCY: 55
LITERACY RATE: 84%

Guess what? *The Republic of the Congo gained independence from France in 1960.*

COSTA RICA

LOCATION: Central America
CAPITAL: San José
AREA: 19,730 sq mi
(51,100 sq km)
POPULATION ESTIMATE (2012):
4,636,348
GOVERNMENT: Democratic republic
LANGUAGES: Spanish (official),
English
MONEY: Costa Rican colón
LIFE EXPECTANCY: 78
LITERACY RATE: 95%

Guess What? *In Spanish,* Costa Rica *means "rich coast."*

COTE D'IVOIRE (IVORY COAST)

LOCATION: Africa
CAPITAL: Yamoussoukro
AREA: 124,502 sq mi
(322,463 sq km)
POPULATION ESTIMATE (2012):
21,952,093
GOVERNMENT: Republic
LANGUAGES: French (official),
various African languages
MONEY: CFA franc
LIFE EXPECTANCY: 57
LITERACY RATE: 49%

Guess What? *Côte d'Ivoire is one of only three African nations to win an Academy Award. It won the Foreign Language Film award in 1977 for* Black and White in Color.

CROATIA

LOCATION: Europe
CAPITAL: Zagreb
AREA: 21,851 sq mi
(56,594 sq km)
POPULATION ESTIMATE (2012):
4,480,043
GOVERNMENT: Presidential
parliamentary democracy
LANGUAGE: Croatian
MONEY: Kuna
LIFE EXPECTANCY: 76
LITERACY RATE: 98%

Guess What? *Croatia is slightly smaller than West Virginia.*

CUBA

LOCATION: Caribbean
CAPITAL: Havana
AREA: 42,803 sq mi
(110,860 sq km)
POPULATION ESTIMATE (2012):
11,075,244
GOVERNMENT: Communist state
LANGUAGE: Spanish
MONEY: Cuban peso
LIFE EXPECTANCY: 78
LITERACY RATE: 100%

Guess What? *When Italian explorer Christopher Columbus landed in Cuba in 1492, he thought he had reached China.*

CYPRUS

LOCATION: Europe
CAPITAL: Nicosia
AREA: 3,571 sq mi (9,250 sq km)
POPULATION ESTIMATE (2012):
1,138,071
GOVERNMENT: Republic
LANGUAGES: Greek and Turkish
(both official), English
MONEY: Euro (formerly Cyprus
pound)
LIFE EXPECTANCY: 78
LITERACY RATE: 98%

Guess What? *One nickname for Cyprus is the "Island of the Gods." According to myth, the Greek goddess Aphrodite was born off the coast of Cyprus.*

CZECH REPUBLIC

LOCATION: Europe
CAPITAL: Prague
AREA: 30,450 sq mi
(78,866 sq km)
POPULATION ESTIMATE (2012):
10,177,300
GOVERNMENT: Parliamentary
democracy
LANGUAGES: Czech, Slovak, others
MONEY: Koruna
LIFE EXPECTANCY: 77
LITERACY RATE: 99%

Guess What? *The first recorded use of the* sugar cube *was in 1843, in the Czech town of Dacice.*

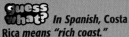

DENMARK

LOCATION: Europe
CAPITAL: Copenhagen
AREA: 16,639 sq mi (43,094 sq km)
POPULATION ESTIMATE (2012): 5,543,453
GOVERNMENT: Constitutional monarchy
LANGUAGES: Danish, Faroese, Greenlandic, German
MONEY: Krone
LIFE EXPECTANCY: 79
LITERACY RATE: 99%

guess what? *Danish author Hans Christian Anderson is well known for writing stories and fairy tales, including "The Ugly Duckling," "The Snow Queen," and "The Little Mermaid."*

DJIBOUTI

LOCATION: Africa
CAPITAL: Djibouti
AREA: 8,958 sq mi (23,200 sq km)
POPULATION ESTIMATE (2012): 774,389
GOVERNMENT: Republic
LANGUAGES: Arabic and French (both official), Somali, Afar
MONEY: Djiboutian franc
LIFE EXPECTANCY: 62
LITERACY RATE: 68%

guess what? *The blue on the Djibouti flag symbolizes the sea and sky, while the green is for the land. The white represents peace, and the red stands for unity.*

DOMINICA

LOCATION: Caribbean
CAPITAL: Roseau
AREA: 291 sq mi (754 sq km)
POPULATION ESTIMATE (2012): 73,126
GOVERNMENT: Parliamentary democracy
LANGUAGES: English (official), French patois
MONEY: East Caribbean dollar
LIFE EXPECTANCY: 76
LITERACY RATE: 94%

guess what? *The World Creole Music Festival, where musicians from around the world perform, is held in Roseau, in southwest Dominica, every year.*

DOMINICAN REPUBLIC

LOCATION: Caribbean
CAPITAL: Santo Domingo
AREA: 18,792 sq mi (48,670 sq km)
POPULATION ESTIMATE (2012): 10,088,598
GOVERNMENT: Democratic republic
LANGUAGE: Spanish
MONEY: Dominican peso
LIFE EXPECTANCY: 77
LITERACY RATE: 87%

guess what? *The first cathedral built in the Americas is the Cathedral de Santa María la Menor in the Dominican Republic's Zona Colonial. It was built from 1514 to 1540.*

EAST TIMOR (TIMOR-LESTE)

LOCATION: Asia
CAPITAL: Dili
AREA: 5,743 sq mi (14,874 sq km)
POPULATION ESTIMATE (2012): 1,201,255
GOVERNMENT: Republic
LANGUAGES: Tetum and Portuguese (both official), Indonesian, English
MONEY: U.S. dollar
LIFE EXPECTANCY: 68
LITERACY RATE: 59%

guess what? *East Timor gained independence from Indonesia in 2002.*

ECUADOR

LOCATION: South America
CAPITAL: Quito
AREA: 109,483 sq mi (283,560 sq km)
POPULATION ESTIMATE (2012): 15,223,680
GOVERNMENT: Republic
LANGUAGES: Spanish (official), Quechua, other Amerindian languages
MONEY: U.S. dollar
LIFE EXPECTANCY: 76
LITERACY RATE: 91%

guess what? *At the festival called Año Viejo (or "old year"), Ecuadorians make puppets that represent the bad things of the past year, then burn them to welcome the new year.*

countries

EGYPT

LOCATION: Africa
CAPITAL: Cairo
AREA: 386,660 sq mi
(1,001,450 sq km)
POPULATION ESTIMATE (2012):
83,688,164
GOVERNMENT: Republic
LANGUAGE: Arabic
MONEY: Egyptian
pound
LIFE EXPECTANCY: 73
LITERACY RATE: 71%

 Ancient Egyptians worshipped cats as sacred. They believed that the animals protected households.

EL SALVADOR

LOCATION: Central America
CAPITAL: San Salvador
AREA: 8,124 sq mi (21,040 sq km)
POPULATION ESTIMATE (2012):
6,090,646
GOVERNMENT: Republic
LANGUAGES: Spanish (official),
Nahua
MONEY: U.S. dollar
LIFE EXPECTANCY: 74
LITERACY RATE: 81%

Guess what? *El Salvador is the smallest and most densely populated country in Central America.*

EQUATORIAL GUINEA

LOCATION: Africa
CAPITAL: Malabo
AREA: 10,830 sq mi
(28,051 sq km)
POPULATION ESTIMATE (2012): 685,991
GOVERNMENT: Republic
LANGUAGES: Spanish and French
(both official), Fang, Bubi
MONEY: CFA franc
LIFE EXPECTANCY: 63
LITERACY RATE: 87%

Guess what? *Equatorial Guinea consists of a small area on mainland Africa and five volcanic islands.*

ERITREA

LOCATION: Africa
CAPITAL: Asmara
AREA: 45,406 sq mi
(117,600 sq km)
POPULATION ESTIMATE (2012):
6,086,495
GOVERNMENT: Transitional
LANGUAGES: Afar, Arabic, Tigre,
Kunama, Tigrinya, others
MONEY: Nakfa
LIFE EXPECTANCY: 63
LITERACY RATE: 59%

Guess what? *To mark special occasions, Eritreans participate in coffee ceremonies. Coffee and popcorn are shared with guests in a ceremony that lasts about an hour.*

ESTONIA

LOCATION: Europe
CAPITAL: Tallinn
AREA: 17,463 sq mi
(45,228 sq km)
POPULATION ESTIMATE (2012):
1,274,709
GOVERNMENT: Parliamentary
republic
LANGUAGES: Estonian (official),
Russian
MONEY: Euro (formerly kroon)
LIFE EXPECTANCY: 74
LITERACY RATE: 100%

Guess what? *Estonia was once part of the Soviet Union and gained its independence in 1991.*

ETHIOPIA

LOCATION: Africa
CAPITAL: Addis Ababa
AREA: 426,373 sq mi
(1,104,300 sq km)
POPULATION ESTIMATE (2012):
93,815,992
GOVERNMENT: Federal republic
LANGUAGES: Amarigna, English,
and Arabic (all official),
Oromigna and Tigrigna (both
regional official), others
MONEY: Birr
LIFE EXPECTANCY: 57
LITERACY RATE: 43%

Guess what? *In 1974, parts of a 3.2-million-year-old skeleton, known as Lucy, were found near Hadar, Ethiopia.*

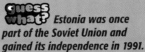

FIJI

LOCATION: Oceania
CAPITAL: Suva
AREA: 7,057 sq mi (18,274 sq km)
POPULATION ESTIMATE (2012): 890,057
GOVERNMENT: Republic
LANGUAGES: Fijian and English (both official), Hindustani
MONEY: Fijian dollar
LIFE EXPECTANCY: 72
LITERACY RATE: 94%

Guess what? *Some Fijians used to engage in cannibalism, or the eating of human flesh. A boot with teeth marks on it that supposedly belonged to the country's last victim can be seen in the Fiji Museum.*

FINLAND

LOCATION: Europe
CAPITAL: Helsinki
AREA: 130,559 sq mi (338,145 sq km)
POPULATION ESTIMATE (2012): 5,262,930
GOVERNMENT: Republic
LANGUAGES: Finnish and Swedish (both official), others
MONEY: Euro (formerly markka)
LIFE EXPECTANCY: 79
LITERACY RATE: 100%

Guess what? *There are more than 2 million saunas in Finland. Traditionally, saunas are steam baths, where the steam comes from water poured over heated rocks. Finns sit in the saunas, then jump into cold lakes, pools, or showers.*

FRANCE

LOCATION: Europe
CAPITAL: Paris
AREA: 248,573 sq mi (643,801 sq km)
POPULATION ESTIMATE (2012): 65,630,692
GOVERNMENT: Republic
LANGUAGE: French
MONEY: Euro (formerly franc)
LIFE EXPECTANCY: 81
LITERACY RATE: 99%

Guess what? *The French greet each other by kissing one another on one cheek, then the other. During the 2009 H1N1 outbreak (a particularly dangerous flu), authorities recommended against this type of greeting.*

GABON

LOCATION: Africa
CAPITAL: Libreville
AREA: 103,346 sq mi (267,667 sq km)
POPULATION ESTIMATE (2012): 1,608,321
GOVERNMENT: Republic
LANGUAGES: French (official), Fang, Myene, Nzebi, Bapounou/Eschira, Bandjabi
MONEY: CFA franc
LIFE EXPECTANCY: 52
LITERACY RATE: 63%

Guess what? *Gabon is one of the few countries that is home to the endangered western lowland gorilla.*

THE GAMBIA

LOCATION: Africa
CAPITAL: Banjul
AREA: 4,361 sq mi (11,295 sq km)
POPULATION ESTIMATE (2012): 1,840,454
GOVERNMENT: Republic
LANGUAGES: English (official), Mandinka, Wolof, Fula, others
MONEY: Dalasi
LIFE EXPECTANCY: 64
LITERACY RATE: 40%

Guess what? *The Stone Circles of Senegambia include four groups of more than 1,000 stone blocks found in the Gambia. They are located near burial mounds that date from the 3rd century B.C. to the 16th century A.D.*

GEORGIA

LOCATION: Asia
CAPITAL: Tbilisi
AREA: 26,911 sq mi (69,700 sq km)
POPULATION ESTIMATE (2012): 4,570,934
GOVERNMENT: Republic
LANGUAGES: Georgian (official), Russian, Armenian, Azeri
MONEY: Lari
LIFE EXPECTANCY: 77
LITERACY RATE: 100%

Guess what? *The five-cross design of the Georgian flag dates back to the 14th century.*

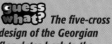

GERMANY

LOCATION: Europe
CAPITAL: Berlin
AREA: 137,847 sq mi
(357,022 sq km)
POPULATION ESTIMATE (2012):
81,305,856
GOVERNMENT: Federal republic
LANGUAGE: German
MONEY: Euro (formerly
deutsche mark)
LIFE EXPECTANCY: 80
LITERACY RATE: 99%

Guess what? *Germany is home to many impressive castles. Neuschwanstein Castle is one of the best known. Sleeping Beauty's castle in Disneyland was modeled after Neuschwanstein.*

GHANA

LOCATION: Africa
CAPITAL: Accra
AREA: 92,098 sq mi
(238,533 sq km)
POPULATION ESTIMATE (2012):
25,241,998
GOVERNMENT: Constitutional
democracy
LANGUAGES: English (official),
Ashanti, Ewe, Fante, Boron,
Dagomba, Dagarte, others
MONEY: Cedi
LIFE EXPECTANCY: 61
LITERACY RATE: 58%

Guess what? *The word ghana means "warrior king" in the Ashanti language.*

GREECE

LOCATION: Europe
CAPITAL: Athens
AREA: 50,949 sq mi
(131,957 sq km)
POPULATION ESTIMATE (2012):
10,767,827
GOVERNMENT: Parliamentary
republic
LANGUAGE: Greek
MONEY: Euro (formerly drachma)
LIFE EXPECTANCY: 80
LITERACY RATE: 96%

Guess what? *The Cretan frog is an endangered frog found only on Crete, Greece's largest island.*

GRENADA

LOCATION: Caribbean
CAPITAL: Saint George's
AREA: 133 sq mi (344 sq km)
POPULATION ESTIMATE (2012): 109,011
GOVERNMENT: Parliamentary
democracy
LANGUAGES: English (official),
French patois
MONEY: East Caribbean dollar
LIFE EXPECTANCY: 73
LITERACY RATE: 96%

Guess what? *One of the local dishes in Grenada is avocado ice cream.*

GUATEMALA

LOCATION: Central America
CAPITAL: Guatemala City
AREA: 42,042 sq mi
(108,889 sq km)
POPULATION ESTIMATE (2012):
14,099,032
GOVERNMENT: Constitutional
democratic republic
LANGUAGES: Spanish, Amerindian
languages
MONEY: Quetzal
LIFE EXPECTANCY: 71
LITERACY RATE: 69%

Guess what? *The quetzal, Guatemala's national bird, has bright green, white, and red feathers. The males have a vibrant tail that is 3 feet (0.9 m) long.*

GUINEA

LOCATION: Africa
CAPITAL: Conakry
AREA: 94,925 sq mi
(245,860 sq km)
POPULATION ESTIMATE (2012):
10,884,958
GOVERNMENT: Republic
LANGUAGES: French (official),
native languages
MONEY: Guinean franc
LIFE EXPECTANCY: 59
LITERACY RATE: 30%

Guess what? *Guinea's 2010 elections were the first free and fair elections held there since the country's independence in 1958.*

GUINEA-BISSAU

LOCATION: Africa
CAPITAL: Bissau
AREA: 13,948 sq mi
(36,125 sq km)
POPULATION ESTIMATE (2012):
1,628,603
GOVERNMENT: Republic
LANGUAGES: Portuguese (official),
Crioulo, African languages
MONEY: CFA franc
LIFE EXPECTANCY: 49
LITERACY RATE: 42%

 Many farmers in Guinea-Bissau follow animism, which is the belief that everything, from rocks and hurricanes to animals and humans, has a soul.

GUYANA

LOCATION: South America
CAPITAL: Georgetown
AREA: 83,000 sq mi
(214,969 sq km)
POPULATION ESTIMATE (2012): 741,908
GOVERNMENT: Republic
LANGUAGES: English (official),
Amerindian dialects, Creole,
Caribbean Hindustani, Urdu
MONEY: Guyanese dollar
LIFE EXPECTANCY: 67
LITERACY RATE: 92%

 The national flower of Guyana is the Victoria amazonica, the largest type of water lily.

HAITI

LOCATION: Caribbean
CAPITAL: Port-au-Prince
AREA: 10,714 sq mi
(27,750 sq km)
POPULATION ESTIMATE (2012):
9,801,664
GOVERNMENT: Republic
LANGUAGES: Creole and French
(both official)
MONEY: Gourde
LIFE EXPECTANCY: 63
LITERACY RATE: 53%

The royal palm tree, pictured on the Haitian coat of arms, can grow to 60 feet (18.3 m) tall in Haiti.

HONDURAS

LOCATION: Central America
CAPITAL: Tegucigalpa
AREA: 43,278 sq mi
(112,090 sq km)
POPULATION ESTIMATE (2012):
8,296,693
GOVERNMENT: Democratic
constitutional republic
LANGUAGES: Spanish (official),
Amerindian dialects
MONEY: Lempira
LIFE EXPECTANCY: 71
LITERACY RATE: 80%

Every year, the "rain of fish" occurs in Honduras. Six-inch (15.2 cm) fish fall from the sky. Scientists are not sure what causes this strange rain.

HUNGARY

LOCATION: Europe
CAPITAL: Budapest
AREA: 35,918 sq mi
(93,028 sq km)
POPULATION ESTIMATE (2012):
9,958,453
GOVERNMENT: Parliamentary
democracy
LANGUAGE: Hungarian
MONEY: Forint
LIFE EXPECTANCY: 75
LITERACY RATE: 99%

Until 1873, Budapest was two distinct cities separated by the Danube River. Buda and Pest merged when a bridge was built over the river.

ICELAND

LOCATION: Europe
CAPITAL: Reykjavík
AREA: 39,768 sq mi
(103,000 sq km)
POPULATION ESTIMATE (2012): 313,183
GOVERNMENT: Constitutional
republic
LANGUAGES: Icelandic, English
MONEY: Icelandic krona
LIFE EXPECTANCY: 81
LITERACY RATE: 99%

The Viking midwinter festival called Thorrablot or Thurseblot is celebrated yearly in Iceland. Traditional foods eaten during the celebration include whale blubber, sheep's head, and rotten shark.

INDIA

LOCATION: Asia
CAPITAL: New Delhi
AREA: 1,269,219 sq mi
(3,287,263 sq km)
POPULATION ESTIMATE (2012):
1,205,073,612
GOVERNMENT: Federal republic
LANGUAGES: Hindi, English,
14 other official languages
MONEY: Indian rupee
LIFE EXPECTANCY: 67
LITERACY RATE: 61%

Guess what? *The Taj Mahal was constructed from 1632 to 1653 by Emperor Shah Jahan as a tribute to his wife, Mumtaz Mahal, who died giving birth to their 14th child.*

INDONESIA

LOCATION: Asia
CAPITAL: Jakarta
AREA: 735,358 sq mi
(1,904,569 sq km)
POPULATION ESTIMATE (2012):
248,216,193
GOVERNMENT: Republic
LANGUAGES: Bahasa Indonesia
(official), Dutch, English,
many local dialects
MONEY: Rupiah
LIFE EXPECTANCY: 72
LITERACY RATE: 90%

Guess what? *Indonesia is one of the largest producers of nutmeg in the world.*

IRAN

LOCATION: Middle East
CAPITAL: Tehran
AREA: 636,372 sq mi
(1,648,195 sq km)
POPULATION ESTIMATE (2012):
78,868,711
GOVERNMENT: Theocratic republic
LANGUAGES: Persian (official),
Turkic, Kurdish, others
MONEY: Rial
LIFE EXPECTANCY: 70
LITERACY RATE: 77%

Guess what? *Iran exports more caviar than any other country. Caviar is an expensive food made of the raw eggs of the sturgeon fish.*

IRAQ

LOCATION: Middle East
CAPITAL: Baghdad
AREA: 169,235 sq mi
(438,317 sq km)
POPULATION ESTIMATE (2012):
31,129,225
GOVERNMENT: Parliamentary
democracy
LANGUAGES: Arabic (official),
Kurdish, Turkoman, Assyrian
MONEY: Iraqi dinar
LIFE EXPECTANCY: 71
LITERACY RATE: 74%

Guess what? *The Hanging Gardens of Babylon, one of the seven wonders of the ancient world, were located in present-day Iraq until an earthquake destroyed them in the 2nd century B.C.*

IRELAND

LOCATION: Europe
CAPITAL: Dublin
AREA: 27,132 sq mi
(70,273 sq km)
POPULATION ESTIMATE (2012):
4,722,028
GOVERNMENT: Republic,
parliamentary democracy
LANGUAGES: Irish (Gaelic) and
English (both official)
MONEY: Euro (formerly Irish
pound, or punt)
LIFE EXPECTANCY: 80
LITERACY RATE: 99%

Guess what? *There are no wild snakes in Ireland. According to legend, Saint Patrick charmed all of the snakes and drove them out of the country.*

ISRAEL

LOCATION: Middle East
CAPITAL: Jerusalem
AREA: 8,019 sq mi (20,770 sq km)
POPULATION ESTIMATE (2012):
7,590,758
GOVERNMENT: Parliamentary
democracy
LANGUAGES: Hebrew (official),
Arabic, English
MONEY: New Israeli shekel
LIFE EXPECTANCY: 81
LITERACY RATE: 97%

Guess what? *The lowest point on Earth is the Dead Sea, in Israel, at 1,286 feet (392 m) below sea level. The Dead Sea is one of the saltiest bodies of water in the world.*

ITALY

LOCATION: Europe
CAPITAL: Rome
AREA: 116,348 sq mi
(301,340 sq km)
POPULATION ESTIMATE (2012):
61,261,254
GOVERNMENT: Republic
LANGUAGES: Italian (official),
German, French, Slovene
MONEY: Euro (formerly lira)
LIFE EXPECTANCY: 82
LITERACY RATE: 98%

Guess what?

The Leaning Tower of Pisa was built on marshy land, which is why the building does not stand straight. It leans a tiny bit more each year.

JAMAICA

LOCATION: Caribbean
CAPITAL: Kingston
AREA: 4,244 sq mi
(10,991 sq km)
POPULATION ESTIMATE (2012):
2,889,187
GOVERNMENT: Constitutional
parliamentary democracy
LANGUAGES: English, English patois
MONEY: Jamaican dollar
LIFE EXPECTANCY: 73
LITERACY RATE: 88%

Guess what? *The Jamaican national fruit, ackee, is poisonous if it is eaten before it is ripe.*

JAPAN

LOCATION: Asia
CAPITAL: Tokyo
AREA: 145,914 sq mi
(377,915 sq km)
POPULATION ESTIMATE (2012):
127,368,088
GOVERNMENT: Parliamentary
government with a
constitutional monarchy
LANGUAGE: Japanese
MONEY: Yen
LIFE EXPECTANCY: 84
LITERACY RATE: 99%

Guess what?

The tallest mountain in Japan is Mount Fuji, which is also an active volcano.

JORDAN

LOCATION: Middle East
CAPITAL: Amman
AREA: 34,495 sq mi
(89,342 sq km)
POPULATION ESTIMATE (2012):
6,508,887
GOVERNMENT: Constitutional
monarchy
LANGUAGE: Arabic (official)
MONEY: Jordanian dinar
LIFE EXPECTANCY: 80
LITERACY RATE: 90%

Guess what? *A white antelope called the Arabian oryx, native to Jordan, was declared extinct in the wild in 1972. Due to breeding programs, there are now about 1,000 animals in the wild.*

KAZAKHSTAN

LOCATION: Asia
CAPITAL: Astana
AREA: 1,052,090 sq mi
(2,724,900 sq km)
POPULATION ESTIMATE (2012):
17,522,010
GOVERNMENT: Republic with
authoritarian presidential rule
LANGUAGES: Russian (official),
Kazakh
MONEY: Tenge
LIFE EXPECTANCY: 70
LITERACY RATE: 100%

Guess what? *The Tian Shan mountain range in Kazakhstan is home to the last wild apple forests in the world.*

KENYA

LOCATION: Africa
CAPITAL: Nairobi
AREA: 224,081 sq mi
(580,367 sq km)
POPULATION ESTIMATE (2012):
43,013,341
GOVERNMENT: Republic
LANGUAGES: English and Kiswahili
(both official), others
MONEY: Kenyan shilling
LIFE EXPECTANCY: 63
LITERACY RATE: 85%

Guess what? *The Great Rift Valley, the largest rift in Earth's surface, was formed in Kenya 20 million years ago.*

KIRIBATI

LOCATION: Oceania
CAPITAL: Tarawa
AREA: 313 sq mi (811 sq km)
POPULATION ESTIMATE (2012): 101,998
GOVERNMENT: Republic
LANGUAGES: English (official), I-Kiribati (Gilbertese)
MONEY: Australian dollar
LIFE EXPECTANCY: 65
LITERACY RATE: Not available

guess what? *Because the islands of Kiribati are so close to sea level, the people of Kiribati are very concerned about climate change. As the world gets warmer, sea levels will rise, putting the country at risk of being submerged.*

KOREA, NORTH

LOCATION: Asia
CAPITAL: Pyongyang
AREA: 46,540 sq mi (120,538 sq km)
POPULATION ESTIMATE (2012): 24,589,122
GOVERNMENT: Communist dictatorship
LANGUAGE: Korean
MONEY: North Korean won
LIFE EXPECTANCY: 69
LITERACY RATE: 99%

guess what? *North Korea is extremely mountainous, and many of the people living in those mountains are very isolated.*

KOREA, SOUTH

LOCATION: Asia
CAPITAL: Seoul
AREA: 38,541 sq mi (99,720 sq km)
POPULATION ESTIMATE (2012): 48,860,500
GOVERNMENT: Republic
LANGUAGE: Korean
MONEY: South Korean won
LIFE EXPECTANCY: 79
LITERACY RATE: 98%

guess what? *Scientists in South Korea developed the world's second female android (a robot designed to be like a human), EveR-1.*

KOSOVO

LOCATION: Europe
CAPITAL: Pristina
AREA: 4,203 sq mi (10,887 sq km)
POPULATION ESTIMATE (2012): 1,836,529
GOVERNMENT: Republic
LANGUAGES: Albanian and Serbian (both official), Bosnian, Turkish, Roma
MONEY: Euro (formerly deutsche mark)
LIFE EXPECTANCY: Not available
LITERACY RATE: 92%

guess what? *The capital of Kosovo, Pristina, translates to "field of blackbirds" in Serbian.*

KUWAIT

LOCATION: Middle East
CAPITAL: Kuwait City
AREA: 6,880 sq mi (17,820 sq km)
POPULATION ESTIMATE (2012): 2,646,314
GOVERNMENT: Constitutional emirate
LANGUAGES: Arabic (official), English
MONEY: Kuwaiti dinar
LIFE EXPECTANCY: 77
LITERACY RATE: 93%

guess what? *The people of Kuwait produce very few agricultural products. Nearly all of the wealth in the country comes from oil.*

KYRGYZSTAN

LOCATION: Asia
CAPITAL: Bishkek
AREA: 77,202 sq mi (199,951 sq km)
POPULATION ESTIMATE (2012): 5,496,737
GOVERNMENT: Republic
LANGUAGES: Kyrgyz and Russian (both official), Uzbek, others
MONEY: Som
LIFE EXPECTANCY: 69
LITERACY RATE: 99%

guess what? *Horses are a huge part of the nomadic lifestyle of the people of Kyrgyzstan.*

LAOS

LOCATION: Asia
CAPITAL: Vientiane
AREA: 91,429 sq mi
(236,800 sq km)
POPULATION ESTIMATE (2012):
6,586,266
GOVERNMENT: Communist state
LANGUAGES: Lao (official), French,
English
MONEY: Kip
LIFE EXPECTANCY: 63
LITERACY RATE: 73%

Guess What? *The red panda, which is more closely related to raccoons than giant pandas, lives in the forests of Laos.*

LATVIA

LOCATION: Europe
CAPITAL: Riga
AREA: 24,938 sq mi
(64,589 sq km)
POPULATION ESTIMATE (2012):
2,191,580
GOVERNMENT: Parliamentary
democracy
LANGUAGES: Latvian, Russian
MONEY: Lats
LIFE EXPECTANCY: 73
LITERACY RATE: 100%

Guess What? *The Riga Castle is now home to the president of Latvia, but it was first constructed by the Livonian Order of Knights in 1330.*

LEBANON

LOCATION: Middle East
CAPITAL: Beirut
AREA: 4,015 sq mi
(10,400 sq km)
POPULATION ESTIMATE (2012):
4,140,289
GOVERNMENT: Republic
LANGUAGES: Arabic (official),
French, English, Armenian
MONEY: Lebanese pound
LIFE EXPECTANCY: 75
LITERACY RATE: 87%

Guess What? *Due to a history of violent clashes between members of different religious sects, there has not been a census in Lebanon since 1932. Leaders agree that a census that records residents' religions might cause trouble.*

LESOTHO

LOCATION: Africa
CAPITAL: Maseru
AREA: 11,720 sq mi
(30,355 sq km)
POPULATION ESTIMATE (2012):
1,930,493
GOVERNMENT: Parliamentary
constitutional monarchy
LANGUAGES: English (official),
Sesotho, Zulu, Xhosa
MONEY: Loti
LIFE EXPECTANCY: 52
LITERACY RATE: 85%

Guess What? *In Lesotho, people can see footprints of a dinosaur called the Lesothosaurus.*

LIBERIA

LOCATION: Africa
CAPITAL: Monrovia
AREA: 43,000 sq mi
(111,369 sq km)
POPULATION ESTIMATE (2012):
3,887,886
GOVERNMENT: Republic
LANGUAGES: English (official),
ethnic dialects
MONEY: Liberian dollar
LIFE EXPECTANCY: 57
LITERACY RATE: 58%

Guess What? *Liberia is home to the only healthy, growing population of pygmy hippos in the world.*

LIBYA

LOCATION: Africa
CAPITAL: Tripoli
AREA: 679,358 sq mi
(1,759,540 sq km)
POPULATION ESTIMATE (2012):
6,733,620
GOVERNMENT: Transitional
LANGUAGES: Arabic (official),
Italian, English
MONEY: Libyan dinar
LIFE EXPECTANCY: 78
LITERACY RATE: 83%

Guess What? *The Sahara desert covers 90% of Libya. In Arabic, Sahara means "desert."*

Countries

LIECHTENSTEIN

LOCATION: Europe
CAPITAL: Vaduz
AREA: 62 sq mi (160 sq km)
POPULATION ESTIMATE (2012): 36,713
GOVERNMENT: Constitutional monarchy
LANGUAGES: German (official), Alemannic dialect
MONEY: Swiss franc
LIFE EXPECTANCY: 82
LITERACY RATE: 100%

Guess What? *Liechtenstein is the only German-speaking country that does not share a border with Germany.*

LITHUANIA

LOCATION: Europe
CAPITAL: Vilnius
AREA: 25,212 sq mi (65,300 sq km)
POPULATION ESTIMATE (2012): 3,525,761
GOVERNMENT: Parliamentary democracy
LANGUAGES: Lithuanian (official), Polish, Russian
MONEY: Litas
LIFE EXPECTANCY: 76
LITERACY RATE: 100%

Guess What? *Trakai Castle, located on an island in Lithuania, used to be a home and a prison, but now it is the site of many music and dance festivals.*

LUXEMBOURG

LOCATION: Europe
CAPITAL: Luxembourg
AREA: 998 sq mi (2,586 sq km)
POPULATION ESTIMATE (2012): 509,074
GOVERNMENT: Constitutional monarchy
LANGUAGES: Luxembourgish, German, French
MONEY: Euro (formerly Luxembourg franc)
LIFE EXPECTANCY: 80
LITERACY RATE: 100%

Guess What? *Luxembourg has the highest minimum wage in the European Union.*

MACEDONIA

LOCATION: Europe
CAPITAL: Skopje
AREA: 9,928 sq mi (25,713 sq km)
POPULATION ESTIMATE (2012): 2,082,370
GOVERNMENT: Parliamentary democracy
LANGUAGES: Macedonian and Albanian (official), Turkish, others
MONEY: Macedonian denar
LIFE EXPECTANCY: 75
LITERACY RATE: 96%

Guess What? *The stone town of Kuklica, in northeast Macedonia, is home to 120 natural stone pillars.*

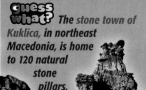

MADAGASCAR

LOCATION: Africa
CAPITAL: Antananarivo
AREA: 226,658 sq mi (587,041 sq km)
POPULATION ESTIMATE (2012): 22,585,517
GOVERNMENT: Republic
LANGUAGES: French and Malagasy (both official), English
MONEY: Malagasy ariary
LIFE EXPECTANCY: 64
LITERACY RATE: 69%

Guess What? *Madagascar is the world's largest exporter of vanilla, which is an expensive spice. So that vanilla plants can reproduce, each vanilla blossom must be pollinated by hand.*

MALAWI

LOCATION: Africa
CAPITAL: Lilongwe
AREA: 45,747 sq mi (118,484 sq km)
POPULATION ESTIMATE (2012): 16,323,044
GOVERNMENT: Multiparty democracy
LANGUAGES: Chichewa (official), Chinyanja, Chiyao, Chitumbuka
MONEY: Kwacha
LIFE EXPECTANCY: 52
LITERACY RATE: 63%

Guess What? *Remains of humans have been found in Malawi dating back to 8000 B.C.*

MALAYSIA

LOCATION: Asia
CAPITAL: Kuala Lumpur
AREA: 127,355 sq mi
(329,847 sq km)
POPULATION ESTIMATE (2012):
29,179,952
GOVERNMENT: Constitutional
monarchy
LANGUAGES: Bahasa Malay
(official), English, Chinese,
Tamil, others
MONEY: Ringgit
LIFE EXPECTANCY: 74
LITERACY RATE: 89%

guess what? *The longest king cobra in the world, measuring more than 18 feet (5.5 m) long, was captured in Malaysia.*

MALDIVES

LOCATION: Asia
CAPITAL: Male
AREA: 116 sq mi (300 sq km)
POPULATION ESTIMATE (2012): 394,451
GOVERNMENT: Republic
LANGUAGES: Dhivehi (official),
English
MONEY: Rufiyaa
LIFE EXPECTANCY: 75
LITERACY RATE: 94%

guess what? *The white crescent moon on the Maldives flag represents Islam.*

MALI

LOCATION: Africa
CAPITAL: Bamako
AREA: 478,841 sq mi
(1,240,192 sq km)
POPULATION ESTIMATE (2012):
14,533,511
GOVERNMENT: Republic
LANGUAGES: French (official),
Bambara, African languages
MONEY: CFA franc
LIFE EXPECTANCY: 53
LITERACY RATE: 46%

guess what? *Timbuktu is home to priceless manuscripts about mathematics, astronomy, philosophy, law, and more, from the Songhai Empire in the 1400s and 1500s.*

MALTA

LOCATION: Europe
CAPITAL: Valletta
AREA: 122 sq mi (316 sq km)
POPULATION ESTIMATE (2012): 409,836
GOVERNMENT: Republic
LANGUAGES: Maltese and English
(both official)
MONEY: Euro (formerly
Maltese lira)
LIFE EXPECTANCY: 80
LITERACY RATE: 93%

guess what? *Traditional Maltese fishing boats, which are very colorful, are symbols of Malta. The luzzu and the dghajsa (di-sa) are two types of these boats.*

MARSHALL ISLANDS

LOCATION: Oceania
CAPITAL: Majuro
AREA: 70 sq mi (181 sq km)
POPULATION ESTIMATE (2012): 68,480
GOVERNMENT: Constitutional
government
LANGUAGES: Marshallese and
English (both official)
MONEY: U.S. dollar
LIFE EXPECTANCY: 72
LITERACY RATE: 94%

guess what? *Enewetak, a chain of coral islands in the Marshall Islands, is where the United States exploded the first hydrogen bomb in 1952.*

MAURITANIA

LOCATION: Africa
CAPITAL: Nouakchott
AREA: 397,953 sq mi
(1,030,700 sq km)
POPULATION ESTIMATE (2012):
3,359,185
GOVERNMENT: Military junta
LANGUAGES: Arabic (official),
French, Pulaar, Soninke, others
MONEY: Ouguiya
LIFE EXPECTANCY: 62
LITERACY RATE: 51%

guess what? *In 1981, Mauritania was one of the last countries in the world to abolish slavery.*

MAURITIUS

LOCATION: Africa
CAPITAL: Port Louis
AREA: 788 sq mi (2,040 sq km)
POPULATION ESTIMATE (2012): 1,313,095
GOVERNMENT: Parliamentary democracy
LANGUAGES: English (official), Creole, Bhojpuri, French
MONEY: Mauritian rupee
LIFE EXPECTANCY: 75
LITERACY RATE: 84%

Guess what? *Naturalist Charles Darwin is credited with being the first person to climb Le Pouce mountain on the volcanic island of Mauritius. Le Pouce means "the thumb" in French.*

MEXICO

LOCATION: North America
CAPITAL: Mexico City
AREA: 758,449 sq mi (1,964,375 sq km)
POPULATION ESTIMATE (2012): 114,975,406
GOVERNMENT: Federal republic
LANGUAGES: Spanish, indigenous languages
MONEY: Peso
LIFE EXPECTANCY: 77
LITERACY RATE: 86%

Guess what? *In 1968, Mexico hosted the first Olympic Games to be held in Latin America.*

MICRONESIA, FEDERATED STATES OF

LOCATION: Oceania
CAPITAL: Palikir
AREA: 271 sq mi (702 sq km)
POPULATION ESTIMATE (2012): 106,487
GOVERNMENT: Constitutional government
LANGUAGES: English (official), Chuukese, Kosraean, Pohnpeian, Yapese, Ulithian, others
MONEY: U.S. dollar
LIFE EXPECTANCY: 72
LITERACY RATE: 89%

Guess what? *There are more than 350 different species of coral surrounding the Micronesian Islands.*

MOLDOVA

LOCATION: Europe
CAPITAL: Chisinau
AREA: 13,070 sq mi (33,851 sq km)
POPULATION ESTIMATE (2012): 3,656,843
GOVERNMENT: Republic
LANGUAGES: Moldovan (official), Russian, Gagauz
MONEY: Leu
LIFE EXPECTANCY: 70
LITERACY RATE: 99%

Guess what? *The Orheiul Vechi cave in Moldova has been home to a monastery since the 14th century.*

MONACO

LOCATION: Europe
CAPITAL: Monaco
AREA: 0.75 sq mi (1.95 sq km)
POPULATION ESTIMATE (2012): 30,510
GOVERNMENT: Constitutional monarchy
LANGUAGES: French (official), English, Italian, Monégasque
MONEY: Euro (formerly French franc)
LIFE EXPECTANCY: 90
LITERACY RATE: 99%

Guess what? *The Monaco Grand Prix is a yearly car race through the tiny country. It began in 1929 and is one of the oldest car races in the world.*

MONGOLIA

LOCATION: Asia
CAPITAL: Ulaanbaatar
AREA: 603,909 sq mi (1,564,116 sq km)
POPULATION ESTIMATE (2012): 3,179,997
GOVERNMENT: Parliamentary republic
LANGUAGES: Khalkha Mongol (official), Turkic, Russian
MONEY: Togrog/tugrik
LIFE EXPECTANCY: 69
LITERACY RATE: 98%

Guess what? *From 1206 to 1227, Genghis Khan, ruler of Mongolia, created the largest empire in the world.*

MONTENEGRO

LOCATION: Europe
CAPITAL: Podgorica
AREA: 5,333 sq mi (13,812 sq km)
POPULATION ESTIMATE (2012): 657,394
GOVERNMENT: Republic
LANGUAGES: Montenegrin (official), Serbian, Bosnian, Albanian, others
MONEY: Euro (formerly deutsche mark)
LIFE EXPECTANCY: Not available
LITERACY RATE: 94%

 *Saint John Fortress, in the seaside village of Kotor, protected the city from pirate attacks for centuries.*

MOROCCO

LOCATION: Africa
CAPITAL: Rabat
AREA: 172,413 sq mi (446,550 sq km)
POPULATION ESTIMATE (2012): 32,309,239
GOVERNMENT: Constitutional monarchy
LANGUAGES: Arabic (official), French, Berber dialects
MONEY: Dirham
LIFE EXPECTANCY: 76
LITERACY RATE: 52%

 Morocco is one of only three countries left in Africa with a monarchy. The others are Swaziland and Lesotho.

MOZAMBIQUE

LOCATION: Africa
CAPITAL: Maputo
AREA: 308,642 sq mi (799,380 sq km)
POPULATION ESTIMATE (2012): 23,515,934
GOVERNMENT: Republic
LANGUAGES: Portuguese (official), Emakhuwa, Xichangana, others
MONEY: Metical
LIFE EXPECTANCY: 52
LITERACY RATE: 48%

 One of the largest exports from Mozambique is the cashew nut.

MYANMAR (BURMA)

LOCATION: Asia
CAPITAL: Nay Pyi Taw
AREA: 261,228 sq mi (676,578 sq km)
POPULATION ESTIMATE (2012): 54,584,650
GOVERNMENT: Parliamentary government with strong military influence
LANGUAGES: Burmese (official), minority languages
MONEY: Kyat
LIFE EXPECTANCY: 65
LITERACY RATE: 90%

The Mingun Bell in Myanmar is one of the largest functioning bells in the world.

NAMIBIA

LOCATION: Africa
CAPITAL: Windhoek
AREA: 318,261 sq mi (824,292 sq km)
POPULATION ESTIMATE (2012): 2,165,828
GOVERNMENT: Republic
LANGUAGES: English (official), Afrikaans, German, native languages
MONEY: Namibian dollar
LIFE EXPECTANCY: 52
LITERACY RATE: 85%

Namibia is home to many large cats, including the world's largest population of cheetahs.

NAURU

LOCATION: Oceania
CAPITAL: Yaren District (unofficial)
AREA: 8.11 sq mi (21 sq km)
POPULATION ESTIMATE (2012): 9,378
GOVERNMENT: Republic
LANGUAGES: Nauruan (official), English
MONEY: Australian dollar
LIFE EXPECTANCY: 66
LITERACY RATE: Not available

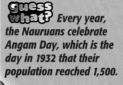 *Every year, the Nauruans celebrate Angam Day, which is the day in 1932 that their population reached 1,500.*

NEPAL

LOCATION: Asia
CAPITAL: Kathmandu
AREA: 56,827 sq mi
(147,181 sq km)
POPULATION ESTIMATE (2012):
29,890,686
GOVERNMENT: Federal democratic
republic
LANGUAGES: Nepali (official),
Maithali, Bhojpuri, Tharu,
Tamang
MONEY: Nepalese rupee
LIFE EXPECTANCY: 67
LITERACY RATE: 49%

guess what? *Nepal's is the only national flag that does not have four sides.*

THE NETHERLANDS

LOCATION: Europe
CAPITAL: Amsterdam
AREA: 16,040 sq mi
(41,543 sq km)
POPULATION ESTIMATE (2012):
16,730,632
GOVERNMENT: Constitutional
monarchy
LANGUAGES: Dutch and Frisian
(both official)
MONEY: Euro (formerly guilder)
LIFE EXPECTANCY: 81
LITERACY RATE: 99%

guess what? *Almost every person in the Netherlands owns a bicycle, and there are two times as many bicycles as cars in the country.*

NEW ZEALAND

LOCATION: Oceania
CAPITAL: Wellington
AREA: 103,363 sq mi
(267,710 sq km)
POPULATION ESTIMATE (2012):
4,327,944
GOVERNMENT: Parliamentary
democracy
LANGUAGES: English, Maori, and
sign language (all official)
MONEY:
New Zealand dollar
LIFE EXPECTANCY: 81
LITERACY RATE: 99%

guess what? *In New Zealand, there are seven sheep for every person.*

NICARAGUA

LOCATION: Central America
CAPITAL: Managua
AREA: 50,336 sq mi
(130,370 sq km)
POPULATION ESTIMATE (2012):
5,727,707
GOVERNMENT: Republic
LANGUAGE: Spanish (official)
MONEY: Córdoba
LIFE EXPECTANCY: 72
LITERACY RATE: 68%

guess what? *Hurricane Mitch in 1998 was Nicaragua's most devastating natural disaster. It killed more than 3,000 people.*

NIGER

LOCATION: Africa
CAPITAL: Niamey
AREA: 489,189 sq mi
(1,267,000 sq km)
POPULATION ESTIMATE (2012):
17,078,839
GOVERNMENT: Republic
LANGUAGES: French (official),
Hausa, Djerma
MONEY: CFA franc
LIFE EXPECTANCY: 54
LITERACY RATE: 29%

guess what? *Niger's nickname is the Frying Pan of the World, because temperatures range from 85°F (24.4°C) to 105°F (40.6°C) year-round.*

NIGERIA

LOCATION: Africa
CAPITAL: Abuja
AREA: 356,667 sq mi
(923,768 sq km)
POPULATION ESTIMATE (2012):
170,123,740
GOVERNMENT: Federal republic
LANGUAGES: English (official),
Hausa, Yoruba, Igbo, Fulani
MONEY: Naira
LIFE EXPECTANCY: 52
LITERACY RATE: 68%

guess what? *Nigeria has a huge film industry that is nicknamed Nollywood. In a 2009 report, UNESCO announced that Nigeria surpassed the United States to become the second-largest movie-producing country. Only India makes more films.*

NORWAY

LOCATION: Europe
CAPITAL: Oslo
AREA: 125,021 sq mi
(323,802 sq km)
POPULATION ESTIMATE (2012):
4,707,270
GOVERNMENT: Constitutional monarchy
LANGUAGES: Two official forms of Norwegian: Bokmal and Nynorsk
MONEY: Krone
LIFE EXPECTANCY: 80
LITERACY RATE: 100%

Guess what? *During the summer in Norway, the sun shines all day and night in the north of the country.*

OMAN

LOCATION: Middle East
CAPITAL: Muscat
AREA: 119,499 sq mi
(309,500 sq km)
POPULATION ESTIMATE (2012):
3,090,150
GOVERNMENT: Monarchy
LANGUAGES: Arabic (official), English, Baluchi, Urdu, Indian dialects
MONEY: Omani rial
LIFE EXPECTANCY: 74
LITERACY RATE: 81%

Guess what? *In the past, Oman made a lot of money exporting incense. Boswellia trees, which produce frankincense, still grow in Oman.*

PAKISTAN

LOCATION: Asia
CAPITAL: Islamabad
AREA: 307,374 sq mi
(790,095 sq km)
POPULATION ESTIMATE (2012):
190,291,129
GOVERNMENT: Federal republic
LANGUAGES: Urdu (official), Punjabi, Sindhi, Siraiki, Pashtu, others
MONEY: Pakistani rupee
LIFE EXPECTANCY: 66
LITERACY RATE: 50%

Guess what? *Although cricket is more popular, the national sport of Pakistan is field hockey.*

PALAU

LOCATION: Oceania
CAPITAL: Melekeok
AREA: 177 sq mi (458 sq km)
POPULATION ESTIMATE (2012): 21,032
GOVERNMENT: Constitutional government
LANGUAGES: Palauan, English, Sonsoralese, Tobi, Anguar, Filipino, Chinese
MONEY: U.S. dollar
LIFE EXPECTANCY: 72
LITERACY RATE: 92%

Guess what? *More than 250 islands make up Palau, but 64% of people live on the island of Koror, where the capital is.*

PANAMA

LOCATION: Central America
CAPITAL: Panama City
AREA: 29,120 sq mi
(75,420 sq km)
POPULATION ESTIMATE (2012):
3,510,045
GOVERNMENT: Constitutional democracy
LANGUAGES: Spanish (official), English
MONEY: Balboa, U.S. dollar
LIFE EXPECTANCY: 78
LITERACY RATE: 92%

Guess what? *More than 20,000 people died constructing the Panama Railroad, which was finished in 1855.*

PAPUA NEW GUINEA

LOCATION: Oceania
CAPITAL: Port Moresby
AREA: 178,703 sq mi
(462,840 sq km)
POPULATION ESTIMATE (2012):
6,310,129
GOVERNMENT: Constitutional parliamentary democracy
LANGUAGES: Tok Pisin, English, and Hiri (all official), about 860 native languages
MONEY: Kina
LIFE EXPECTANCY: 66
LITERACY RATE: 57%

Guess what? *The southwest coast of Papau New Guinea is home to one of the world's largest swamps.*

PARAGUAY

LOCATION: South America
CAPITAL: Asunción
AREA: 157,046 sq mi (406,750 sq km)
POPULATION ESTIMATE (2012): 6,541,591
GOVERNMENT: Constitutional republic
LANGUAGES: Spanish and Guaraní (both official)
MONEY: Guaraní
LIFE EXPECTANCY: 76
LITERACY RATE: 94%

Guess What? *One of Paraguay's major exports is soybeans.*

PERU

LOCATION: South America
CAPITAL: Lima
AREA: 496,223 sq mi (1,285,220 sq km)
POPULATION ESTIMATE (2012): 29,549,517
GOVERNMENT: Constitutional republic
LANGUAGES: Spanish and Quechua (both official), Aymara, others
MONEY: Nuevo sol
LIFE EXPECTANCY: 73
LITERACY RATE: 93%

Guess What? *The Moche people, who lived in Peru before Columbus arrived in the Americas in 1492, practiced ritualized combat. They'd offer the blood of the people they defeated in battle to their gods.*

PHILIPPINES

LOCATION: Asia
CAPITAL: Manila
AREA: 115,830 sq mi (300,000 sq km)
POPULATION ESTIMATE (2012): 103,775,002
GOVERNMENT: Republic
LANGUAGES: Filipino (based on Tagalog) and English (both official), regional languages
MONEY: Philippine peso
LIFE EXPECTANCY: 72
LITERACY RATE: 93%

Guess What? *The endangered tamaraw, a buffalo, is only found on the island of Mindoro in the Philippines.*

POLAND

LOCATION: Europe
CAPITAL: Warsaw
AREA: 120,728 sq mi (312,685 sq km)
POPULATION ESTIMATE (2012): 38,415,284
GOVERNMENT: Republic
LANGUAGE: Polish
MONEY: Zloty
LIFE EXPECTANCY: 76
LITERACY RATE: 100%

Guess What? *Poland is known for its sausage, called kielbasa, and its dumplings, called pierogi, which are stuffed with meat, cheese, potatoes, onion, cabbage, or other vegetables and boiled.*

PORTUGAL

LOCATION: Europe
CAPITAL: Lisbon
AREA: 35,556 sq mi (92,090 sq km)
POPULATION ESTIMATE (2012): 10,781,459
GOVERNMENT: Republic, parliamentary democracy
LANGUAGES: Portuguese and Mirandese (both official)
MONEY: Euro (formerly escudo)
LIFE EXPECTANCY: 79
LITERACY RATE: 93%

Guess What? *In 1488, Portuguese explorer Bartholomeu Dias was the first to sail around the southern tip of Africa, which is named the Cape of Good Hope.*

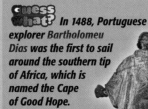

QATAR

LOCATION: Middle East
CAPITAL: Doha
AREA: 4,473 sq mi (11,586 sq km)
POPULATION ESTIMATE (2012): 1,951,591
GOVERNMENT: Traditional monarchy (emirate)
LANGUAGES: Arabic (official), English
MONEY: Qatari rial
LIFE EXPECTANCY: 78
LITERACY RATE: 89%

Guess What? *Qatar is scheduled to host the FIFA World Cup, the world's biggest international soccer competition, in 2022.*

ROMANIA

LOCATION: Europe
CAPITAL: Bucharest
AREA: 92,043 sq mi (238,391 sq km)
POPULATION ESTIMATE (2012): 21,848,504
GOVERNMENT: Republic
LANGUAGES: Romanian (official), Hungarian, Romany
MONEY: Leu
LIFE EXPECTANCY: 74
LITERACY RATE: 97%

Guess what? *Monks and nuns at Romania's painted monasteries strike wooden beams as a call to prayer, a tradition that started when invading Turks forbade the ringing of bells.*

RUSSIA

LOCATION: Europe and Asia
CAPITAL: Moscow
AREA: 6,601,668 sq mi (17,098,242 sq km)
POPULATION ESTIMATE (2012): 138,082,178
GOVERNMENT: Federation
LANGUAGES: Russian, others
MONEY: Ruble
LIFE EXPECTANCY: 66
LITERACY RATE: 99%

Guess what? *Russia is the largest country in the world. It covers one-seventh of the total land on Earth.*

RWANDA

LOCATION: Africa
CAPITAL: Kigali
AREA: 10,169 sq mi (26,338 sq km)
POPULATION ESTIMATE (2012): 11,689,696
GOVERNMENT: Republic
LANGUAGES: Kinyarwanda, French, and English (all official)
MONEY: Rwandan franc
LIFE EXPECTANCY: 58
LITERACY RATE: 70%

Guess what? *Rwanda is Africa's most densely populated country.*

SAINT KITTS AND NEVIS

LOCATION: Caribbean
CAPITAL: Basseterre
AREA: 101 sq mi (261 sq km)
POPULATION ESTIMATE (2012): 50,726
GOVERNMENT: Parliamentary democracy
LANGUAGE: English
MONEY: East Caribbean dollar
LIFE EXPECTANCY: 75
LITERACY RATE: 98%

Guess what? *Both the islands of Saint Kitts and Nevis, seperated by only a 1.9-mile (3.1 km) stretch of water, are home to large volcanoes. However only Mount Nevis, located on Nevis, may still be active.*

SAINT LUCIA

LOCATION: Caribbean
CAPITAL: Castries
AREA: 238 sq mi (616 sq km)
POPULATION ESTIMATE (2012): 162,178
GOVERNMENT: Parliamentary democracy
LANGUAGES: English (official), French patois
MONEY: East Caribbean dollar
LIFE EXPECTANCY: 77
LITERACY RATE: 90%

Guess what? *The Saint Lucia parrot is native only to Saint Lucia island. It is the country's national bird.*

SAINT VINCENT AND THE GRENADINES

LOCATION: Caribbean
CAPITAL: Kingstown
AREA: 150 sq mi (389 sq km)
POPULATION ESTIMATE (2012): 103,537
GOVERNMENT: Parliamentary democracy
LANGUAGES: English, French patois
MONEY: East Caribbean dollar
LIFE EXPECTANCY: 74
LITERACY RATE: 96%

Guess what? *Kingstown is known as the "City of Arches" because of the decorations found on the buildings and walkways there.*

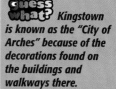

SAMOA

LOCATION: Oceania
CAPITAL: Apia
AREA: 1,093 sq mi (2,831 sq km)
POPULATION ESTIMATE (2012): 194,320
GOVERNMENT: Parliamentary democracy
LANGUAGES: Samoan, English
MONEY: Tala
LIFE EXPECTANCY: 73
LITERACY RATE: 100%

Guess what? *Samoa, now independent, was once ruled by Germany and New Zealand.*

SAN MARINO

LOCATION: Europe
CAPITAL: San Marino
AREA: 24 sq mi (61 sq km)
POPULATION ESTIMATE (2012): 32,140
GOVERNMENT: Republic
LANGUAGE: Italian
MONEY: Euro (formerly Italian lira)
LIFE EXPECTANCY: 83
LITERACY RATE: 96%

Guess what? *According to legend, San Marino was founded by a stonemason who wanted religious freedom in 301 A.D.*

SAO TOME AND PRINCIPE

LOCATION: Africa
CAPITAL: São Tomé
AREA: 372 sq mi (964 sq km)
POPULATION ESTIMATE (2012): 183,176
GOVERNMENT: Republic
LANGUAGE: Portuguese (official)
MONEY: Dobra
LIFE EXPECTANCY: 63
LITERACY RATE: 85%

Guess what? *Cocoa is the most important crop to the economy of São Tomé and Prícipe.*

SAUDI ARABIA

LOCATION: Middle East
CAPITAL: Riyadh
AREA: 830,000 sq mi (2,149,690 sq km)
POPULATION ESTIMATE (2012): 26,534,504
GOVERNMENT: Monarchy
LANGUAGE: Arabic
MONEY: Saudi riyal
LIFE EXPECTANCY: 74
LITERACY RATE: 79%

Guess what? *Mecca and Medina are the two holiest sites in the Islamic religion. Both places are in Saudi Arabia.*

SENEGAL

LOCATION: Africa
CAPITAL: Dakar
AREA: 75,955 sq mi (196,722 sq km)
POPULATION ESTIMATE (2012): 12,969,606
GOVERNMENT: Republic
LANGUAGES: French (official), Wolof, Pulaar, Jola, Mandinka
MONEY: CFA franc
LIFE EXPECTANCY: 60
LITERACY RATE: 39%

Guess what? *About 94% of the population of Senegal is Muslim. But the country's first president, Leopold Senghor, who was elected in 1960, was Catholic.*

SERBIA

LOCATION: Europe
CAPITAL: Belgrade
AREA: 29,913 sq mi (77,474 sq km)
POPULATION ESTIMATE (2012): 7,276,604
GOVERNMENT: Republic
LANGUAGES: Serbian (official), Hungarian, others
MONEY: Serbian dinar
LIFE EXPECTANCY: 75
LITERACY RATE: 96%

Guess what? *The terrain of Serbia varies. It includes mountains, fertile plains, and limestone ranges.*

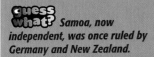

SEYCHELLES

LOCATION: Africa
CAPITAL: Victoria
AREA: 176 sq mi (455 sq km)
POPULATION ESTIMATE (2012): 90,024
GOVERNMENT: Republic
LANGUAGES: Creole, English (official), other
MONEY: Seychelles rupee
LIFE EXPECTANCY: 74
LITERACY RATE: 92%

guess what? *The rare Seychelles bulbul, a small bird, is found only on the islands of Seychelles.*

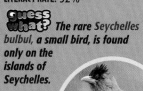

SIERRA LEONE

LOCATION: Africa
CAPITAL: Freetown
AREA: 27,699 sq mi (71,740 sq km)
POPULATION ESTIMATE (2012): 5,485,998
GOVERNMENT: Constitutional democracy
LANGUAGES: English (official), Mende, Temne, Krio
MONEY: Leone
LIFE EXPECTANCY: 56
LITERACY RATE: 35%

guess what? *The Star of Sierra Leone is the world's third largest high-quality diamond, and is worth several million dollars.*

SINGAPORE

LOCATION: Asia
CAPITAL: Singapore
AREA: 269 sq mi (697 sq km)
POPULATION ESTIMATE (2012): 5,353,494
GOVERNMENT: Parliamentary republic
LANGUAGES: Chinese (Mandarin), English, Malay, Hokkien, Cantonese, others
MONEY: Singapore dollar
LIFE EXPECTANCY: 84
LITERACY RATE: 93%

guess what?
The national flower of Singapore is the Vanda Miss Joaquim, a type of orchid. It was discovered in the garden of Miss Agnes Joaquim in 1893.

SLOVAKIA

LOCATION: Europe
CAPITAL: Bratislava
AREA: 18,933 sq mi (49,035 sq km)
POPULATION ESTIMATE (2012): 5,483,088
GOVERNMENT: Parliamentary democracy
LANGUAGES: Slovak (official), Hungarian, Roma, Ukranian
MONEY: Euro (formerly koruna)
LIFE EXPECTANCY: 76
LITERACY RATE: 100%

guess what? *Slovaks usually serve fried carp in their traditional Christmas meals.*

SLOVENIA

LOCATION: Europe
CAPITAL: Ljubljana
AREA: 7,827 sq mi (20,273 sq km)
POPULATION ESTIMATE (2012): 1,996,617
GOVERNMENT: Parliamentary republic
LANGUAGES: Slovenian (official), Serbo-Croatian
MONEY: Euro (formerly Slovenian tolar)
LIFE EXPECTANCY: 77
LITERACY RATE: 100%

guess what? *Lipizzan horses, known for performing, come from Lipica in Slovenia.*

SOLOMON ISLANDS

LOCATION: Oceania
CAPITAL: Honiara
AREA: 111,517 sq mi (28,896 sq km)
POPULATION ESTIMATE (2012): 584,578
GOVERNMENT: Parliamentary democracy
LANGUAGES: English (official), Melanesian pidgin, more than 120 local languages
MONEY: Solomon Islands dollar
LIFE EXPECTANCY: 74
LITERACY RATE: Not available

guess what? *Kavachi, an active underwater volcano, is part of the Solomon Islands.*

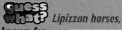

SOMALIA

LOCATION: Africa
CAPITAL: Mogadishu
AREA: 246,199 sq mi
(637,657 sq km)
POPULATION ESTIMATE (2012):
10,085,638
GOVERNMENT: Transitional,
parliamentary federal
government
LANGUAGES: Somali (official),
Arabic, English, Italian
MONEY: Somali shilling
LIFE EXPECTANCY: 51
LITERACY RATE: 38%

guess what? *Somali pirates are a major problem in the waters off East Africa. They take over boats and force people or companies to pay to get their boats or merchandise back.*

SOUTH AFRICA

LOCATION: Africa
CAPITALS: Pretoria (administrative),
Cape Town (legislative),
Bloemfontein (judicial)
AREA: 471,008 sq mi
(1,219,090 sq km)
POPULATION ESTIMATE (2012):
48,810,427
GOVERNMENT: Republic
LANGUAGES: Zulu, Xhosa, Afrikaans,
Sepedi, English, Setswana,
Sesotho, Tsonga, others
MONEY: Rand
LIFE EXPECTANCY: 49
LITERACY RATE: 86%

guess what? *Actress Charlize Theron is from South Africa.*

SPAIN

LOCATION: Europe
CAPITAL: Madrid
AREA: 195,124 sq mi
(505,370 sq km)
POPULATION ESTIMATE (2012):
47,042,984
GOVERNMENT: Parliamentary
monarchy
LANGUAGES: Castilian Spanish
(official), Catalan, Galician,
Basque
MONEY: Euro (formerly peseta)
LIFE EXPECTANCY: 81
LITERACY RATE: 98%

guess what? *Paella, a popular Spanish dish, is made with rice, seafood, sausage, and saffron. One of the world's most expensive spices, saffron is grown in Spain.*

SRI LANKA

LOCATION: Asia
CAPITAL: Colombo
AREA: 25,332 sq mi
(65,610 sq km)
POPULATION ESTIMATE (2012):
21,481,334
GOVERNMENT: Republic
LANGUAGES: Sinhala (official),
Tamil, English
MONEY: Sri Lankan rupee
LIFE EXPECTANCY: 76
LITERACY RATE: 91%

guess what? *Cinnamon originated in Sri Lanka and was first mentioned in writings that date back to 2800 B.C.*

SUDAN

LOCATION: Africa
CAPITAL: Khartoum
AREA: 718,723 sq mi
(1,861,484 sq km)
POPULATION ESTIMATE (2012):
25,946,220
GOVERNMENT: Federal republic
LANGUAGES: Arabic and English
(both official), Nubian, Ta
Bedawie, others
MONEY: Sudanese pound
LIFE EXPECTANCY: 63
LITERACY RATE: 61%

guess what? *Sudan is home to the Sudd marshes, the largest inland wetland in the world.*

SUDAN, SOUTH

LOCATION: Africa
CAPITAL: Juba
AREA: 284,777 sq mi
(644,329 sq km)
POPULATION ESTIMATE (2012):
10,625,176
GOVERNMENT: Republic
LANGUAGES: Arabic and English
(both official), others
MONEY: South Sudanese pound
LIFE EXPECTANCY: Not available
LITERACY RATE: 27%

guess what? *After 98% of participants voted to separate from northern Sudan in January 2011, South Sudan finally became an independent country on July 9, 2011.*

SURINAME

LOCATION: South America
CAPITAL: Paramaribo
AREA: 63,251 sq mi (163,820 sq km)
POPULATION ESTIMATE (2012): 560,157
GOVERNMENT: Constitutional democracy
LANGUAGES: Dutch (official), Surinamese, English, others
MONEY: Surinamese dollar
LIFE EXPECTANCY: 71
LITERACY RATE: 90%

Guess What? *The British traded Suriname to the Dutch in exchange for New Amsterdam, the island now known as Manhattan, part of modern-day New York City.*

SWAZILAND

LOCATION: Africa
CAPITAL: Mbabane
AREA: 6,704 sq mi (17,360 sq km)
POPULATION ESTIMATE (2012): 1,386,914
GOVERNMENT: Monarchy
LANGUAGES: Swati and English (both official)
MONEY: Lilangeni
LIFE EXPECTANCY: 49
LITERACY RATE: 82%

Guess What? *The shield on the Swaziland flag is a traditional Zulu shield. Zulus are an ethnic group of Bantu-speaking people from southeastern Africa.*

SWEDEN

LOCATION: Europe
CAPITAL: Stockholm
AREA: 173,860 sq mi (450,295 sq km)
POPULATION ESTIMATE (2012): 9,103,788
GOVERNMENT: Constitutional monarchy
LANGUAGE: Swedish
MONEY: Krona
LIFE EXPECTANCY: 81
LITERACY RATE: 99%

Guess What? *Sweden's Ice Hotel in the village of Jukkasjarvi is made entirely of snow and ice.*

SWITZERLAND

LOCATION: Europe
CAPITAL: Bern
AREA: 15,937 sq mi (41,277 sq km)
POPULATION ESTIMATE (2012): 7,655,628
GOVERNMENT: Confederation (similar to a federal republic)
LANGUAGES: German, French, Italian, and Romansh (all official), others
MONEY: Swiss franc
LIFE EXPECTANCY: 81
LITERACY RATE: 99%

Guess What? *The alpenhorn, a 9-foot-long (3 m) instrument made of a single log of wood, was used by communities in the Swiss Alps to signal one another.*

SYRIA

LOCATION: Middle East
CAPITAL: Damascus
AREA: 71,498 sq mi (185,180 sq km)
POPULATION ESTIMATE (2012): 22,530,746
GOVERNMENT: Republic under an authoritarian regime
LANGUAGES: Arabic (official), Kurdish, Armenian, Aramaic, Circassian
MONEY: Syrian pound
LIFE EXPECTANCY: 75
LITERACY RATE: 80%

Guess What? *Latakia, a port in western Syria, is thought to have existed since 400 B.C.*

TAIWAN

LOCATION: Asia
CAPITAL: Taipei
AREA: 13,892 sq mi (35,980 sq km)
POPULATION ESTIMATE (2012): 23,113,901
GOVERNMENT: Multiparty democracy
LANGUAGES: Chinese (Mandarin), Taiwanese, Hakka dialects
MONEY: New Taiwan dollar
LIFE EXPECTANCY: 78
LITERACY RATE: 96%

Guess What? *The Formosan black bear is found only in Taiwan.*

Countries

TAJIKISTAN

LOCATION: Asia
CAPITAL: Dushanbe
AREA: 55,251 sq mi
(143,100 sq km)
POPULATION ESTIMATE (2012):
7,768,385
GOVERNMENT: Republic
LANGUAGES: Tajik (official),
Russian
MONEY: Somoni
LIFE EXPECTANCY: 66
LITERACY RATE: 100%

Guess What? *The Silk Road, a major trade route used between the 5th and 12th centuries, passed through Tajikistan.*

TANZANIA

LOCATION: Africa
CAPITALS: Dar es Salaam
(commercial), Dodoma
(political)
AREA: 365,755 sq mi
(947,300 sq km)
POPULATION ESTIMATE (2012):
43,601,796
GOVERNMENT: Republic
LANGUAGES: Swahili and English
(both official), Arabic, others
MONEY: Tanzanian shilling
LIFE EXPECTANCY: 53
LITERACY RATE: 69%

Guess What? *Kilimanjaro, the tallest African mountain, is located in northeastern Tanzania.*

THAILAND

LOCATION: Asia
CAPITAL: Bangkok
AREA: 198,117 sq mi
(513,120 sq km)
POPULATION ESTIMATE (2012):
67,091,089
GOVERNMENT: Constitutional
monarchy
LANGUAGES: Thai (Siamese),
English, regional dialects
MONEY: Baht
LIFE EXPECTANCY: 74
LITERACY RATE: 93%

Guess What? *Muay Thai, a form of boxing, is Thailand's national sport.*

TOGO

LOCATION: Africa
CAPITAL: Lomé
AREA: 21,925 sq mi
(56,785 sq km)
POPULATION ESTIMATE (2012):
6,961,049
GOVERNMENT: Republic, under
transition to multiparty
democratic rule
LANGUAGES: French (official), Ewe,
Mina, Kabye, Dagomba
MONEY: CFA franc
LIFE EXPECTANCY: 63
LITERACY RATE: 61%

Guess What? *Cocoa, coffee, and cotton are the most important crops in Togo.*

TONGA

LOCATION: Oceania
CAPITAL: Nuku'alofa
AREA: 289 sq mi (748 sq km)
POPULATION ESTIMATE (2012): 106,146
GOVERNMENT: Constitutional
monarchy
LANGUAGES: Tongan, English
MONEY: Pa'anga
LIFE EXPECTANCY: 75
LITERACY RATE: 99%

Guess What? *Juggling with tuitui, or candlenuts, is a popular activity for Tongan women.*

TRINIDAD AND TOBAGO

LOCATION: Caribbean
CAPITAL: Port-of-Spain
AREA: 1,980 sq mi (5,128 sq km)
POPULATION ESTIMATE (2012):
1,226,383
GOVERNMENT: Parliamentary
democracy
LANGUAGES: English (official),
Hindi, French, Spanish, Chinese
MONEY: Trinidad and
Tobago dollar
LIFE EXPECTANCY: 72
LITERACY RATE: 99%

Guess What? *The limbo, where a person leans backward and dances under a gradually lowered horizontal pole, was first danced in Trinidad and Tobago.*

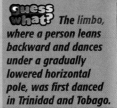

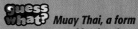

TUNISIA

LOCATION: Africa
CAPITAL: Tunis
AREA: 63,170 sq mi
(163,610 sq km)
POPULATION ESTIMATE (2012):
10,732,900
GOVERNMENT: Republic
LANGUAGES: Arabic (official),
French
MONEY: Tunisian dinar
LIFE EXPECTANCY: 75
LITERACY RATE: 74%

Guess what? *Carthage, a city in northern Tunisia, was an important port until the Romans destroyed it in 146 B.C. Roman ruins can still be seen there today.*

TURKEY

LOCATION: Europe and Asia
CAPITAL: Ankara
AREA: 302,535 sq mi
(783,562 sq km)
POPULATION ESTIMATE (2012):
79,749,461
GOVERNMENT: Republican
parliamentary democracy
LANGUAGES: Turkish (official),
Kurdish, others
MONEY: New Turkish lira
LIFE EXPECTANCY: 73
LITERACY RATE: 87%

Guess what? *Bursa, in northwestern Turkey, was the first capital of the Ottoman Empire. There are more mosques and tombs in Bursa than in any other Turkish city.*

TURKMENISTAN

LOCATION: Asia
CAPITAL: Ashgabat
AREA: 188,455 sq mi
(488,100 sq km)
POPULATION ESTIMATE (2012):
5,054,828
GOVERNMENT: Republic with
authoritarian presidential rule
LANGUAGES: Turkmen (official),
Russian, Uzbek, others
MONEY: Manat
LIFE EXPECTANCY: 69
LITERACY RATE: 99%

Guess what? *The Karakumskiy Canal, which runs through Turkmenistan, is one of the longest irrigation canals in the world.*

TUVALU

LOCATION: Oceania
CAPITAL: Funafuti
AREA: 10 sq mi (26 sq km)
POPULATION ESTIMATE (2012): 10,619
GOVERNMENT: Parliamentary
democracy
LANGUAGES: Tuvaluan and
English (both official),
Samoan, Kiribati
MONEY: Australian dollar,
Tuvaluan dollar
LIFE EXPECTANCY: 65
LITERACY RATE: Not available

Guess what? *The highest point in Tuvalu is only 15 feet (4.6 m) above sea level. Global warming and rising sea levels are a constant concern.*

UGANDA

LOCATION: Africa
CAPITAL: Kampala
AREA: 93,065 sq mi
(241,038 sq km)
POPULATION ESTIMATE (2012):
35,873,253
GOVERNMENT: Republic
LANGUAGES: English (official),
Luganda, Swahili, others
MONEY: Ugandan shilling
LIFE EXPECTANCY: 53
LITERACY RATE: 67%

Guess what? *On the Ugandan flag, the red color represents the brotherhood of man. Black represents the African people, and yellow stands for the sun.*

UKRAINE

LOCATION: Europe
CAPITAL: Kiev
AREA: 233,032 sq mi
(603,550 sq km)
POPULATION ESTIMATE (2012):
44,854,065
GOVERNMENT: Republic
LANGUAGES: Ukrainian, Russian
MONEY: Hryvnia
LIFE EXPECTANCY: 69
LITERACY RATE: 99%

Guess what? *Borscht, a soup made from beets, is the national dish of Ukraine.*

UNITED ARAB EMIRATES

LOCATION: Middle East
CAPITAL: Abu Dhabi
AREA: 32,278 sq mi
(83,600 sq km)
POPULATION ESTIMATE (2012):
5,314,317
GOVERNMENT: Federation
LANGUAGES: Arabic (official),
Persian, English, Hindi, Urdu
MONEY: U.A.E. dirham
LIFE EXPECTANCY: 77
LITERACY RATE: 78%

Guess What? *The 2,717-foot-tall (828 m) Burj Khalifa in Dubai is the tallest building in the world.*

UNITED KINGDOM

LOCATION: Europe
CAPITAL: London
AREA: 94,058 sq mi
(243,610 sq km)
POPULATION ESTIMATE (2012):
63,047,162
GOVERNMENT: Constitutional
monarchy
LANGUAGES: English, Scots,
Scottish Gaelic, Welsh, Irish
MONEY: British pound
LIFE EXPECTANCY: 80
LITERACY RATE: 99%

Guess What? *Big Ben is not the name of the famous clock in London. It is actually the name of the bell inside the clock tower.*

UNITED STATES

LOCATION: North America
CAPITAL: Washington, D.C.
AREA: 3,794,100 sq mi
(9,826,675 sq km)
POPULATION ESTIMATE (2012):
313,847,465
GOVERNMENT: Constitution-based
federal republic
LANGUAGES: English, Spanish
(spoken by a sizable minority)
MONEY: U.S. dollar
LIFE EXPECTANCY: 78
LITERACY RATE: 99%

Guess What? *The first capital city of the United States was New York City.*

URUGUAY

LOCATION: South America
CAPITAL: Montevideo
AREA: 68,039 sq mi
(176,220 sq km)
POPULATION ESTIMATE (2012):
3,316,328
GOVERNMENT: Constitutional
republic
LANGUAGES: Spanish (official),
Portuñol, Brazilero
MONEY: Uruguayan peso
LIFE EXPECTANCY: 76
LITERACY RATE: 98%

Guess What? *About 93% of Uruguayans live in cities, and one-third of those live in the capital.*

UZBEKISTAN

LOCATION: Asia
CAPITAL: Tashkent
AREA: 172,741 sq mi
(447,400 sq km)
POPULATION ESTIMATE (2012):
28,394,180
GOVERNMENT: Republic with
authoritarian presidential rule
LANGUAGES: Uzbek (official),
Russian, Tajik, others
MONEY: Uzbekistani soum
LIFE EXPECTANCY: 73
LITERACY RATE: 99%

Guess What? *In the Kashkadarya and Samarkand regions, 2,700-year-old pyramids were discovered.*

VANUATU

LOCATION: Oceania
CAPITAL: Port-Vila
AREA: 4,710 sq mi (12,200 sq km)
POPULATION ESTIMATE (2012): 227,574
GOVERNMENT: Parliamentary
republic
LANGUAGES: Most people speak
one of more than 100 local
languages; Bislama, English
MONEY: Vatu
LIFE EXPECTANCY: 65
LITERACY RATE: 74%

Guess What? *Pigs are symbols of wealth in Vanuatu. Some banks even accept pig tusks as they would money.*

VATICAN CITY (HOLY SEE)

LOCATION: Europe
CAPITAL: Vatican City
AREA: 0.17 sq mi (0.44 sq km)
POPULATION ESTIMATE (2012): 836
GOVERNMENT: Ecclesiastical
LANGUAGES: Italian, Latin, French
MONEY: Euro
LIFE EXPECTANCY: Not available
LITERACY RATE: 100%

guess what? *Vatican City is the smallest country in the world. The post office there issues official Vatican City stamps.*

VENEZUELA

LOCATION: South America
CAPITAL: Caracas
AREA: 352,143 sq mi (912,050 sq km)
POPULATION ESTIMATE (2012): 28,047,938
GOVERNMENT: Federal republic
LANGUAGES: Spanish (official), native languages
MONEY: Bolivar
LIFE EXPECTANCY: 74
LITERACY RATE: 93%

guess what? *At 3,212 feet tall (979 m), Angel Falls in Venezuela is the world's tallest waterfall.*

VIETNAM

LOCATION: Asia
CAPITAL: Hanoi
AREA: 127,881 sq mi (331,210 sq km)
POPULATION ESTIMATE (2012): 91,519,289
GOVERNMENT: Communist state
LANGUAGES: Vietnamese (official), French, English, Khmer, Chinese
MONEY: Dong
LIFE EXPECTANCY: 72
LITERACY RATE: 94%

guess what? *In Vietnam, people usually eat a soup called pho for breakfast. It consists of broth, rice noodles, bean sprouts, and slices of beef or chicken.*

YEMEN

LOCATION: Middle East
CAPITAL: Sanaa
AREA: 203,849 sq mi (527,970 sq km)
POPULATION ESTIMATE (2012): 24,771,809
GOVERNMENT: Republic
LANGUAGE: Arabic
MONEY: Yemeni rial
LIFE EXPECTANCY: 64
LITERACY RATE: 50%

guess what? *The Romans called Yemen Arabia Felix, or "Happy Arabia," in 26 B.C., because the area was beautiful, rich, and powerful. Much of its wealth came from growing spices.*

ZAMBIA

LOCATION: Africa
CAPITAL: Lusaka
AREA: 290,584 sq mi (752,614 sq km)
POPULATION ESTIMATE (2012): 14,309,466
GOVERNMENT: Republic
LANGUAGES: Bemba, Nyanja, Tonga, Lozi, Lunda, Kaonde, Luvale, and English (all official), others
MONEY: Kwacha
LIFE EXPECTANCY: 53
LITERACY RATE: 81%

guess what? *There are 19 national parks in Zambia. Walking, canoeing, and river-rafting safaris are offered year-round so visitors may see the abundant wildlife there.*

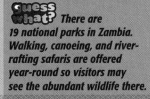

ZIMBABWE

LOCATION: Africa
CAPITAL: Harare
AREA: 150,872 sq mi (390,757 sq km)
POPULATION ESTIMATE (2012): 12,619,600
GOVERNMENT: Parliamentary democracy
LANGUAGES: English (official), Shona, Ndebele (Sindebele)
MONEY: Zimbabwean dollar
LIFE EXPECTANCY: 52
LITERACY RATE: 91%

guess what? *Zimbabwe was known as Southern Rhodesia until its independence from Britain in 1964.*

Countries

COOL LANDMARKS AROUND THE WORLD

La Sagrada Família, Spain

Statue of Liberty, United States

Golden Gate Bridge, United States

Teotihuacán, Mexico

Machu Picchu, Peru

Iguazú Falls, Argentina/Brazil

Leptis Magna, Libya

Colosseum, Italy

St. Basil's Cathedral, Russia

Temple of Apollo, Greece

Sultan Ahmet Mosque (The Blue Mosque), Turkey

Petronas Twin Towers, Malaysia

Pyramids of Giza, Egypt

Taj Mahal, India

Uluru (Ayers Rock), Australia

Dance and Drama

Real-Life *Glee*

By Vickie An

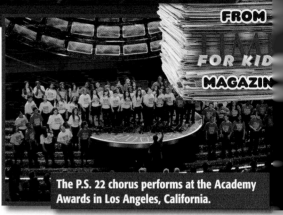

FROM TIME FOR KIDS MAGAZIN

The fifth-grade chorus from Public School 22, in Staten Island, New York, closed out the 2011 Academy Awards on a high note. Most of the kids in the P.S. 22 chorus had never set foot outside of their hometown before, let alone flown on a plane. But, in February 2011, all 65 fifth graders flew across the country to perform at the Academy Awards, in Los Angeles, California.

In December 2010, the kids learned they would be singing at the show. Producer Bruce Cohen and Oscar cohost Anne Hathaway surprised them at P.S. 22's annual winter concert. "You guys have brought such joy to my heart," Hathaway said when she told them the news.

After all the gold statues had been handed out, the singers filed onto the Oscar stage. They swayed as they sang "Over the Rainbow," from *The Wizard of Oz*. The soulful rendition earned a standing ovation from the star-studded crowd.

The P.S. 22 chorus performs at the Academy Awards in Los Angeles, California.

NO STRANGERS TO FAME

P.S. 22 singers are used to the spotlight. Over the years, the chorus has performed for Oprah Winfrey, Lady Gaga, and the Obama family. The glee club is known for its rousing performances of popular tunes. "I always knew the chorus was special," P.S. 22 music teacher Gregg Breinberg said. "I'm thrilled people see in them what I see." Breinberg began posting online videos of the chorus in 2006. Five years later, the videos had been viewed nearly 30 million times. "People give up their free time to listen to us," fifth grader Adham told TIME. "We're pretty proud of that."

All the World's a Stage

Performing on stage can be incredibly rewarding—and incredibly fun.

DANCING From ballet to jazz, tap to hip-hop, there is a type of movement for everyone. Find the style that is perfect for you.

BAND AND ORCHESTRA Do you play an instrument? Marching bands perform at sports games, parades, and other events. Orchestras play at assemblies, concerts, musicals, and more.

SINGING Add your voice to the chorus. Some school singing groups—choirs, choruses, glee clubs—perform at schools, nursing homes, and assemblies.

ACTING Are you a *High School Musical* fan? Maybe the stage is the place for you. School plays and musicals offer tons of great opportunities. Memorizing lines, remembering blocking (onstage movement and positioning), and learning dance numbers can be challenging, but working with your fellow actors can be a blast. You may also find a film club where you can play

Let's Dance

On stage or in your bedroom, dancing is an excellent form of exercise and a way to creatively express yourself. There's a type of movement for every period in history, every age group, and every level of physical strength. Find one that you like and give it a try.

BALLET is a classical dance form that uses precise, formal movements. It started in the royal courts of Europe in the 1600s. Ballet requires dancers to practice many different steps and to hold positions. Learning ballet can make you graceful and strong.

Guess what?

In ballet, a dance for two people is called a "pas de deux," which means "steps for two."

HIP-HOP DANCING, which accompanies hip-hop and rap music, became popular in the 1970s when musicians and dance crews created an exciting and vibrant new culture based on African rhythms and traditions. Most hip-hop dancing is free-style, which means it does not follow any set patterns. Breakdancing, which started in New York's South Bronx neighborhood, is especially athletic. It combines acrobatic moves with freezes that show off a dancer's strength and control. Krumping uses wild, expressive moves of arms and legs. Popping and locking (sometimes called poplocking), were first done in Fresno, California. These movements are more controlled. Dancers lock their joints in fixed positions for a few seconds, sometimes while breakdancing.

Two popular forms of **STEP DANCING** are African stepping (often just called stepping), in which a dancer's whole body is used almost like an instrument to keep beats, and Irish step dancing, which started in Ireland, and features quick, complicated foot movements. African stepping includes steps, words, and handclaps. Steppers use incredibly precise moves and usually perform in groups and sometimes in competition with other groups. Stepping follows other African and Caribbean dance traditions and sometimes includes elements of hip-hop dance and gymnastics.

In Irish step dancing, dancers keep their upper body stiff.

Steppers show off their moves.

JAZZ DANCE is a broad category of movement that includes many styles that are performed to jazz music, show tunes, and pop songs. In general, it is less formal than ballet.

BALLROOM DANCING is done by couples and combines fast and slow steps. The fox trot, waltz, and cha-cha are ballroom dances.

TAP DANCE is all about fancy footwork. Metal taps on the bottom of tap shoes add sounds to dancers' movements.

Dance and Drama

The Play's the Thing

There are many, many plays available for school performances. Choices include full-length and short plays, comedies and dramas, musicals and straight plays, shows with lots of roles (including dancing and choruses), and shows with just a few parts.

SOME POPULAR PLAYS INCLUDE:

Our Town, by Thornton Wilder, follows everyday life in Grover's Corners, a small town in New Hampshire. The two main characters are a young couple, George Gibbs and Emily Webb. A stage manager explains some of the action to the audience.

Mortals and fairies join in the wedding of the Duke of Athens and the Queen of the Amazons in William Shakespeare's *A Midsummer Night's Dream.* Among the players are Oberon and Titania (the King and Queen of the Fairies), a troublemaking fairy named Puck, and an actor named Bottom who has been turned into a donkey.

In *Peter Pan,* by J.M. Barrie, Wendy and her brothers fly to Neverland to help Peter Pan and his lost boys battle Captain Hook. A fairy named Tinker Bell, a Native American princess called Tiger Lily, a ticking crocodile, and a gang of bumbling pirates join the action.

HERE ARE A FEW FAVORITE MUSICALS:

Follow the yellow brick road with Dorothy Gale, the Tin Man, the Scarecrow, and the Cowardly Lion as they visit the Great Wizard to get the things they need most. *The Wizard of Oz,* by L. Frank Baum, includes great songs like "Over the Rainbow" and "Ding Dong, the Witch Is Dead."

The characters from Maurice Sendak's beloved Nutshell Library (*Alligators All Around, Pierre, Chicken Soup with Rice,* and *One Was Johnny*) come to life in The action is directed by sassy Rosie from *The Sign on Rosie's Door.*

The Disney Company turned the fairy tale *Beauty and the Beast* into a spectacular musical with book-loving Belle as the heroine who helps the Beast turn back into a prince. A chorus of household objects join in the musical numbers.

> **Guess what?** Some famous actors who acted in school plays include Morgan Freeman, Emma Watson, Rupert Grint, Zac Efron, and many others.

? MYSTERY PERSON

I wrote plays in England in the 16th and early 17th centuries. Some people call me the greatest writer in the English language. My plays are divided into comedies, tragedies, and histories. I also wrote poetry, including 154 sonnets. My plays have many famous lines, such as: "That which we call a rose by any other name would smell as sweet," "To thine own self be true," and "To be, or not to be, that is the question."

WHO AM I? _____

Answer on page 242.

Other Ways to Shine

Performing on stage is not for everyone, but there are many other ways to participate in the arts. Every one of these jobs is important for a successful show. You may be interested in finding out more about these tasks as a way to join in your school's productions—or as a career for the future.

Costume designers decide what each character in a play will wear. They collect appropriate clothing for performers and sometimes sew new pieces.

Set designers design and paint scenery.

Directors rehearse with the performers and work with them on how best to move around the stage and speak their lines.

Stagehands prepare props and move them on and off the stage between scenes.

Publicists and **marketing people** spread the word about the show and help get audience members excited to see it.

Ticket sellers sell tickets to the performances.

Ushers help the audience find their seats.

ADMIT
★ ONE ★
15174A15A

TIPS FOR BEING YOUR BEST

Research. Find videos of singers, dancers, and actors who have done performances similar to yours. Look for inspiration in their work, but don't just copy someone else. Make every performance your own. If you can, talk to other performers about your role. Read about the time period and traditions of people whose lives you are recreating.

Think. What is making your characters do what they do? How would you react in a similar situation?

Practice, practice, practice. Performing is not easy. Every time you rehearse, you get a little bit better. And practice helps you to avoid getting stage fright.

Deal with stage fright. Most performers get stage fright sometimes. Make sure to do some run-throughs of your performance in front of people so you can get accustomed to an audience.

Focus. Before your performance, take a few minutes to concentrate on what you are doing and put aside any other day-to-day issues that might be on your mind.

Have fun!

WHO DOES WHAT?

TIME FOR KIDS
GAME

There are special titles for some of the people who work in the performing arts. Can you match the titles to their job descriptions?

Someone who writes music		Someone who writes scripts for plays

Conductor

Choreographer

Composer

Playwright

A leader of an orchestra		A person who creates steps for dances

Answer on page 242.

Dance and Drama

Rain Forests at Risk

By Vickie An

Not too long ago, hundreds of thousands of orangutans could be found swinging through the rain forests of Southeast Asia. Today, there are fewer than 60,000 of the great apes left in the wild. Orangutans are listed as endangered. Their home is also in danger of being destroyed.

FROM TIME FOR KIDS MAGAZINE

THE SHRINKING JUNGLE

About 90% of all orangutans live on the island of Borneo, which is divided among the countries of Brunei, Indonesia, and Malaysia. The rest of the apes live on the Indonesian island of Sumatra. Orangutans spend most of their lives climbing, eating, and sleeping in the forest canopy. In the past 30 years, deforestation has destroyed nearly 80% of the orangutan's habitat. As the rain forests disappear, so do the species that rely on them for their survival.

Forestry expert Amity Doolittle says illegal logging and the growth of the palm-oil industry are the main culprits. Palm-oil companies cut down large areas of forest to plant oil-palm trees. Palm oil can be found in everything from cookies to soap. One recent study shows that 20 million Indonesians earn their living through palm oil. This economic growth has consequences. Environmentalists and others are demanding that palm-oil companies follow guidelines to protect forestland. Biruté Mary Galdikas, whose 40 years of studying orangutans is featured in the film *Born to Be Wild*, says the best thing we can do to help orangutans is to be aware of palm-oil use. "Read product labels," she says. "Be responsible."

Rain forests once covered 14% of Earth's land surface. They now cover only 6%. We lose 1.5 acres (6,070 sq m) of rain forest every second.

Rain forests are a critical part of the way the oxygen we breathe is created. Rain forests absorb a huge amount of carbon dioxide and turn it into oxygen. This process helps to regulate the temperature of the world.

Some of the many things that come from rain forests include chocolate, bananas and other fruits, medicines, fibers, plastics, and coffee.

Rain forests are home to more than half of the species in the world. When rain forests die, incredible animals and plants die as well.

THE WORLD'S LAST WILD PLACES

Today, it's rare to find a truly wild part of the world, but there are still pockets of relatively unspoiled land. Conservation International (*conservation.org*) compiled a list of 37 of the Earth's last wild places. These are places that cover at least 3,860 square miles (10,000 sq km) and have fewer than five humans per square kilometer. In these areas, the majority of the original vegetation exists and has not been cut down. Here are a few of these environmental wonders.

Amazonia refers to the Amazon rain forest, which covers parts of Bolivia, Brazil, Colombia, Ecuador, French Guiana, Guyana, Peru, Suriname, and Venezuela.

The Mojave Desert is a dry, arid region mostly found in Southern California. It also includes parts of Arizona, Nevada, and Utah.

The Serengeti, in Kenya and Tanzania, is famous for the overland migration of its wildlife (see also page 23). Parts of the Serengeti are national parks and game reserves.

The Congo Forests of Central Africa spread over parts of Angola, Cameroon, Central African Republic, Democratic Republic of the Congo, Equatorial Guinea, Gabon, and the Republic of the Congo.

The Gran Chaco includes parts of northern Argentina, southeastern Bolivia, and northwestern Paraguay, as well as a tiny portion of Brazil.

The Sundarbans, a mangrove forest and group of forested islands in Bangladesh and India, is home to many endangered species, including the Bengal tiger.

Patagonia, the southernmost region of South America, lies mostly in Argentina and partly in southern Chile.

The Arctic Tundra is found in Canada, Finland, Greenland, Iceland, Norway, Russia, Sweden, and in the U.S. state of Alaska.

Kimberley is a remote region in the northwest of Australia.

The Sudd is a large swamp in Sudan. The White Nile runs through the wetlands of the Sudd.

going green

HELP SAVE THE RAIN FORESTS
Join the fight to help save wild places.

• Educate yourself! Visit the Rainforest Action Network (RAN) at *rainforestheroes.com* for helpful ideas, reading lists, and other information.

• Use less paper. When you buy books, look for those that are printed on recycled paper.

• Try not to use disposable products like paper plates and bags.

• Use less gasoline and plastic. Products from the rain forest are used in making them.

• When your family buys wood products, such as furniture or wall paneling, look for the Forest Stewardship Council (FSC) logo. This group checks to make sure that the wood was harvested with as little damage to the rain forest as possible.

Energy and the Environment

POLLUTION

The Earth is constantly changing. Earthquakes, volcanoes, floods, and other natural forces can alter the planet. Humans also leave their mark on Earth through industrial development, over-farming, and overpopulation. Here are some of the ways human actions pollute the environment.

ACID RAIN

Many pollutants, including sulfur dioxide (SO_2) and nitrogen dioxide (NO_2), are released when fossil fuels such as coal and petroleum are burned. Acid rain is formed when water vapor in the air combines with SO_2 and NO_2 to form sulfuric and nitric acids. Acid rain falls to the ground, damaging trees and other plants. It poisons streams, rivers, and lakes. Fish and other aquatic animals fall ill or die in the poisoned water. Acid rain eats away at stone, destroying buildings and monuments.

TRASH

In 2009, more than 243 million tons of garbage were produced in the United States. That comes to about 4.3 pounds (1.95 kg) of waste per person each day. The greatest danger to wildlife is caused by nonorganic trash, such as plastics, metal, Styrofoam, and glass that take months, years, or even centuries to break down.

SMOG

The word *smog* is a combination of the words *smoke* and *fog*. Car and truck exhaust, the burning of wood, factory emissions, and certain chemical processes release particles into the air. These particles contain pollutants, which can get trapped in the air close to the ground. This smog can be especially harmful to the elderly and people with asthma or other breathing problems.

Smog in some areas of China gets so thick that people often wear masks.

WHAT ARE FOSSIL FUELS?

Most of the energy used in the world today is made by burning fossil fuels. Fossil fuels are found in many places on Earth, usually deep under the Earth's surface. They were formed millions of years ago, when prehistoric plants and animals died and what was left over turned into gooey oil, hard coal, or natural gas. There are two big problems with fossil fuels. The first is that they emit carbon dioxide (CO_2) when they are burned and that CO_2 causes climate change. The second is that fossil fuels are not a renewable resource. At some point, there will be no more fossil fuels left. The more fossil fuels we use up, the harder we have to work to find more.

CHEMICAL CONTAMINATION

Chemical contamination of the Earth comes in different forms, the most common being agricultural pesticides (used to kill insects), herbicides (which kill weeds), and fertilizers (used to enrich the soil), as well as the chemical waste products of factories, especially those that work with metals and plastics. In large amounts, these contaminants can hurt people and wildlife.

Cleaning up after oil spills is time-consuming, difficult work.

OIL SPILLS

Oil poisons, blinds, suffocates, and kills sea creatures. It also harms the birds and land animals that come into contact with polluted water or food sources.

THE DANGERS OF FOSSIL FUELS

About 85% of the energy used in the United States today is supplied by fossil fuels. Unearthing these fuels and using them to create electricity has negative effects on humans, wildlife, and the environment. For example, burning fossil fuels contributes to global warming, causes acid rain, and makes water dirty and air unhealthy. Mining coal damages the land, destroys water supplies, and harms the health of miners.

THE GREENHOUSE EFFECT

Burning fossil fuels creates the energy that can be used to power manufacturing plants, enable you to ride in a car, and keep the lights on in your home. But it also releases carbon dioxide (CO_2) and other gases into Earth's atmosphere, which is made up of layers of gases that surround the planet and protect it from extreme heat and cold.

Gases such as CO_2 and methane trap the heat of the sun in the atmosphere just like the walls of a greenhouse trap heat and moisture inside. In this way, gases like CO_2 and methane help keep the temperature of the planet warm enough for living things. But scientists believe that humans are producing far more CO_2 and methane than the atmosphere needs. As a result, the world is getting warmer.

CLIMATE CHANGE

Earth has gotten more than 1°F (0.6°C) warmer over the past century. That may not seem like a big difference, but even the difference of a single degree can have a devastating effect on the planet:

➡ Warmer air causes wind patterns to shift, leading to climate changes around the world. Some areas are experiencing longer droughts, while others are getting too much rain and flooding. This results in a loss of crops and wildlife.

➡ The surface waters of Earth's oceans are getting warmer. Hurricanes, which feed on warm water, are getting stronger and more numerous.

➡ Tropical diseases are spreading into temperate regions that are becoming warmer.

➡ Glaciers are melting, causing sea levels to rise. This destroys the habitat for polar bears and other animals.

A melting glacier

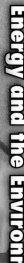
Energy and the Environment

SOURCES OF ENERGY

The energy used to heat homes, manufacture goods, grow and harvest food, transport products, and more comes from two kinds of sources. Renewable energy sources are created continually and are not in danger of running out. Nonrenewable sources, also called fossil fuels, are in limited supply and will be used up entirely.

NONRENEWABLE SOURCES

COAL is a hard rock made of carbon. Many millions of years ago, decaying plant matter underwent a change and transformed into coal. Coal is the largest source of fossil fuel in the United States.

PETROLEUM is found deep within the Earth and has to be drilled and piped up to the surface. It began as decaying plant and animal remains. Like coal, it was formed from pressure and heat over many millions of years. In its "crude" state, before it is refined, it is known as petroleum. Petroleum can be refined into oil, gasoline, or diesel fuel.

NUCLEAR ENERGY was developed in the 20th century. In nuclear fission, the atoms of an element, most often Uranium-235, are hit with atomic particles called neutrons. The uranium atoms are split and give off lots of heat, which is used to boil water. The steam from this water powers electrical generators.

NATURAL GAS was formed in the same way as coal and petroleum, except that it is the odorless by-product of the decaying matter. The bubbles of gas are trapped underground and can be piped to the surface. Natural gas is used as a source of home heating as well as for grilling and cooking.

FINDING FOSSIL FUELS

There are still huge deposits of coal, oil, and natural gas all over the world. The problem is that it is getting very dangerous to access them. For example, companies have been using offshore drilling stations to find oil deep under the ocean floor. Recently, an explosion on an oil rig in the Gulf of Mexico allowed millions of gallons of oil to spew into the ocean, killing marine life and causing enormous environmental damage.

There's a process that some energy companies would like to use to capture natural gas. It's called hydraulic fracturing, or fracking for short. In this process, millions of gallons of fresh water and chemicals are shot down into the Earth, breaking up shale rock and forcing the gas to come up. If the process works, it will give us clean, cheap energy. But it can cause terrible problems. The water used in fracking becomes polluted and can contaminate clean water and soil. The chemicals that are used might get into nearby drinking water. The equipment used for fracking pollutes the air.

Many people object to fracking.

RENEWABLE SOURCES

BIOMASS is an energy source found in plants and animals, such as **switchgrass,** corn, sugar cane, manure, and plant and animal fats.

GEOTHERMAL energy uses the heat that rises from the Earth's core, located about 4,000 miles (6,400 km) under the planet's surface. The most common way of harnessing geothermal energy involves capturing steam that emerges from deep in the Earth by way of volcanoes, fumaroles (vents in ground that give off steam), hot springs, and **geysers** (fountainlike bursts of shooting water). The steam, heat, or hot water can be trapped in pipes that lead directly to electrical power plants and even to homes.

HYDROGEN is the most common element in the universe. It is everywhere, but it doesn't exist on its own. Instead, hydrogen atoms bind with the atoms of other elements to form such compounds as water (hydrogen + oxygen), methane (hydrogen + carbon), and ammonia (hydrogen + nitrogen). Up-to-date technology is being used to separate hydrogen molecules and turn the hydrogen gas into a liquid that can be used in fuel cells. These fuel cells can power vehicles and electrical generators.

WIND farms use huge **turbines** to transform the power of wind into usable energy. Wind turns a turbine's giant blades, which are connected to a long shaft that moves up and down to power an electrical generator.

guess what? The windiest places in the world are not near the cities where people need power. Engineers are working on a high-voltage electrical superhighway that will move the electricity generated by wind to the places where it's needed.

WATER can produce energy called hydropower. Water pressure can turn the shafts of powerful electrical generators, making electricity. Waterfalls and fast-running rivers are major sources of hydropower because their natural flow creates pressure. Another way to harness hydropower is the "storage" method, in which **dams** are used to trap water in large reservoirs. When power is needed, the dams are opened and the water flows out. The water pressure created is then converted into energy.

SUNLIGHT can be converted into heat and electricity. Solar cells absorb the heat from the sun and convert it to energy. Solar power plants collect the sun's heat onto huge **solar panels,** which then heat water to produce steam. This steam powers an electrical generator.

Energy and the Environment

KEEPING WATER CLEAN AND SAFE

About three-quarters of the Earth is covered by water—mostly oceans, but also seas, rivers, lakes, and streams. These bodies of water are habitats for a vast number of animal and plant species, which are important sources of food. And water is a critical part of the way the oxygen we breathe is created. But human activity is harming our waters in many ways.

OVERFISHING Taking fish out of the water faster than they can reproduce puts them in danger of becoming extinct. Some species, like the **bluefin tuna,** are already in danger.

TRAWLING Some commercial fishermen catch fish by dragging nets and other machinery through the water. A practice called bottom trawling involves dragging equipment along the seafloor, which can destroy coral, kill organisms, rip up seaweed, and harm the ocean floor.

SPILLS AND SEEPAGE Substances, such as oil from spills and fertilizer that runs off farmland or seeps into the ground, get into the water. These pollutants can be deadly to the plants and animals that live there.

Many government and private organizations are watching our waters, but there are things the average person can do to help out, such as eating only fish that are not endangered. Throwing away all trash in garbage cans with lids helps to prevent household junk from ending up in waterways. Be sure to conserve water when showering, doing dishes, brushing teeth, and washing the car.

Guess what? The United Nations Food and Agriculture Organization reports that 70% of fish species are being caught at a rate that makes them unable to replenish their populations. Some of the most overfished species are bluefin tuna, swordfish, and Chilean sea bass.

SUSTAINABLE SEAFOOD

Supporting ocean health doesn't mean giving up on your favorite dishes. Here are some fish that are okay to eat:

➡ Shellfish that are grown on fish farms, such as clams, mussels, and crabs

➡ Species that have large populations, such as tilapia (from the U.S.), wild Alaskan salmon, cobia (from the U.S.), catfish, and mackerel

➡ Small fish such as sardines and anchovies

See the list of safe-to-eat fish compiled by the Monterey Bay Aquarium Seafood Watch (*montereybayaquarium.org*).

WHAT'S A DEAD ZONE?

Water is a combination of hydrogen and oxygen. Fish and other marine life need oxygen to live. If the oxygen level in a body of water is drastically reduced, nothing can live in that water. It becomes what is called a "dead zone." Dead zones can happen naturally. More often, they are caused by humans, when nitrogen-rich wastes flow or are dumped into oceans, seas, rivers, streams, and lakes. The nitrogen causes tiny plantlike organisms called phytoplankton to multiply rapidly. When these huge blooms of phytoplankton die, they decompose, which removes oxygen from the water and attracts bacteria, which removes even more oxygen.

To prevent dead zones, farmers should use fewer fertilizers, keep animal waste from reaching waterways, and plant crops that prevent soil from running off into the water. Factories should also work to lessen air pollution.

ENERGY USE AT HOME

The average U.S. household produces more than 26,000 pounds (12,000 kg) of carbon dioxide per year. Here are the activities and objects that use the most energy in the home, along with a few tips on how to cut down your energy use.

Heating the home: 46%
Instead of turning up the heat in the winter, put on a sweatshirt.

Heating water: 14%
Take shorter showers.

Other: 12%
Switch off power strips at night when you go to sleep.

Cooling the home: 7%
Use a fan instead of turning on the air-conditioning.

Computers: 1%
Turn off your computer when you are going to be away from it for more than 45 minutes.

Lighting: 6%
Switch to compact fluorescent lightbulbs (CFLs).

Electronics (such as TVs): 3%
Spend one night a week electronics-free. Read a book or play a board game with your family.

Washing machines: 4%
Wait until you have a full load of laundry before running the washing machine.

Cooking/Cleanup: 3%
Allow dishes to air-dry rather than using the dishwasher's drying cycle.

Refrigeration: 4%
Only open the refrigerator door to get something. Don't let the door hang open while you think about a snack.

Energy and the Environment

89

HOPE FOR THE PLANET

Environmentalists and everyday citizens do their part to combat pollution and to conserve the planet's natural resources. Protecting the environment is an ongoing task, but there have been some great successes in the recent past. Take a minute to read about some environmental efforts that have really paid off.

HEALING THE OZONE LAYER

A layer of gas called ozone protects Earth from the sun's ultraviolet (UV) radiation. Without this layer, everything on Earth would die. In the past century, a huge hole developed in this layer, caused by chemicals such as chlorofluorocarbons (CFCs), which are used in refrigeration and aerosol spray cans. Then scientists and environmental activists convinced the world to take action. In 1987, the Montreal Protocol, an international treaty to phase out use of ozone-depleting chemicals, was signed. The damage has stopped, and the ozone layer is healing. With careful monitoring, the ozone hole will recover in another 50 or more years.

A National Oceanic and Atmospheric Administration researcher launches a weather balloon carrying instruments that measure ozone.

CLEANER CARS

Until recently, most automobiles ran on internal combustion engines, which use large quantities of petroleum and pollute the air with harmful emissions (the gases that are given off by the engines). Spurred by laws that limit the amount of harmful emissions allowed, car manufacturers have developed electric cars and hybrid vehicles (which use a small amount of gas along with electricity). These cars, and the charging stations that power them, are now available throughout the country. Smog and other pollution caused by gas-driven cars has already begun to drop.

A ROARING RETURN

Bald eagles, tigers, and grizzly bears were all in danger. Their habitats were shrinking, and hunters were killing them. But now these amazing animals are bouncing back.

After a united effort by 13 countries to protect them, a recent count of tigers in Asia showed that there are 300 more of them than there were four years ago.

The U.S. Fish and Wildlife Service started the Grizzly Bear Recovery Plan in 1993, which brought these animals back from the brink of extinction. They are still threatened but not endangered.

Bald eagle populations have been on the rise ever since the Migratory Bird Treaty Act and the Bald and Golden Eagle Protection Act helped them increase from only 450 nesting pairs in the early 1960s to an estimated 9,789 nesting pairs today.

EDIBLE SCHOOLYARDS

An Edible Schoolyard in New Orleans

In 1995, chef Alice Waters started "a delicious revolution" in Berkeley, California, near her restaurant Chez Panisse. On a one-acre (4,047 sq m) plot of land, kids learn how to grow and cook food. The Edible Schoolyard has expanded to several schools around the country, teaching thousands of students about the connection between food, the environment, and feeling good. Many more schools have followed Waters's lead and are growing produce on rooftops and working with local farmers to make school lunches fresher, more nutritious, and tastier.

RECYCLE AND SAVE

Before the 1970s, few people recycled. Today, 34% of our waste goes to recycling centers instead of landfills. That represents 85 million tons (77 million metric tons) of garbage that becomes useful again—every single year!

Guess what? In Costa Rica, a 2.5-million-acre (10,117 sq km) marine reserve was established in 2011.

Guess what? After a campaign by Rainforest Action Network, eight children's book publishers pledged not to use any paper that comes from the rain forest in their books.

THE FIRE IN THE RIVER

Forty years ago, Ohio's Cuyahoga River was so full of debris, toxic chemicals, and oil slicks that on June 22, 1969, it burst into flames. Politicians and activists were outraged by the neglected state of rivers throughout the country. The Cuyahoga fire was one of the events that sparked the creation of the U.S. Environmental Protection Agency (EPA). In 1972, the EPA helped get the Clean Water Act passed by Congress. Today, the Cuyahoga River—and other waterways throughout the country—is clean, healthy, and full of fish and other wildlife.

THE REUSABLE BAG CHALLENGE

About 90 billion plastic grocery bags are used in the United States every year. Production of these bags uses huge amounts of petroleum, and the bags create about 9% of the debris found along our coasts. A campaign is now going strong to get people to rely only on reusable bags. The success of this campaign is up to us!

A Balanced Food Plate

By Kelli Plasket

The U.S. Department of Agriculture (USDA) is serving Americans a new plate. To help consumers better balance their meals, the USDA and First Lady Michelle Obama announced in June 2011 that the government is throwing out its familiar but complicated food pyramid. The pyramid had been used to represent nutritional guidelines. It will be replaced by a symbol that the USDA hopes is easier to understand: a food plate.

"When it comes to eating, what's more useful than a plate?" Mrs. Obama said during a news conference unveiling the new icon, called MyPlate. The USDA, which provides nutritional guidelines to consumers, first introduced the food pyramid icon in 1992. The USDA revised the symbol in 2005 to reduce the significance of grains and include exercise. Many nutrition experts had criticized the pyramid-shaped guide. It was too complicated for people to easily understand when making food choices, they said. So the USDA partnered with Michelle Obama and her Let's Move campaign to better show consumers how to build a healthy meal. The Let's Move initiative aims to "put children on the path to a healthy future."

"This is a quick, simple reminder for all of us to be more mindful of the foods that we're eating," the First Lady said at the conference. She emphasized the importance of having a kid-friendly nutrition symbol. "[Children] can learn to use this tool now and use it for the rest of their lives," she said.

IT'S NOT A "PIE" CHART!

The plate icon is a colorful circle graph divided into four sections representing fruits, vegetables, protein, and grains, plus an additional small circle on the side for dairy. It illustrates that half your meals should be fruits and vegetables, a little more than a quarter should be whole grains, and a bit less than a quarter should be protein, plus a small amount of dairy. The symbol also serves as a reminder to control portion sizes and to consider various options for each category.

First Lady Michelle Obama unveils MyPlate at a news conference in Washington, D.C., on June 4, 2011.

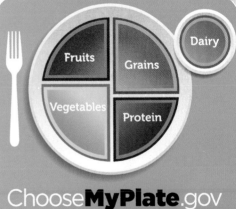

ChooseMyPlate.gov

MyPlate aims to help Americans make healthier food choices.

TIPS FOR HEALTHY EATING

On the MyPlate website, *choosemyplate.gov*, the USDA provides a tool to determine more specific serving sizes based on your age and health. Other dietary guidelines from the USDA include eating whole grains for at least half your grain servings, choosing water and low-fat or fat-free milk over sugary drinks, and selecting soups, bread, and frozen meals with lower sodium, or salt, levels.

Michael Pollan, author of many books about food, including *Food Rules: An Eater's Manual,* offers this short and easy advice about eating: Eat food. Not too much. Mostly plants.

EAT FOOD

A lot of the products on supermarket shelves contain ingredients, such as preservatives, coloring, and artificial flavors, that aren't really food. Some food is processed to make it easy to ship and store for long periods of time. It's best to eat food that has been processed as little as possible.

NOT TOO MUCH

Our bodies tell us when we have had enough food, but we sometimes eat so fast that our brains can't catch up with the signals that our stomachs send them. Eating too much can lead to obesity and contribute to ill health. Eating more slowly is one way to combat overeating.

MOSTLY PLANTS

Meat, poultry, fish, and dairy products can be healthy, but it's a good idea to limit them. Eating foods that started out as plants—fruits, vegetables, grains, nuts, and seeds— will provide you with the nutrients you need and will keep you feeling good.

TRY SOMETHING NEW

Familiar dishes are comforting. But it can be lots of fun to try out new foods.

Here are three fabulous fruits that are worth a try.

Pomegranates have a tart taste. You cut them open and eat the seeds.

Ugli fruit is sweeter and less bitter than grapefruit. It is very juicy.

A **pluot** (*ploo*-ot; also called an aprium) is a cross between a plum and an apricot.

Have you eaver heard of these great grains?

Quinoa (*keen*-wa) is packed with protein.

Couscous (*koos*-koos) is a tiny pasta.

Farro is dense and chewy.

Try these lesser-known (but very tasty) veggies.

Ground cherries are small and sweet. They come wrapped in their own paper casing.

Edamame (ed-uh-*ma*-may) are fresh soybeans. Just pop them out of their shells and into your mouth.

Romanesco broccoli looks a lot like pointy cauliflower. It tastes like a cross between broccoli and cauliflower.

NUTRITION BASICS

Food provides the human body with the nutrients it needs to grow, repair itself, and keep fit and healthy. These nutrients include proteins, carbohydrates, fats, vitamins, and minerals.

PROTEINS

Proteins, found in fish, meat, poultry, eggs, nuts, dairy products, and legumes (such as peanuts, lentils, and beans), keep us strong. They help the body build new cells and repair damaged ones. Most Americans eat much more protein than they actually need. Excess protein is often stored in our bodies as fat.

EAT THE RAINBOW!
Consuming many different-colored foods in a day helps ensure that you get lots of different vitamins and minerals.

CARBOHYDRATES

Carbohydrates are the body's main source of fuel. Your body breaks down carbohydrates into glucose (blood sugar), which travels through your bloodstream and supplies your cells with energy. **Simple carbohydrates**, which are found in fruits, soda, candy, and table sugar, are digested quickly. **Complex carbohydrates** (fiber and starches), which are found in rice, bread, whole grains, pasta, and vegetables, take longer for the body to digest.

FATS

Not only do fats help your body grow, but they also help protect your internal organs and your skin. They should be eaten only in small quantities. There are different types of fats, and some are better for you than others. **Saturated fats** are considered "bad" fats, as they increase your risk for diseases. Saturated fats are most often found in foods that come from animals, including meat, cheese, and butter. **Monounsaturated fats** and **polyunsaturated fats** are considered "good" fats. They lower your risk for disease. These fats are found in olive, safflower, and canola oils, among others. They are also found in fish and nuts.

KEEP MOVING!
In addition to eating healthfully, exercise regularly to stay fit. Playing basketball, tennis, and soccer are great ways to get your heart rate up.

CALORIES

Calories measure how much energy we get from food. You can tell how many calories a food has by looking at the nutrition facts label. Girls ages 9 through 13 need between 1,600 and 2,200 calories a day, while boys of the same age need between 1,800 and 2,600. Eating too many calories can lead to weight gain.

VITAMINS AND MINERALS

Vitamins and minerals are micronutrients that help regulate body processes.

VITAMIN A, found in milk, many greens, carrots, and egg yolks, benefits your skin and eyes.

VITAMIN C, found in many fruits and vegetables, is good for skin, teeth, gums, and the immune system.

VITAMIN D, found in fish, eggs, milk, yogurt, and cheese, helps promote strong bones and teeth, and regulates cell growth.

VITAMIN E, found in spinach, nuts, and olives, has great **antioxidant** properties, and it may lower your risk for heart disease.

MINERALS such as potassium, calcium, iron, and magnesium are necessary for healthy bones, blood, and muscles. Minerals are found naturally in many foods. For example, milk, yogurt, broccoli, and leafy greens like spinach are good sources of calcium, and red meat is high in iron. Minerals are sometimes added to foods to make them more nutritious. You may see calcium-fortified orange juice at the grocery store.

WHAT ARE ANTIOXIDANTS?

Antioxidants are substances in foods that prevent or repair damage to your cells.

GET TO KNOW YOUR FOOD

Growing and cooking food are two wonderful ways to learn more about what you eat.

GROW IT! Does your school have an edible schoolyard (see page 91)? If not, ask your teachers if you can start one. Talk to your parents about growing some veggies or herbs in the backyard—or setting up a pot of lettuce or cherry tomatoes on a windowsill.

COOK IT! One of the best ways to learn about food is to cook it yourself (with a parent's help and permission, of course). Read up on new recipes and try out a few. Ask your parents, grandparents, and neighbors to share kitchen tips with you. For more information, sign up for a cooking class.

FOOD FIRSTS

FROZEN FOOD Clarence Birdseye, a Brooklyn businessman, read about how people in the Arctic froze fish in seawater. He bought a $7 electric fan and some ice and invented the first system for freezing food in 1924. He later packed his frozen food into waxed cardboard boxes and sold his idea to General Foods for $22 million. Birdseye frozen vegetables are still sold in grocery stores today.

BANANAS Bananas were introduced to U.S. consumers at the 1876 Philadelphia Centennial Exposition. They were sold for 10 cents each and became a crowd favorite.

PIZZA People have been eating foods that are sort of like pizza (bread baked with a topping) for many centuries. But the pizza we see so often today—with tomato sauce, mozzarella cheese, and basil (or other herbs)—has an official story. In 1899, Italian King Umberto and Queen Margherita visited a restaurant in Naples and were served three special pizzas. The queen said she liked the one that was red, white, and green best because it reminded her of the Italian flag.

POTATO CHIPS In 1853, George Crum, a Native American chef, was working in a restaurant in Saratoga Springs, New York, when a customer sent back his french fries because they were too thick. George was annoyed and decided to make the fries so thin that they couldn't be picked up with a fork. He sent these ultrathin fries out to the customer—who loved them. Soon, everyone in the restaurant was asking for chips, and the craze spread throughout the country.

POPSICLES In 1905, an 11-year-old boy named Fred Epperson left his glass of lemonade, with a stirrer in it, on his windowsill on a cold night. The next morning, he tasted the frozen results and loved it. Eighteen years later, he began selling frozen treats. At first he called them Epsicles, but he soon changed the name to Popsicles.

CANDY CANES Christmas trees became popular in Europe in the 17th century, and people usually decorated them with food such as cookies and stick candies. In 1670, the choirmaster at the Cologne Cathedral in Germany bent some of the stick candies to make them look like shepherds' staffs. It became a custom to give these to children.

SANDWICHES John Montagu (1718–1792), the fourth Earl of Sandwich, loved to play cards. He didn't want to leave his games to eat. So he invented a dish that could be eaten with one hand. He put roast beef between two slices of bread and ate while he played.

MYSTERY PERSON

I was born in Missouri in 1864. In the years following the Civil War, I realized that cotton should not be the only crop grown in the South because it took all the nutrients out of the soil. I became a botanist and experimented with different crops, such as soybeans, sweet potatoes, and peanuts. These became major crops in the South and helped southern farmers and the whole region.

WHO AM I? _____

Answer on page 242.

The term *organic* usually refers to food that has been processed or cultivated without the use of any chemicals such as fertilizers, pesticides, or artificial additives. Organic farmers believe that these materials are harmful to the environment and bad for the consumer. Organic foods are more expensive to produce and therefore cost more. Many people believe that organic food is safer to eat than food exposed to chemicals.

BUY LOCAL

A lot of our food is grown by huge companies on very big farms and sent across the country by train and truck. This transportation burns a lot of gas, causing air pollution. We can avoid this by buying food that is grown closer to us. To find local food, visit farmstands or go online and see if there is a farmers' market near you. Some supermarkets label the local food.

AROUND-THE-WORLD DISHES

In some countries, a particular food is part of the way people think of their homeland. For example, in the United States, we say that some things are "as American as apple pie." Draw lines to connect each of these foods to its picture and to the name of the country where it is often eaten.

GADO GADO
Salad with hard-boiled egg and peanut sauce

TOM-YUM
Fish soup with seafood, lime, lemongrass, herbs, and spices

MOUSSAKA
Ground lamb with eggplant, tomato sauce, and custard

COLCANNON
Mashed potatoes with cabbage and/or kale

CREPE
A thin pancake with sweet or savory fillings

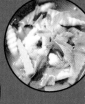

THAILAND   **INDONESIA**   **IRELAND**   **GREECE**   **FRANCE**

Answers on page 242.

Food and Nutrition

Geography

Geography is a science that studies the physical features of planet Earth and the ways human beings interact with and change the world. Geographers study the people and places that make up our planet—including mountains and maps, explorers and the countries they discovered, cities and seas, continents and cultures.

THE CONTINENTS

ANTARCTICA
How big is it? 5,100,000 square miles (13,209,000 sq km)
Highest point Vinson Massif—16,066 feet (4,897 m)
Lowest point Bentley Subglacial Trench—8,383 feet (2,555 m) below sea level

NORTH AMERICA *(including Central America and the Caribbean)*
How big is it? 9,449,460 square miles (24,474,000 sq km)
Highest point Mount McKinley—20,322 feet (6,194 m)
Lowest point Death Valley—282 feet (86 m) below sea level

SOUTH AMERICA
How big is it? 6,879,000 square miles (17,819,000 sq km)
Highest point Mount Aconcagua—22,834 feet (6,960 m)
Lowest point Valdés Peninsula—131 feet (40 m) below sea level

AFRICA
How big is it? 11,608,000 square miles (30,065,000 sq km)
Highest point Kilimanjaro—19,341 feet (5,895 m)
Lowest point Lake Assal—512 feet (156 m) below sea level

EUROPE
How big is it? 3,837,000 square miles (9,938,000 sq km)
Highest point Mount Elbrus—18,481 feet (5,642 m)
Lowest point Caspian Sea—92 feet (28 m) below sea level

ASIA *(including the Middle East)*
How big is it? 17,212,000 square miles (44,579,000 sq km)
Highest point Mount Everest—29,035 feet (8,850 m)
Lowest point Dead Sea—1,286 feet (392 m) below sea level

AUSTRALIA/OCEANIA
How big is it? 3,132,000 square miles (8,112,000 sq km)
Highest point Mount Wilhelm—14,794 feet (4,509 m)
Lowest point Lake Eyre—52 feet (16 m) below sea level

EARTH ON THE MOVE

The Earth's rocky crust is not a solid piece. It's broken into seven major plates and several minor ones. These plates all move across, under, or over one another. The breakup and movement of different plates is called plate tectonics.

DIVERGENT movements occur when plates are pushed apart from one another by magma rushing to the surface. Pieces from each plate sink toward the Earth's core, forming a valley, or rift.

The Great Rift Valley in East Africa is the result of diverging plates.

CONVERGENT movements occur when plates crash into one another. Converging plates can form trenches and mountains, such as the Andes Mountains in South America.

Andes Mountains

LATERAL (also called transforming) movements occur when plates move alongside one another in different directions. This sideswiping motion causes earthquakes. The San Andreas Fault, in California, is a place where laterally moving plates meet. It is often struck by earthquakes.

THE OCEANS

More than 70% of the surface of the Earth is made up of water. Here are the five oceans that cover much of the planet.

1. PACIFIC OCEAN
Area: 60,060,700 square miles
(155,557,000 sq km)
Average depth: 15,215 feet (4,638 m)

2. ATLANTIC OCEAN
Area: 29,637,900 square miles
(76,762,000 sq km)
Average depth: 12,880 feet (3,926 m)

3. INDIAN OCEAN
Area: 26,469,500 square miles
(68,556,000 sq km)
Average depth: 13,002 feet (3,963 m)

4. SOUTHERN OCEAN
Area: 7,848,300 square miles
(20,327,000 sq km)
Average depth: 13,100–16,400 feet*
(4,000–5,000 m)

5. ARCTIC OCEAN
Area: 5,427,000 square miles
(14,056,000 sq km)
Average depth: 3,953 feet
(1,205 m)

*Official depths of the Southern Ocean are in dispute.

guess what? The Pacific Ocean covers about one-third of Earth's surface.

TIME ZONES

Earth spins as it moves around the sun. For part of the day, each area of the Earth is facing away from the sun. That's why it is dark at night. As an area comes back into view of the sun, morning light arrives. But it doesn't arrive for all parts of the world at the same time.

Before there were telephones, telegraphs, fast cars, and airplanes, a person couldn't communicate quickly with someone in another part of the world. But as transportation and communication improved, people needed to standardize time schedules. In 1879, Canadian engineer Sir Sandford Fleming convened several conferences to create a standard world clock that would divide the day into 24 time zones. By the early 1900s, the 24-hour day and 40 land time zones were accepted by most countries.

When it is 5:00 pm on Monday in New York City, it is . . .

2:00 p.m. Monday in **Las Vegas, NV**
4:00 p.m. Monday in **Minneapolis, MN**
5:00 p.m. Monday in **Cleveland, OH**
7:00 p.m. Monday in **Buenos Aires, Argentina**
10:00 p.m. Monday in **Accra, Ghana**
11:00 p.m. Monday in **Paris, France**
12:00 a.m. Tuesday in **Johannesburg, South Africa**
1:00 a.m. Tuesday in **Kuwait City, Kuwait**
2:00 a.m. Tuesday in **Moscow, Russia**
5:00 a.m. Tuesday in **Hanoi, Vietnam**
7:00 a.m. Tuesday in **Tokyo, Japan**
9:00 a.m. Tuesday in **Melbourne, Australia**

guess what?
China officially uses only one time. The country is huge and covers the area of five time zones, but the government decreed that the time would be the same all over China.

Archipelago in New Zealand

Faafu Atoll, Maldives

Bay on the Côte d'Azur, France

Buttes in Utah

Zion Canyon, Utah

WORLDLY WORDS

Altitude is the height of an object above sea level. It tells you how tall a mountain or other area is.

A group of scattered islands is called an **archipelago.** Many archipelagoes have formed in isolated parts of the ocean. Examples include Hawaii, the Philippines, Indonesia, and Fiji.

An **atoll** is a coral island or group of coral islands, often made up of a reef surrounding a lagoon.

A **bay** is a section of an ocean or lake that fills an indentation in the coastline. Large bays are usually called **gulfs.** Examples include San Francisco Bay and the Gulf of Mexico.

A **butte** is a flat-topped hill or rock formation with steep sides. Many buttes are found in the southwestern United States.

A **canal** is a man-made waterway. The Suez and Panama Canals are two well-known examples built to provide shorter passageways for people and goods.

A **canyon** is a deep, narrow valley with steep sides. The Grand Canyon in the United States and the Copper Canyon in Mexico are well-known examples.

EARTH FACTS

Estimated weight (mass): 13 septillion pounds (6 septillion kg)
Estimated age: 4.6 billion years
Current population: Approximately 7 billion
Surface area: 196,936,994 sq mi (510,064,472 sq km)

Plateau in Newfoundland, Canada

The **equator** is an imaginary line drawn all the way around the world. It is located halfway between the North and South Poles. Above the equator, you will find the Northern Hemisphere, and below, the Southern Hemisphere.

A **fjord** is a narrow inlet of sea that is bordered by steep cliffs. There are many fjords along the coastline of Norway.

An **isthmus** is a narrow piece of land that connects two larger land areas.

An **oasis** is a small green area in a desert region. Water is usually present at an oasis.

The state of Florida is an example of a **peninsula,** which is a piece of land that juts into the water.

A **plateau** is a mountain with a wide, flat top. Plateaus are a common in the U.S. Southwest.

A **sea** is an inland body of water. It is often filled with salt water and is sometimes connected to the ocean. The Red Sea and the Caspian Sea are examples.

A **strait,** sometimes called a **channel,** is a narrow strip of water connecting two larger bodies of water. The Bering Strait is between Alaska and Russia. The English Channel separates Great Britain and France.

Isthmus in Montenegro

Huacachina Oasis, Peru

1. Largest freshwater lake (by surface area) Lake Superior, on the United States–Canada border, has the largest surface area.

2. Largest freshwater lake (by volume) Lake Baikal, in southern Russia, has the greatest amount of water.

3. Largest saltwater lake The landlocked Caspian Sea has a greater volume of water than any other lake, including all freshwater lakes.

4. Lowest place Deep in the Pacific Ocean is the Mariana Trench, which is 35,827 feet (10,920 m) below sea level.

5. Highest place Mount Everest in Nepal, the world's tallest mountain, stands 29,035 feet (8,850 m) above sea level.

WHERE IN THE WORLD?

6. Largest rain forest The Amazon in South America covers parts of Brazil, Bolivia, Ecuador, Peru, Colombia, Venezuela, Suriname, French Guiana, and Guyana.

7. Largest desert Stretching across most of North Africa, the Sahara desert covers 3.5 million square miles (9 million sq km).

8. Longest river The Nile runs for 4,145 miles (6,654 km).

9. Largest volcano At about 50,000 feet (15,240 m) from tip to base, Mauna Loa in Hawaii is actually taller than Mount Everest. But most of the volcano is under the sea.

10. Hottest place On September 13, 1922, the temperature reached 136°F (57.8°C) in El Azizia, Libya.

11. Coldest place Vostok, Antarctica, reached a low of −129°F (−89°C) on July 21, 1983.

12. Most populous city Shanghai, located on the Yangtze River Delta in eastern China is home to more than 17 million people.

Goreme, Turkey, was built on volcanic rock left over from ancient volcanic eruptions. The houses in Goreme are built around caves, pointy rock peaks (known as fairy chimneys), and other unique and colorful rock formations. About 2,500 people live there.

STRANGE CITIES

Most cities are built in areas that make life easy—with flat land, big harbors, and access to neighboring communities. But others are built on top of water, in the desert, or deep in the forest. Here are a few of the world's unusual cities.

All the homes in **Ganvie, Benin** (West Africa), are built on stilts above Lake Nakoué. The town was settled 400 years ago by the Tofinu people, who believed their enemies wouldn't pursue them over water. Today, the 30,000 residents of this lake-top city get around in hand-carved boats. The only building on dry land is the town school.

Iquitos, Peru, is home to about 370,000 people. It is located in a rain forest on the banks of the Amazon River. The city looks pretty ordinary, but if you venture outside, you're in deep jungle, with exotic tropical animals and vegetation so thick you'd need a strong knife, like a machete, to cut a path. Other than one small route to a neighboring town, there are no roads into Iquitos. Everything and everybody comes and goes by helicopter, airplane, or boat.

Matera was one of the first settlements in **Italy**. It dates back to the Stone Age. The ancient city was built on top of a small canyon, and the houses are carved right into the soft stone. These cave dwellings were slums for several hundred years, but in the 1950s, the government began renovating the area.

Venice, Italy, has been called the most beautiful city in the world. It has intricate architecture, museums, restaurants, and art galleries. What it doesn't have is streets. Venice is built on 117 small islands that dot a marshy lagoon. The waterways have been turned into canals, and people travel them by boat or big canoes called gondolas.

MYSTERY PERSON

I am a Portuguese explorer. In 1519, I began the first journey to circumnavigate, or travel around, the world. My crew and I were the first Europeans to cross the Pacific Ocean. I died before the end of the voyage. A strait in South America bears my name.

WHO AM I? _____

Answer on page 242.

Geography

103

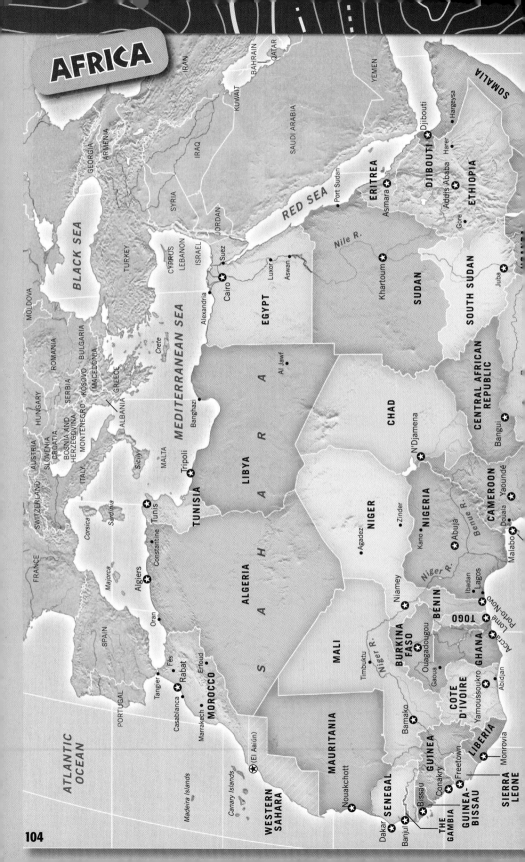

AFRICA

GEORGIA
ARMENIA
IRAN
KUWAIT
BAHRAIN
QATAR
SAUDI ARABIA
YEMEN

SOMALIA

Djibouti
DJIBOUTI
Hargeysa
Harer
Addis Ababa
ETHIOPIA
Gore

ERITREA
Asmara
Port Sudan
RED SEA

BLACK SEA
MOLDOVA
ROMANIA
BULGARIA
KOSOVO
MACEDONIA
SERBIA
MONTENEGRO
BOSNIA AND HERZEGOVINA
CROATIA
SLOVENIA
HUNGARY
AUSTRIA
SWITZERLAND
ITALY
ALBANIA
GREECE
MALTA
Sicily
Sardinia
Corsica
Majorca
FRANCE
SPAIN
PORTUGAL
Madeira Islands
Canary Islands

TURKEY
CYPRUS
LEBANON
ISRAEL
SYRIA
IRAQ
JORDAN

Crete
MEDITERRANEAN SEA

Alexandria
Cairo
Suez
Luxor
Aswan
Nile R.
Khartoum
SUDAN
SOUTH SUDAN
Juba

EGYPT

Al Jawf

S   A   H   A   R   A

Banghazi
Tripoli
LIBYA

CHAD
N'Djamena

CENTRAL AFRICAN REPUBLIC
Bangui

TUNISIA
Tunis
Constantine

NIGER
Agadez
Zinder
Kano
NIGERIA
Abuja
Ibadan
Lagos
Benue R.
CAMEROON
Yaoundé
Douala
Malabo

Algiers
Oran
ALGERIA

MALI
Timbuktu
Niger R.
Niamey
BURKINA FASO
Ouagadougou
Gaoua
BENIN
TOGO
Lomé
Porto-Novo
Accra
GHANA
Abidjan
COTE D'IVOIRE
Yamoussoukro
Niger R.

Tangier
Fès
Rabat
Casablanca
Marrakech
Erfoud
MOROCCO
(El Aaiún)

WESTERN SAHARA

MAURITANIA
Nouakchott
Bamako
Dakar
SENEGAL
Banjul
THE GAMBIA
Bissau
GUINEA-BISSAU
Conakry
GUINEA
Freetown
SIERRA LEONE
Monrovia
LIBERIA

ATLANTIC OCEAN

INDIAN
OCEAN

Mombasa

Dar es Salaam

Nacala

MADAGASCAR

Antananarivo

Moroni

COMOROS

Mozambique Channel

BURUNDI

Bujumbura

Kigoma

Lake
Tanganyika

THE CONGO

Kananga

Kinshasa

Brazzaville

Pointe-Noire

Luanda

ANGOLA

Lubango

Namibe

Walvis Bay

NAMIBIA

Windhoek

Lubumbashi

Kitwe

ZAMBIA

Lusaka

BOTSWANA

Gaborone

Dodoma

TANZANIA

Zanzibar

Lake
Nyasa

MALAWI

Lilongwe

Blantyre

MOZAMBIQUE

ZIMBABWE

Harare

Beira

Maputo

Pretoria

Johannesburg

Mbabane

SWAZILAND

LESOTHO

Maseru

Bloemfontein

SOUTH
AFRICA

Durban

Port Elizabeth

Cape Town

ATLANTIC
OCEAN

0 mi   500 mi   1,000 mi

0 km   500 km   1,000 km

Geography

ASIA AND THE MIDDLE EAST

IRELAND
UNITED KINGDOM
NETHERLANDS
BELGIUM
FRANCE LUXEMBOURG
GERMANY
SWITZERLAND
AUSTRIA
SLOVENIA
ITALY
CROATIA
BOSNIA AND
HERZEGOVINA
MONTENEGRO
ALBANIA
MACEDONIA
GREECE
NORWAY SWEDEN
DENMARK
FINLAND
ESTONIA
RUSSIA LATVIA
LITHUANIA
POLAND
BELARUS
CZECH
REPUBLIC
SLOVAKIA
HUNGARY
UKRAINE
MOLDOVA
ROMANIA
YUGOSLAVIA
KOSOVO
BULGARIA

RUSSIA

Khanty-Mansiysk
Yakaterinburg
Chelyabinsk
Magnitogorsk
Omsk
Novosibirs
K

Imeni Gastello
Astana
KAZAKHSTAN
Qaraghandy
(Karaganda)

Istanbul
Black
Sea
Izmir
Ankara
GEORGIA
Caspian
Sea
T'bilisi
Tyuratam
Aral
Sea
TURKEY
ARMENIA
Yerevan
Adana
Baku
Nukus
UZBEKISTAN
Bishkek
Almaty
CYPRUS
Nicosia
Aleppo
AZERBAIJAN
Tashkent
KYRGYZSTAN
LEBANON
Beirut
Mosul
Tabriz
TURKMENISTAN
Samarkand
Fergana
ISRAEL SYRIA
Irbil
Tehran
Ashgabat
Dushanbe
TAJIKISTAN
Tel Aviv
Damascus
Kirkuk
Mashhad
Jerusalem
Amman
Baghdad
Kermanshah
Herat
Claimed
by India
JORDAN
Esfahan
Kabul
Tabuk
IRAQ
Islamabad
Mediterranean
Sea
LIBYA
EGYPT
Kuwait City
Shiraz
IRAN
Kerman
AFGHANISTAN
Srinagar
Faisalabad
Quetta
Multan
KUWAIT
Persian
Gulf
Manama
BAHRAIN
PAKISTAN
Delhi
NEPAL
Kath
Red
Sea
Jidda
Mecca
Riyadh
Doha
Abu Dhabi
QATAR
Kanpur
INDIA
A F R I C A
SAUDI ARABIA
Abha
Muscat
Karachi
Arabian Sea
Nagpur
Kolkata
SUDAN
OMAN
Hyderabad
ERITREA
Sanaa
UNITED ARAB
EMIRATES
Mumbai
(Bombay)
Pune
SOUTH
SUDAN
Taizz
YEMEN
Al Mukalla
DJIBOUTI
Aden
Bay
Ben
Bangalore
Chennai
(Madras)
ETHIOPIA
Cochin
Madurai
Jaffna
UGANDA
KENYA
SOMALIA
INDIAN OCEAN
Colombo
SRI LAN
MALDIVES
Male

0 mi   500 mi   1,000 mi

0 km   500 km   1,000 km

ARCTIC OCEAN

Bering
Sea

Cherskiy

Tiksi

Verkhoyansk

Magadan

Kamchatka
Peninsula

RUSSIA

Yakutsk

Petropavlovsk-
Kamchatskiy

Sea of
Okhotsk

IBERIA

oyarsk

Sakhalin

tsk

Irkutsk

Khabarovsk

Sapporo

Harbin

Ulaanbaatar

Changchun

Vladivostok

MONGOLIA

Gobi

Shenyang

JAPAN

Hohhot

Jinxi

N. KOREA

P'yongyang

Tokyo

Beijing

Nagoya

Tianjin

Seoul

Kyoto

Taiyuan

Jinan

Taegu

Kobe

Osaka

Pusan

S. KOREA

Lanzhou

Qingdao

Hiroshima

Xi'an

Fukuoka

CHINA

Hefei

Nagasaki

Wuhan

Shanghai

PACIFIC
OCEAN

Chengdu

Chongqing

UTAN

Fuzhou

Naha

NGLADESH

Taipei

aka

Xiamen

Mandalay

TAIWAN

hittagong

Liuzhou

Kao-hsiung

NMAR
RMA)

Nanning

Guangzhou

Nay Pyi Taw

Macao
(special
admin.
region)

Hong Kong (special admin. region)

Hanoi

LAOS

Chang Mai

Vientiane

Luzon

THAILAND

Da Nang

Baguio

Quezon City

Bangkok

VIETNAM

Manila

CAMBODIA

PHILIPPINES

Phnom
Penh

Ho Chi Minh City

Cebu

Phuket

Songkhla

Davao

Ipoh

Bandar Seri Begawan

MALAYSIA

BRUNEI

Kota Kinabalu

Medan

Kuching

Manado

Sorong

Jayapura

Kuala Lumpur

Borneo

Irian
Jaya

SINGAPORE

Pontianak

Palu

New Guinea

Singapore

Samarinda

Celebes

Pakanbaru

INDONESIA

Sumatra

Banjarmasin

Palembang

Ujungpandang

AUSTRALIA AND OCEANIA

JAPAN

CHINA

TAIWAN

PHILIPPINE SEA

LAOS

VIETNAM

THAILAND

PHILIPPINES

CAMBODIA

NORTHERN MARIANA ISLANDS
Saipan ★ (U.S.)

Agana ★ *Guam*
(U.S.)

Yap Islands

Caroline Islands

Koror
⊙

MICRONESIA

Palikir ★

PALAU

BRUNEI

M A L A Y S I A

Borneo

SINGAPORE

Celebes

Irian Jaya

Wewak

PAPUA NEW GUI

I N D O N E S I A

New Guinea

Honiara ⊙

Sumatra

Dili

Java

EAST TIMOR

Port Moresby

Guadalcan

Timor Sea

Darwin

West Island •

Ashmore and Cartier Islands
(Australia)

Gulf of Carpentaria

Great Barrier Reef

Coral Sea Islands (Australia)

CORAL SEA

Cairns

INDIAN OCEAN

Derby

Townsville

Mackay

Alice Springs

Rockhampton • Gladstone

A U S T R A L I A

Brisbane •

Tropic of Capricorn

Geraldton •

Broken Hill •

Lord Ho Island (Austral

Kalgoorlie •

Whyalla •

Sydney •

Perth •

Esperance •

Adelaide •

Canberra ⊙

Bunbury •

Melbourne •

TASMAN SEA

Hobart •

Tasmania

guess what? The term *Oceania* refers to the islands in the Pacific Ocean, such as New Zealand, Micronesia, French Polynesia, Tonga, and more. Some geographers consider Australia part of Oceania, but others do not.

108

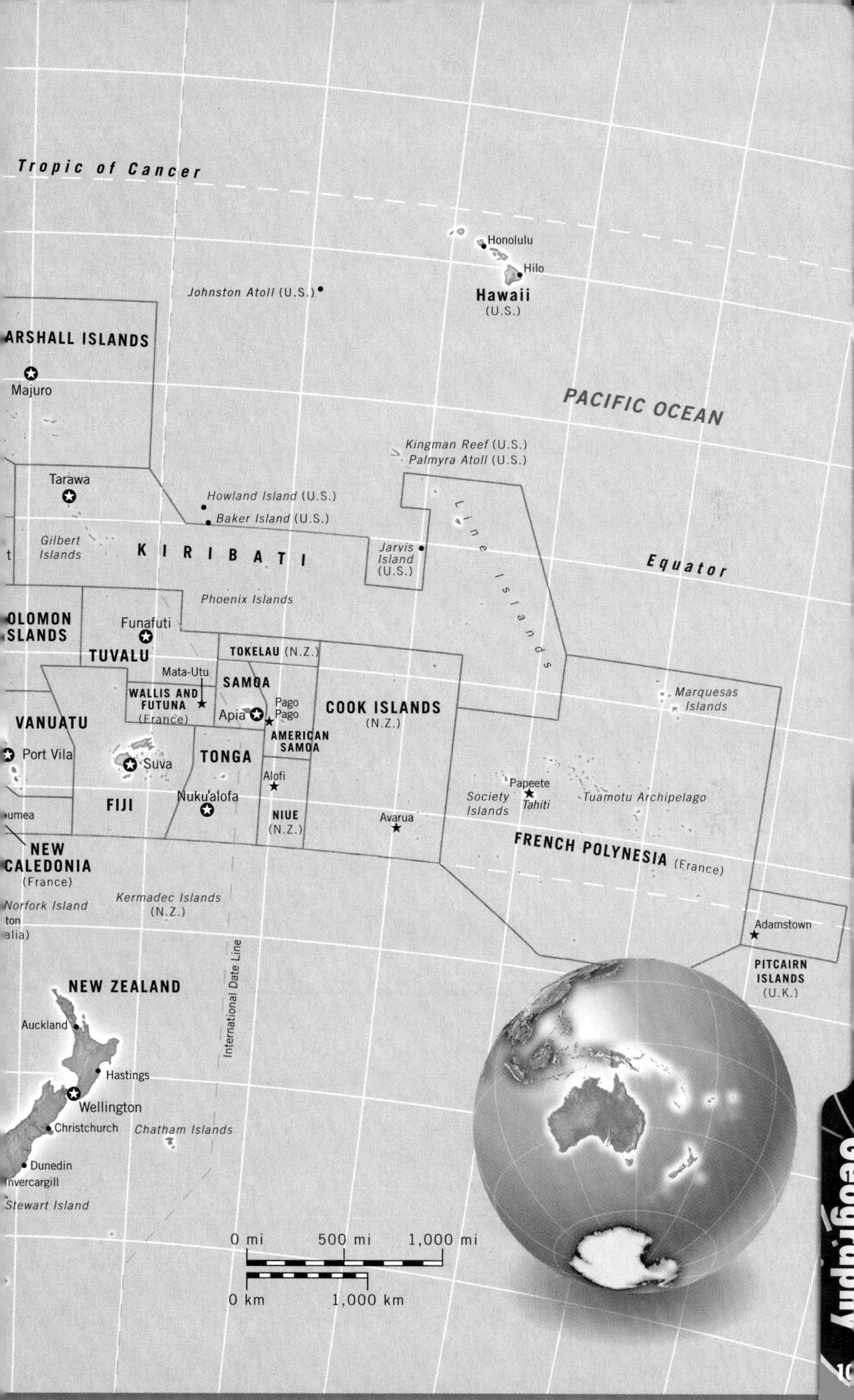

Tropic of Cancer

Honolulu

Hilo

Johnston Atoll (U.S.)

Hawaii
(U.S.)

PACIFIC OCEAN

ARSHALL ISLANDS

Majuro

Kingman Reef (U.S.)
Palmyra Atoll (U.S.)

Tarawa

Howland Island (U.S.)

Baker Island (U.S.)

*Gilbert
Islands*

K I R I B A T I

Jarvis
Island
(U.S.)

Line Islands

Equator

Phoenix Islands

Marquesas
Islands

**OLOMON
SLANDS**

Funafuti

TUVALU

TOKELAU (N.Z.)

Mata-Utu

SAMOA

Pago
Pago

COOK ISLANDS
(N.Z.)

**WALLIS AND
FUTUNA**
(France)

Apia

VANUATU

**AMERICAN
SAMOA**

Port Vila

Suva

TONGA

Alofi

Papeete

*Society
Islands*

Tahiti

Tuamotu Archipelago

umea

FIJI

Nuku'alofa

NIUE
(N.Z.)

Avarua

FRENCH POLYNESIA (France)

**NEW
CALEDONIA**
(France)

Norfork Island
ton
alia)

Kermadec Islands
(N.Z.)

Adamstown

**PITCAIRN
ISLANDS**
(U.K.)

NEW ZEALAND

International Date Line

Auckland

Hastings

Wellington

Christchurch

Chatham Islands

Dunedin

nvercargill

Stewart Island

| 0 mi | 500 mi | 1,000 mi |

| 0 km | 1,000 km |

Geography

109

EUROPE

Reykjavík
ICELAND

Arctic Circle

FAROE ISLANDS
(Denmark)
Torshavn

Trondheim

SHETLAND ISLANDS

HEBRIDES   ORKNEY
ISLANDS   Bergen   NORWAY
                                                  Oslo   Ga
Stavanger

0 mi   300 mi   600 mi

0 km   300 km   600 km

Aberdeen
Glasgow   SWEDEN
Belfast   Edinburgh   DENMARK   Göteborg
Dublin   Ålborg
UNITED   NORTH   Copenhagen
KINGDOM   SEA
IRELAND   Liverpool Leeds   Malmö
Manchester
Sheffield
Birmingham   NETHERLANDS
London   Amsterdam   Hamburg
The Hague   Bremen
GUERNSEY (U.K.)   Rotterdam   Berlin
Calais Lille   Essen
JERSEY (U.K.)   Antwerp   Düsseldorf   Poznan
Le Havre Brussels   Cologne
BELGIUM   Bonn   Frankfurt
ATLANTIC OCEAN   LUXEMBOURG
Paris   Luxembourg   GERMANY   Prague
Nantes   CZECH   Brno
Strasbourg   Stuttgart   REPUBLIC
Dijon   LIECHTENSTEIN Munich
FRANCE   Zürich Vaduz   Vienna
Bordeaux   Geneva Bern   AUSTRIA
Lyon SWITZERLAND   HU
BAY OF   Ljubljana SLOVENIA
BISCAY   Turin Milan   Trieste   Zagre
Porto   Genoa   CROATIA
Bilbao   SAN   BOSNIA
Toulouse   Florence MARINO HERZEGO
Lisbon   Marseille   MONACO   Sarajev
PORTUGAL Madrid   Andorra   Bastia ITALY   ADRIATIC SEA
la Vella   Barcelona MONACO
SPAIN   ANDORRA   Corsica   Rome   Bari
Faro Seville   Valencia Majorca   VATICAN
Málaga   Palma   CITY   Naples
Gibraltar   Sardinia
MEDITERRANEAN SEA   Cagliari
Palermo Messina
MOROCCO   ALGERIA   Sicily

AFRICA   TUNISIA   Valletta
MALTA

110

Murmansk

Pechora

ASIA

Arkhangel'sk

Oulu

A

FINLAND

S
R
U
S
S
I
A

Izhevsk

Tampere

ku Helsinki

St. Petersburg

Kazan

Tallinn

Nizhniy Novgorod

ESTONIA

iga LATVIA

Moscow

Samara

HUANIA

Vilnius

Smolensk

Saratov

ND

Minsk

Lipetsk

KAZAKHSTAN

BELARUS

Homyel'

Voronezh

Brest

Kiev

Kharkiv

Volgograd

Lviv

Derazhnya

Voroshilovgrad

UKRAINE

Gorlovka

Makeyevka

Chisinau

Zhdanov

Rostov

Iasi

Odessa

Mykolayiv

MOLDOVA

Kerch

Grozny

ROMANIA

Simferopol

e

Sevastopol'

Craiova

Bucharest

Constanta

BLACK SEA

Sofia

Varna

na

BULGARIA

opje

EDONIA

Istanbul

essaloniki

T

U

R

K

E

Y

Volos

ECE

Izmir

IRAN

Athens

SYRIA

Crete

CYPRUS

IRAQ

LEBANON

NORTH AMERICA AND CENTRAL AMERICA

Ålesund
ICELAND
Greenland Sea
Longyearbyen
GREENLAND
(Denmark)
Tasiilaq
(Ammassalik)
Narsarsuaq
Nuuk (Godthab)
Davis Strait
Labrador
Sea
St. John's
Island of
Newfoundland
Happy Valley
Goose Bay
CANADA
Qaanaaq (Thule)
Baffin Bay
Baffin Island
Iqaluit
Alert
Queen Elizabeth Islands
Chisasibi
(Fort George)
HUDSON
BAY
Moosonee
Kaujuitoq (Resolute)
Churchill
Arctic Circle
Victoria Island
Banks Island
ARCTIC
OCEAN
Beaufort
Sea
Echo Bay
Yellowknife
Winnipeg
Regina
Saskatoon
Inuvik
Prudhoe Bay
Barrow
Edmonton
Calgary
Helena
Alaska (U.S.)
Whitehorse
Fairbanks
Juneau
Vancouver
Seattle
Victoria
Olympia
Portland
Salem
Boise
RUSSIA
Nome
Anchorage
Valdez
Bethel
Kodiak
Bering
Sea
Aleutian Islands

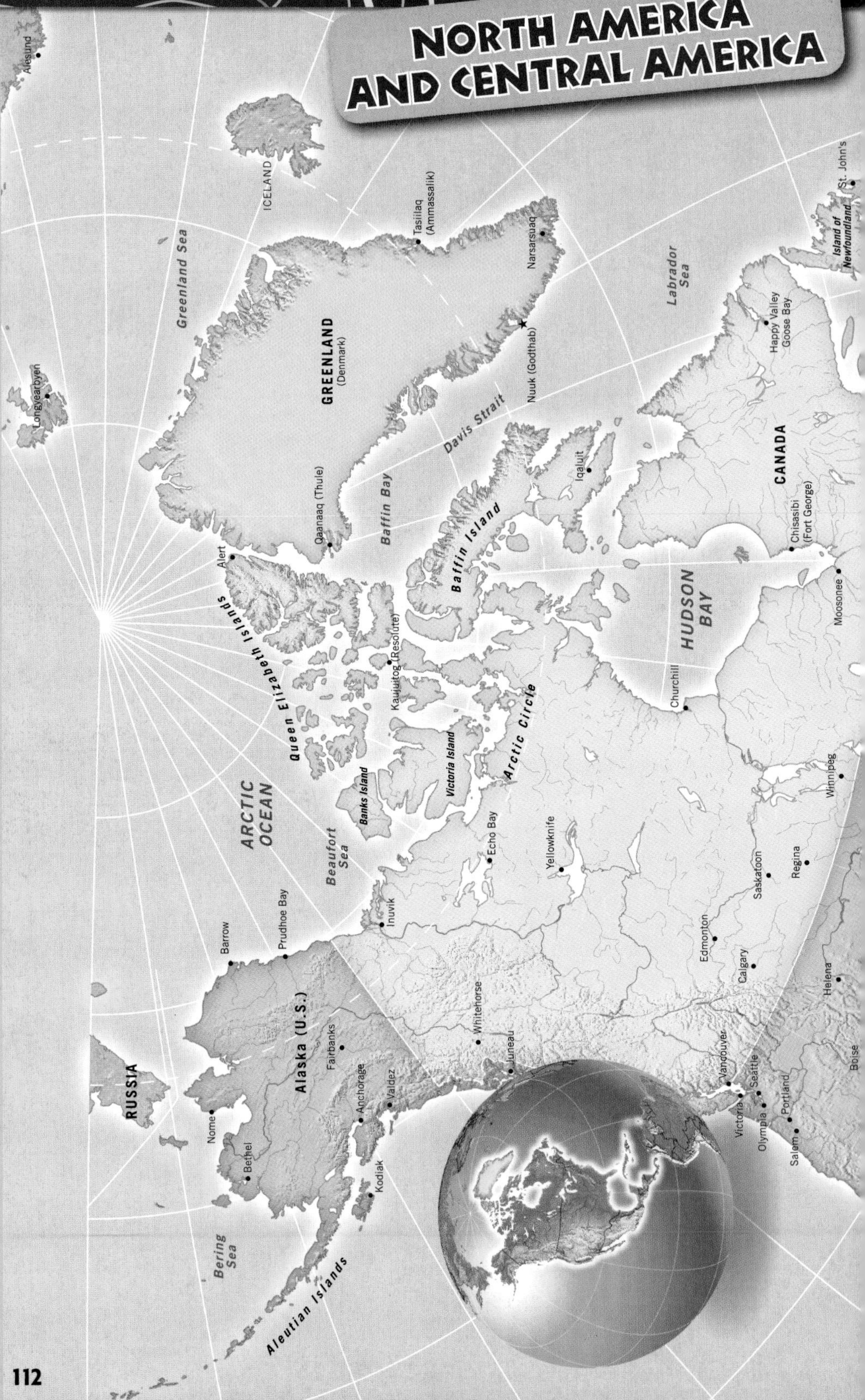

ATLANTIC
OCEAN

BERMUDA (U.K.)

Hamilton

UNITED STATES

Denver

Santa Fe

Phoenix

El Paso

Ciudad Juárez

Hermosillo

MEXICO

Los Angeles

San Diego

Tijuana

La Paz

Mazatlán

Puerto Vallarta

Gulf of California

Tropic of Cancer

PACIFIC
OCEAN

Acapulco

Guadalajara

León

Mexico City

Puebla

Oaxaca

Veracruz

Tampico

Monterrey

San Antonio

Houston

Austin

Dallas

Oklahoma City

Little Rock

Jefferson City

Topeka

Kansas City

Lincoln

Des Moines

Omaha

Madison

Chicago

Springfield

Saint Louis

Memphis

Jackson

Baton Rouge

New Orleans

Birmingham

Montgomery

Mobile

Milwaukee

Detroit

Toledo

Indianapolis

Cincinnati

Louisville

Nashville

Frankfort

Atlanta

Columbia

Tallahassee

Savannah

Jacksonville

Raleigh

Richmond

Charleston

Norfolk

Washington, D.C.

Baltimore

Harrisburg

Philadelphia

New York

Dover

Hartford

Providence

Boston

Albany

Concord

Augusta

Montpelier

Buffalo

Toronto

Cleveland

Pittsburgh

Columbus

GULF OF
MEXICO

Mérida

Cancún

Belize City

BELIZE

Belmopan

GUATEMALA

Guatemala City

San Salvador

EL SALVADOR

Tegucigalpa

HONDURAS

NICARAGUA

Managua

COSTA RICA

San José

Panama City

PANAMA

CARIBBEAN SEA

BAHAMAS

Nassau

Freeport

Miami

Havana

CUBA

Camagüey

CAYMAN ISLANDS (U.K.)

George Town

JAMAICA

Montego Bay

Kingston

Guantánamo

Santiago

HAITI

Port-au-Prince

DOMINICAN
REPUBLIC

Santo
Domingo

San Juan

Puerto
Rico (U.S.)

TURKS AND
CAICOS ISLANDS
(U.K.)

Grand
Turk

VIRGIN
ISLANDS
(U.S., U.K.)

SAINT MAARTEN/
SAINT MARTIN
(Neth. Antilles)/(France)

SAINT
BARTHÉLEMY
(France)

ANGUILLA
(U.K.)

ANTIGUA AND
BARBUDA

SAINT KITTS AND NEVIS

MONTSERRAT (U.K.)

GUADELOUPE (France)

DOMINICA

MARTINIQUE (France)

SAINT LUCIA

SAINT VINCENT AND
THE GRENADINES

BARBADOS

GRENADA

NETHERLANDS ANTILLES (Neth.)

ARUBA (Neth.)

TRINIDAD
AND
TOBAGO

VENEZUELA

COLOMBIA

GUYANA

0 mi   500 mi   1,000 mi

0 km   500 km   1,000 km

SOUTH AMERICA

CARIBBEAN SEA

ATLANTIC OCEAN

PACIFIC OCEAN

ATLANTIC OCEAN

BELIZE
HONDURAS
NICARAGUA
COSTA RICA
PANAMA
JAMAICA
HAITI
Puerto Rico (U.S.)
ANTIGUA AND BARBUDA
SAINT KITTS AND NEVIS
GUADELOUPE
DOMINICA
SAINT LUCIA
BARBADOS
SAINT VINCENT AND THE GRENADINES
GRENADA
TRINIDAD AND TOBAGO

Aruba
Barranquilla
Cartagena
Maracaibo
Lake Maracaibo
Caracas
Orinoco River
Ciudad Guayana
Georgetown
Paramaribo
Cayenne

Medellín
Bogotá
Cali
VENEZUELA
GUYANA
SURINAME
FRENCH GUIANA

Esmeraldas
Quito
Equator
COLOMBIA
Negro River
Macapá

ECUADOR
Guayaquil
Putumayo River
Manaus
Amazon River
Belém
São Luís
Parnaíba
Fortaleza

Iquitos
Benjamin Constant
AMAZON BASIN
Santarém

Piura
PERU
Amazon River
Selvas
Natal

Trujillo
Cruzeiro do Sul
Madeira River
BRAZIL
Recife
Maceió

Lima
Cuzco
Cobija
Riberalta
Pôrto Velho
Xingu River
Araguaia River
Tocantins River
São Francisco River
Salvador

Arequipa
Lake Titicaca
La Paz
Cochabamba
BOLIVIA
Santa Cruz
Sucre
Brasília
Brazilian Highlands
Belo Horizonte

Arica
Iquique
Antofagasta
Paraguay River
PARAGUAY
Asunción
Formosa
Ciudad del Este
Encarnación
São Paulo
Curitiba
Rio de Janeiro

San Miguel de Tucumán
Resistencia
Paraná River
Pôrto Alegre

CHILE
Córdoba
Salto
URUGUAY

Valparaíso
Santiago
Rosario
Buenos Aires
Montevideo

Concepción
ARGENTINA
Río de la Plata
Mar del Plata

Bahía Blanca

Puerto Montt

Comodoro Rivadavia

Strait of Magellan
Río Gallegos
Stanley
Punta Arenas
Ushuaia
Falkland Is.
(Islas Malvinas)
(Administered by U.K.; claimed by Argentina)
Cape Horn

Andes Mts.
Ucayali River
Marañón River
Magdalena River

0 mi   500 mi   1,000 mi
0 km   500 km   1,000 km

114

ANTARCTICA

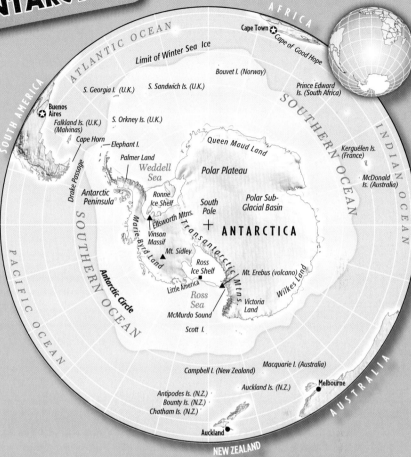

- ATLANTIC OCEAN
- Limit of Winter Sea Ice
- AFRICA
- Cape Town
- Cape of Good Hope
- Bouvet I. (Norway)
- Prince Edward Is. (South Africa)
- S. Georgia I. (U.K.)
- S. Sandwich Is. (U.K.)
- SOUTHERN OCEAN
- SOUTH AMERICA
- Buenos Aires
- Falkland Is. (U.K.) (Malvinas)
- S. Orkney Is. (U.K.)
- Kerguélen Is. (France)
- INDIAN OCEAN
- Cape Horn
- Elephant I.
- Palmer Land
- Queen Maud Land
- McDonald Is. (Australia)
- Weddell Sea
- Polar Plateau
- Drake Passage
- Antarctic Peninsula
- Ronne Ice Shelf
- South Pole
- Polar Sub-Glacial Basin
- Ellsworth Mtns.
- Vinson Massif
- Transantarctic Mtns.
- ANTARCTICA
- SOUTHERN OCEAN
- PACIFIC OCEAN
- Marie-Byrd Land
- Mt. Sidley
- Ross Ice Shelf
- Mt. Erebus (volcano)
- Wilkes Land
- Antarctic Circle
- Little America
- Ross Sea
- Victoria Land
- McMurdo Sound
- Scott I.
- Campbell I. (New Zealand)
- Macquarie I. (Australia)
- Melbourne
- AUSTRALIA
- Antipodes Is. (N.Z.)
- Bounty Is. (N.Z.)
- Chatham Is. (N.Z.)
- Auckland Is. (N.Z.)
- Auckland
- NEW ZEALAND

TIME FOR KIDS
GAME

JUMBLED GEOGRAPHY

The names of all the continents and oceans in the world are listed below. But they have gotten jumbled. Unscramble each word. Then, write the letters in the red spaces in order to uncover a special phrase.

SHOUT RAIMEAC   _ _ _ _ _ _ _ _ _ _ _ _

SAAI   _ _ _ _

FACCIPI   _ _ _ _ _ _ _

CLANATTI   _ _ _ _ _ _ _ _

ISALUTARA   _ _ _ _ _ _ _ _ _

CITCRA   _ _ _ _ _ _

THRON CREAMIA   _ _ _ _ _ _ _ _ _ _ _ _

REEPOU   _ _ _ _ _ _

CIRAFA   _ _ _ _ _ _

TRAINACCAT   _ _ _ _ _ _ _ _ _ _

TROUSHEN   _ _ _ _ _ _ _ _

DANINI   _ _ _ _ _ _

ANSWER:
_ _ _ _ _ _ _ _ _ _!

Answers on page 242.

Geography

Government and Law

TYPES OF GOVERNMENT

There are many kinds of governments in the world. Monarchies, like the ones in Norway, Monaco, and Jordan, have a ruler who usually inherits the position and rules for life. Communist states, such as Cuba and China, plan and control the country's businesses. There is no private ownership of land in a communist state. A few countries, including Belarus and North Korea, have dictatorships in which one person controls the whole country.

The United States is a federal republic. That means that the powers of the central government are limited, and the states keep some powers. But the United States is also a democracy, so the final power belongs to the citizens who vote for government representatives. Most countries, including monarchies, have a constitution, which is a set of rules that describe how the country is to be run.

Dictator Kim Jong Il ruled North Korea until his death in December 2011. His son, Kim Jong Un, then took over.

The United Kingdom is a constitutional monarchy. Elizabeth II is the queen, but the government is run by the Prime Minister and the Parliament.

SEPARATION OF POWERS IN THE UNITED STATES

The U.S. government is divided into three branches. The purpose of this structure is to provide a separation of powers among three equally important branches.

The LEGISLATIVE branch makes the laws. It is made up of a bicameral, or two-chambered, legislature. The two chambers are the Senate and the House of Representatives.

The EXECUTIVE branch carries out those laws. This branch is made up of the President, the Vice President, and the Cabinet.

The JUDICIAL branch determines whether the laws created by the legislature and enforced by the executive branch are constitutional. The judicial branch is made up of the Supreme Court and the courts of law found all over the country.

For a time, the Supreme Court Justices worked in the basement of the Capitol building, where the legislature is. But, members of the government knew it was important for this branch of government to have its own space like the other two did. The Supreme Court building (left) was completed in 1935.

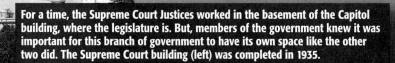

THE U.S. CONSTITUTION

In May 1787, a convention was held in Philadelphia, Pennsylvania, to create the most important document in the formation of the United States government, the U.S. Constitution. George Washington was voted to preside over the gathering of 55 representatives from 12 states. Ratified on March 4, 1789, the Constitution lays out the organization of the federal government and explains the relationship between the federal and state governments and the citizens of the United States.

Many people with different opinions contributed to the Constitution. For example, Federalists wanted to have a strong central government, while Anti-Federalists wanted the strongest powers to remain with the states.

To keep large states from having too much power over smaller states, two delegates from Connecticut proposed that part of the government (the Senate) would include the same number of senators (two from each state) whether the state was large or small, and another part of the government (the House of Representatives) would include a number of representatives that reflected the population of the state. This is called the Great Compromise.

There were many angry debates and arguments, but the Constitution was approved unanimously by the members of the Constitutional Convention. Those members then took the document back to their home states. By July 1788, it was ratified by three-quarters of the states. On March 4, 1789, the Constitution took its place as the supreme law of the land.

We the People of the United States, in order to form a more perfect union, establish justice, insure domestic tranquility, provide for the common defense, promote the general welfare, and secure the blessings of liberty to ourselves and our posterity, do ordain and establish this Constitution for the United States of America.

The Constitution begins with a passage called the preamble, which states the document's purpose.

James Madison was a major force behind the success of the convention. He is sometimes called the Father of the Constitution.

The signing of the U.S. Constitution

Guess what? Rhode Island refused to take part in the Constitutional Convention because the state's leaders did not want a national government interfering in the state's affairs.

THE LEGISLATIVE BRANCH

In general, the Senate determines many national and foreign policies, and the House is in charge of finding ways to carry out these policies in an effective, financially responsible manner. Both chambers have the power to hold hearings to gather information on the bills they are considering and to investigate wrongdoings relating to any issues they are responsible for. Every bill must be approved by both chambers to become a law. The political party with the most members in either chamber is called the majority party. The other is called the minority party.

The SENATE CHAMBER is on the north side of the Capitol building.

The HOUSE CHAMBER is on the south side of the Capitol building.

Members of the House and the Senate both meet in the Capitol building.

THE SENATE

This chamber includes 100 senators, two for each state. Senators are elected to six-year terms, with one-third of the Senate being elected every even-numbered year. The Vice President (or president pro tempore, in the Vice President's absence) presides over the sessions. The Senate has the following special powers and responsibilities:

• Ratify, or approve, treaties made by the President. This requires a two-thirds vote of all senators.

• Accept or reject (by majority vote of all senators) the President's appointments of Supreme Court Justices and federal judges, ambassadors, Cabinet secretaries, and other high-level executive-branch officials.

• Hold trials of officials impeached by the House of Representatives and convict or acquit them. A two-thirds vote of all senators is needed for conviction.

THE HOUSE OF REPRESENTATIVES

This chamber includes 435 representatives. The larger a state's population, the more representatives it has. For example, California has 53 representatives, and Montana has one. Representatives are elected to two-year terms. The Speaker of the House presides over the sessions. The House of Representatives has the following special powers and responsibilities:

• Create bills that allow the government to collect taxes.

• Create bills that empower the government to spend money.

• Elect the President in the event that no candidate receives a majority of electoral votes.

• Vote to impeach the President, Vice President, or other elected official. This means to formally charge a public official with wrongdoing.

HOW A BILL BECOMES A LAW

Every law in the United States starts as a bill. It often has to follow a long and winding path to gain enough support to become a law. This chart shows the straightest, simplest route a bill can take.

YEA 74 NAY 26
Motion to Concur in the House Amdt. to S. 365, the Legislative Vehicle for the Debt Limit Increase Bill

This television image shows the floor of the Senate moments after the senators passed a bill to increase government debt limits.

CHECKS AND BALANCES

The three branches of government have different responsibilities, but they work together to keep any one branch from becoming too powerful. For example, the legislative branch creates laws, but the judicial branch can strike down a law if it conflicts with the spirit of the Constitution.

To keep Congress in check, the President has the power to veto, or refuse to approve, bills that have been written and okayed by both houses of Congress. In return, if two-thirds of the lawmakers in the house that wrote the original bill can agree, then the bill can be considered for passage without the President's signature.

President Obama signs the Civil Rights History Project Act into law in May 2009.

THE BILL IS INTRODUCED.
A member of Congress introduces the bill to the Senate or the House of Representatives. If there is enough support for the idea, then the bill goes to a committee for review.

THE COMMITTEE WEIGHS IN.
If the committee votes yes on the bill, the bill is sent back to the original chamber (House of Representatives or Senate) for debate.

THE ORIGINAL CHAMBER CONSIDERS THE BILL.
The House of Representatives or Senate debates the bill. If they vote yes, the bill is sent to the other chamber.

THE OTHER CHAMBER CONSIDERS THE BILL.
The other chamber debates the bill and votes.

IF THERE ARE NO CHANGES...
The bill goes to the President. If the President signs the bill, then it becomes a law. If the President vetoes the bill, it can still become a law—but only if two-thirds of the House and Senate vote to approve it.

IF THERE ARE CHANGES...
The bill goes back to the original chamber, which votes whether to approve the changes.

THE EXECUTIVE BRANCH

When George Washington became President of the United States on April 30, 1789, it was the beginning of the executive branch of the U.S. government as outlined in Article II of the Constitution. The President, Vice President, and Cabinet make up this branch.

THE PRESIDENT

The President serves a term of four years, with a maximum of two terms. A President must be a native-born U.S. citizen, must be at least 35 years old, and must have lived in the United States for at least 14 years. The President has the following powers and responsibilities:

- Carry out the laws of the land
- Appoint U.S. ambassadors, Supreme Court Justices, federal judges, and Cabinet secretaries (who then must be approved by the Senate)
- Give the annual State of the Union address to Congress
- Receive foreign ambassadors, thus recognizing their governments
- Propose treaties with other nations
- Serve as Commander in Chief of the armed forces; send troops overseas (but Congressional approval is needed to declare war)
- Call both houses of Congress to meet in a special session
- Approve or veto bills passed by Congress
- Grant pardons for federal crimes

President Obama

President Obama welcomes the ambassador from Malaysia in the White House.

THE VICE PRESIDENT

Under Article I of the Constitution, the Vice President presides over the Senate, but casts a vote only in the event of a tie. Article XXV allows the Vice President to assume the office of President if the President dies, resigns, or is removed from office. The Vice President must also be a native-born U.S. citizen and meet the same age and residential qualifications as the President.

Vice President Biden

THE CABINET

Since 1789, Presidents have designated certain responsibilities to members of their Cabinet, who oversee separate executive departments. The first Cabinet consisted of the heads of four departments: foreign affairs, treasury, war, and justice. Today the President's Cabinet consists of the Vice President and the heads of the 15 Cabinet departments, listed below in the order of their creation.

Secretary of State Clinton and Treasury Secretary Geithner applaud before the State of the Union address.

DEPARTMENT	DEPARTMENT HEAD	WEBSITE
STATE	Hillary Rodham Clinton	state.gov
TREASURY	Timothy Geithner	treasury.gov
INTERIOR	Ken Salazar	doi.gov
AGRICULTURE	Tom Vilsack	usda.gov
JUSTICE (ATTORNEY GENERAL)	Eric Holder	usdoj.gov
COMMERCE	John Bryson	commerce.gov
LABOR	Hilda Solis	dol.gov
DEFENSE	Leon Panetta	defenselink.mil
HOUSING AND URBAN DEVELOPMENT	Shaun Donovan	hud.gov
TRANSPORTATION	Ray LaHood	dot.gov
ENERGY	Steven Chu	energy.gov
EDUCATION	Arne Duncan	ed.gov
HEALTH AND HUMAN SERVICES	Kathleen Sebelius	hhs.gov
VETERANS AFFAIRS	Ret. Gen. Eric Shinseki	va.gov
HOMELAND SECURITY	Janet Napolitano	dhs.gov

CABINET-LEVEL POSITIONS

In addition to the Cabinet, there are several other Cabinet-level positions in the executive branch, including the White House chief of staff, the administrator of the Environmental Protection Agency, the director of the Office of Management and Budget, the U.S. trade representative, and the U.S. ambassador to the United Nations.

Guess what?

In January 2012, President Obama elevated the head of the Small Business Administration to a cabinet-level position.

Homeland Security Secretary Napolitano meets with President Obama in the Oval Office.

Sonia Sotomayor
Stephen Breyer
Samuel Alito Jr.
Elena Kagan
Antonin Scalia
Anthony Kennedy
Clarence Thomas
Chief Justice John Roberts
Ruth Bader Ginsburg

THE JUDICIAL BRANCH

On February 1, 1790, the U.S. Supreme Court held its first session. As part of the checks and balances and the separation of powers built into the nation's governmental structure, the main task of the judicial branch, and of the Supreme Court in particular, is to make sure that the Constitution and the laws formed under its provisions are preserved and followed. The U.S. Supreme Court and federal courts interpret the way an established law must be carried out. The Supreme Court also has the power to declare a law unconstitutional.

Supreme Court Justices and federal judges are appointed by the President and confirmed by the Senate. They serve for life or until they decide to resign or retire. The Supreme Court consists of eight Associate Justices and a Chief Justice. All decisions are made by a majority vote of the Justices.

guess what?

In 1789, the Chief Justice of the U.S. Supreme Court made $3,500 a year. By 2011, the salary had risen to $223,500.

IMPORTANT SUPREME COURT CASES

Dred Scott v. Sandford (1857) said that a slave was not a U.S. citizen. It also established that all residents (including slaveholders) in a U.S. territory must be treated equally and that Congress could not outlaw slavery in the U.S. territories.

Plessy v. Ferguson (1896) upheld a Louisiana court decision that racial segregation was legal.

Brown v. Board of Education (1954) declared that racial segregation in public schools is unconstitutional, overturning *Plessy v. Ferguson.*

Miranda v. Arizona (1966) determined that suspected criminals must be read their constitutional rights before being questioned by law enforcement officers.

An integrated classroom in Washington, D.C., in 1954

Massachusetts et al. v. Environmental Protection Agency et al. (2007) declared that greenhouse gases are pollutants and that the EPA has the power to regulate them.

Dred Scott

LOCAL LAWS

Most laws are written by state, city, county, and town governments—and even neighborhood and school boards.

MARRIAGE LAWS are primarily handled by the states. In most states, anyone over age 18 can get married without their parents' consent. In Mississippi, people under age 21 need parental permission; in Nebraska, 17- and 18-year-olds do. In New Hampshire, 13-year-old girls and 14-year-old boys can marry if their parents permit it.

DRIVING LAWS, including speed limits, are usually made by states. The lowest limit is in Hawaii, where cars cannot legally go more than 60 mph (96 kph). When a new law goes into effect (scheduled to be sometime in 2013), the fastest U.S. drivers will be in Texas, where they can legally drive up to 85 mph (137 kph) in some areas. State laws also regulate driving age. In Idaho, Montana, and North Dakota, teenagers can get an unrestricted driver's license at 16. In Washington, D.C., young people have to wait until age 21.

In Wisconsin, a couple must wait six days to get a marriage license. In some states, there is no wait at all.

Some states, including South Dakota, give driving permits to 14-year-olds.

CRIMINAL LAW is handled at all levels of government. In some cases, states decide how criminals are punished. For some crimes, cities, counties, or towns decide on punishments and run prisons. There are only a few crimes, such as treason, civil rights violations, and crimes that cross state lines that the federal government controls.

HEALTH AND SAFETY laws are passed by federal, state, and local governments. These laws range from how stores and farms are inspected to how food and water are stored and how hospitals are run.

EDUCATION is mostly handled at the local and state levels. Usually, counties and cities run schools and raise money through taxes to pay for them. States decide on a minimum number of days for the school year, but some towns or cities increase them. Every school in Missouri must be open for at least 174 days. The state of Virginia requires schools to be open for 180 days. But in the city of Virginia Beach, schools are open for 183 days.

Most school decisions are made on a state or local level, but the federal government provides billions of dollars every year for special teachers, reading programs, and other school improvements.

NEW LAWS ON BULLYING

Many children have suffered terribly from bullying. In the past decade, lawmakers have begun to address the issue. There are laws in 47 states that ban bullying. Behavior such as teasing, name-calling, hitting, and sending threatening or insulting messages are now illegal. But, as with all laws, it's up to all of us to do the right thing!

Bully Free Zone

Government and Law

History

The period before human beings began keeping records is called prehistory. Scientists examine fossils and rock formations to make educated guesses about what happened on Earth.

PRECAMBRIAN ERA

4.5 BILLION YEARS AGO Earth is formed from the dust and debris thrown off by an exploding star.

3.8 BILLION YEARS AGO The first rocks on Earth—chunks of Earth's crust—appear. There is evidence of bacteria in these rocks.

2.5 BILLION YEARS AGO Single-celled cynobacteria use the sun's power to create oxygen. The process is similar to the way plants create oxygen in photosynthesis.

CAMBRIAN PERIOD

570 MILLION YEARS AGO Very simple creatures appear. Made of just a few cells, they have shells and can move about. Over the next 20 to 30 million years, early fish, shellfish, and corals are born.

ORDOVICIAN PERIOD

440–450 MILLION YEARS AGO A mass extinction occurs during the Ordovician period. Many scientists think Earth may have suddenly cooled, killing off huge amounts of marine life (animals and plants that live in water).

This fossil is evidence of a 460-million-year-old animal that resembles a modern sea lily. It looks a lot like a plant, but it is not. It's a sea creature.

SILURIAN PERIOD

430 MILLION YEARS AGO The first plants start growing in water. Later, they develop root systems that let them live on dry land.

DEVONIAN PERIOD

370 MILLION YEARS AGO Fish leave the water and begin to breathe on land. These early amphibians look a little like crocodiles. Some insects come into existence.

CARBONIFEROUS PERIOD

300–360 MILLION YEARS AGO During the Carboniferous period, all the land areas on Earth join into one supercontinent known as Pangaea. The land is mostly marshy swamp, covered with plants such as tree ferns, mosses, cycads, and giant trees. This vegetation absorbs lots of carbon dioxide and creates an oxygen-rich atmosphere.

Eurasia

North America

Africa

South America

India

Antarctica

Australia

Pangaea

PALEOZOIC ERA

A 350-million-year-old fossil of a trilobite, which was a hard-shelled marine animal

251–300 MILLION YEARS AGO The first reptiles appear. They evolve slowly into sluggish creatures, some with odd-looking sails on their backs.

245–251 MILLION YEARS AGO The Great Dying occurs during the Triassic period. About 95% of marine life and 70% of the plants and animals on land are wiped out. Some scientists think that the climate may have changed because of volcanic eruptions or gases released from the ocean floor.

One early reptile with a sail on its back was the dimetrodon.

200–240 MILLION YEARS AGO The first dinosaurs appear. The earliest are about the size of kangaroos and are called prosauropods. Diplodocus, stegosaurus, and brachiosaurus are some of the dinosaurs that lived during this time. During this period, Pangaea breaks into separate continents, with oceans and seas between them.

145–200 MILLION YEARS AGO During the Jurassic period, the landscape is lush and green, with palm trees and lots of shrubs. Plant-eating dinosaurs, like the apatosaurus and the seismosaurus, thrive and become gigantic. The seismosaurus is about 148 feet (45 m) long. It has a tiny head and swallows rocks to help process all the leaves it eats. Meat-eating dinosaurs also roam the Earth, eating everything in sight. Cryolophosaurus is the fastest. Gasosaurus has incredibly powerful jaws.

65–145 MILLION YEARS AGO There are even more dinosaurs in the Cretaceous period than in the Jurassic period. Different dinosaurs develop different features that help protect them from predators and help them kill their prey. For example, the horns on a triceratops's head could gore other dinosaurs. The biggest and most fierce of all Cretaceous meat eaters is the *Tyrannosaurus rex,* or T. rex.

The fossilized bones of an Albertosaurus, a meat eater

65 MILLION YEARS AGO About 65 million years ago, something happens that kills all the dinosaurs. Some think that deadly germs were to blame. Others believe that dinosaurs killed and ate each other. There is also a theory that a huge asteroid slammed into Earth and created walls of water and dust that killed the dinosaurs. It's one of the great mysteries of world history.

65 MILLION YEARS AGO–THE PRESENT The continents reach their current positions. New life evolves. Many mammals, including humans, appear in this period. Around 6,000 years ago, humans start leaving records, which marks the end of prehistory and the beginning of history.

Stegosaurus, a plant-eating dinosaur

History

TIME LINES OF HISTORY

ANCIENT HISTORY

5000–3500 B.C. Sumer, located in what is now Iraq, becomes the earliest known civilization. Among other innovations, Sumerians develop a written alphabet.

3500–2600 B.C. People settle in the Indus River Valley, in what is now India and Pakistan.

2600 B.C. Minoan civilization begins on the island of Crete, in the Mediterranean Sea.

Circa 2560 B.C. The Egyptian king Khufu finishes building the Great Pyramid at Giza. The Great Sphinx is completed soon after by his son Khaefre.

2000 B.C. Babylonians develop a system of mathematics.
• The kingdom of Kush, in Africa, becomes a major center of trade and learning.

1792 B.C. Hammurabi becomes the ruler of Babylonia. He creates the first set of laws, now known as Hammurabi's Code.

Circa 1600–1050 B.C. The Shang Dynasty is the first Chinese dynasty to leave written records.

1200 B.C. The Trojan War is fought between the Greeks and the Trojans.

814 B.C. The city of Carthage, located in what is now Tunisia, is founded by the Phoenicians.

753 B.C. According to legend, Rome is founded by Romulus.

563 B.C. Siddhartha Gautama, who becomes the Buddha, or Enlightened One, is born. He will become the founder of the Buddhist religion.

551 B.C. Chinese philosopher Confucius is born. His teachings on honesty, humanity, and how people should treat one another are the foundations of Confucianism.

510 B.C. Democracy is established in Athens, Greece.

438 B.C. Construction of the Parthenon on the Acropolis (the highest hill in Athens) is completed.

431 B.C. The Peloponnesian War breaks out between Sparta and Athens. In 404 B.C., Sparta finally wins the war and takes over Athens.

334 B.C. Alexander the Great invades Persia. He eventually conquers lands from Greece to India. He even crosses into North Africa.

100 B.C. The great city of Teotihuacán flourishes in Mexico.

Alexander the Great

58 B.C. Julius Caesar leaves Rome for Gaul (France) and spends nine years conquering much of central Europe. He is murdered in 44 B.C.

27 B.C. Octavian becomes the first Roman emperor, ushering in a long period of peace. He is also known by the title Augustus.

The Great Sphinx

Buddha statue

The Parthenon

WORLD HISTORY

Circa 1 A.D. Jesus Christ is born. He is crucified by the Romans around 30 A.D.

66 Jews rebel against Roman rule. The revolution is put down by the Romans, who destroy Jerusalem (in present-day Israel) in 70 A.D. and force many Jews into slavery.

79 Mount Vesuvius erupts, destroying the city of Pompeii (in present-day Italy).

122 Construction on Hadrian's Wall begins. It spans northern England and offers protection from the tribes to the north.

Circa 250 The classic period of Mayan civilization begins. It lasts until about 900. The Maya erect impressive stone buildings and temples in areas that are now part of Mexico and Central America.

330 Constantine the Great chooses Byzantium as the capital of the Roman Empire, and the city becomes known as Constantinople.

476 The Roman Empire collapses.

622 Muhammad, the founder of Islam, flees from Mecca to Medina in what is now Saudi Arabia. This journey is called the Hegira. After the death of Muhammad in 632, Muslims conquer much of North Africa and the Middle East. In 711, Muslims also conquer Spain.

800 Charlemagne is crowned the first Holy Roman Emperor by Pope Leo III.

960 The Song Dynasty begins in China. This dynasty is known for its advances in art, poetry, and philosophy.

Circa 1000—1300 During the classic period of their culture, Anasazi people build homes and other structures in the sides of cliffs in what is now the southwestern United States.

1066 At the Battle of Hastings, the Norman king William the Conqueror invades England and defeats English king Harold II.

1095 Pope Urban II delivers a speech urging Christians to capture the Holy Land from the Muslims. The fighting between 1096 and 1291 is known as the Crusades.

Circa 1200 The Inca Empire begins, and elaborate stone structures are eventually built in Cuzco and Machu Picchu, Peru. The Incas flourish until Francisco Pizarro, a Spaniard, conquers them in 1533.

1206 A Mongolian warrior named Temujin is proclaimed Genghis Khan. He expands his empire so that it includes most of Asia.

1215 A group of barons in England force King John to sign the Magna Carta, a document limiting the power of the king.

1271—1295 Marco Polo, a Venetian merchant, travels throughout Asia. His book, *Il Milione* (*The Million*), is a major European source of information about Asia.

1273 The Habsburg Dynasty begins in Eastern Europe. It will remain a powerful force in the region until World War I.

1325 Aztecs begin building Tenochtitlán on the site of modern Mexico City.

1337 The Hundred Years' War starts between the English and French. France finally wins in 1453.

Mount Vesuvius

Battle of Hastings

Genghis Khan

1347 The Black Death, or bubonic plague, breaks out in Europe. It spreads quickly, killing more than one-third of Europe's population.

1368 The Ming Dynasty is founded in China by Buddhist monk Zhu Yuanzhang (or Chu Yuan-Chang).

1433 Portuguese explorer Gil Eannes sails past Cape Bojador, in western Africa, which was thought to be the end of the world.

1453 Constantinople falls to the Ottoman Turks, ending the Byzantine Empire.

1455 Johannes Gutenberg invents the printing press. The Gutenberg Bible is the first book printed on the press.

1478 The Spanish Inquisition begins.

1487–1488 Bartholomeu Dias of Portugal leads the first European expedition around the Cape of Good Hope, at the southern tip of Africa, opening up a sea route to Asia.

1492 Christopher Columbus leaves Spain, hoping to sail to the East Indies. Instead, he and his crew land in the Bahamas and visit Cuba, Hispaniola (which is now Haiti and the Dominican Republic), and other small islands.

1497–1499 Portuguese explorer Vasco da Gama leads the first European expedition to India by sea via the Cape of Good Hope.

1517 Martin Luther protests the abuses of the Catholic Church, which leads to a religious split and the rise of the Protestant faith.

1519 While exploring Mexico, Spanish adventurer Hernán Cortés conquers the Aztec Empire.

1519–1522 Portuguese explorer Ferdinand Magellan's expedition circumnavigates, or sails around, the globe.

1532–1533 Spanish explorer Francisco Pizarro conquers the Inca Empire in South America.

1543 Polish astronomer Copernicus shares his theory that the sun, not the Earth, is the center of the universe.

1547 Ivan the Terrible becomes the first czar, or ruler, of Russia.

1588 The English defeat the Spanish Armada, or fleet of warships, when Spain attempts to invade England.

1618 The Thirty Years' War breaks out between Protestants and Catholics in Europe.

1620 English Pilgrims aboard the *Mayflower* land at Plymouth Rock.

1632 Italian astronomer Galileo, the first person to use a telescope to look into space, confirms Copernicus's theory that Earth revolves around the sun.

1642 The English Civil War, sometimes called the Puritan Revolution, begins in Britain.

1688 The Glorious Revolution, or Bloodless Revolution, takes place in England. James II is removed from the throne, and William and Mary become the heads of the country.

1721 Peter the Great becomes czar of Russia.

1789 An angry mob storms the Bastille, a prison in Paris, setting off the French Revolution.

Gutenberg's press

The storming of the Bastille

Mayflower landing

1819 Simón Bolívar crosses the Andes to launch a surprise attack against the Spanish, liberating New Granada (now Colombia, Venezuela, Panama, and Ecuador) from Spain.

1824 Mexico becomes independent from Spain.

1845 A blight ruins the potato crop in Ireland. More than 1 million Irish starve to death, and another million leave for the United States to escape the Irish potato famine.

1848 This is known as the year of revolutions in Europe, as there is upheaval in France, Italy, Germany, Hungary, and elsewhere.

1859 Charles Darwin publishes *On the Origin of Species.*

1871 A group of independent states unifies, creating the German Empire.

1876 Alexander Graham Bell invents the telephone.

1884 Representatives of 14 European countries meet at the Berlin West Africa Conference and divide Africa into areas of control.

1892 The diesel engine is invented by Parisian Rudolf Diesel.

1893 New Zealand becomes the first country to give women the right to vote.
• The Columbian Exposition, also known as the Chicago World's Fair, is held.

1894 The Sino-Japanese War breaks out between China and Japan, who are fighting for control of Korea. An 1895 treaty declares Korea independent.

1898 The Spanish-American War begins.

1899 During the Boxer Rebellion, the Chinese fight against Christian and foreign influences in

their country. American, Japanese, and European forces help stop the fighting by 1901.

1904 Japan declares war on Russia, beginning the Russo-Japanese War. The countries clash over influence in Manchuria and Korea. Japan wins the conflict and becomes a world power.

1909 Robert Peary is credited as the first to reach the North Pole, although recent evidence suggests he might have been as far as 30 to 60 miles (48 to 97 km) away.

1911 Roald Amundsen, the first man to travel the Northwest Passage, reaches the South Pole.

1914 Austro-Hungarian archduke Franz Ferdinand is assassinated, setting off the chain of events that starts World War I.

1917 The United States enters World War I.
• Led by socialist Vladimir Lenin, the Russian Revolution begins. The czarist government is overthrown and, in 1922, the Soviet Union is formed.

1918 A flu epidemic spreads quickly around the world, killing more than 20 million people.

1919 The Treaty of Versailles ends World War I.

1927 Philo Farnsworth invents the television.

1928 Alexander Fleming discovers penicillin accidentally after leaving a dish of staphylococcus bacteria uncovered and finding mold.

1929 The U.S. stock market collapses, beginning the Great Depression.

1933 Adolf Hitler becomes chancellor of Germany.
• Frequency modulation, or FM, radio is developed by Edwin Armstrong.

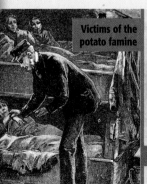
Victims of the potato famine

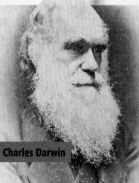
Charles Darwin

Vladimir Lenin

1936 The Spanish Civil War breaks out.

1939 World War II begins when Germany invades Poland. Britain responds by declaring war on Germany. The United States declares neutrality.

1941 The Japanese launch a surprise attack on the United States, bombing U.S. ships docked in Hawaii's Pearl Harbor. In response, the United States declares war on Japan, and both Germany and Italy declare war on the United States.

1945 Germany surrenders on May 7, ending the war in Europe. In August, the United States drops two atomic bombs on the Japanese cities Hiroshima and Nagasaki. Japan surrenders, ending World War II.

1947 India and Pakistan become free of British colonial rule.

1948 Israel becomes a nation.

1949 Following China's civil war, Mao Zedong sets up the Communist People's Republic of China.
• South Africa enacts apartheid laws, which make discrimination against nonwhite people part of public policy.

1950 North Korean communist forces invade South Korea, beginning the Korean War. U.S. forces support South Korea. China backs North Korea. The war ends three years later.
• Frank McNamara develops the first credit card, the Diners' Club.

1952 The hydrogen bomb is developed by Edward Teller and a team at a laboratory in Los Alamos, New Mexico.

1953 Edmund Hillary and Tenzing Norgay climb to the top of Mount Everest.

1955 Jonas Salk's polio vaccine is introduced.

1961 A group of Cuban exiles, supported by the United States, invades Cuba at the Bay of Pigs. The invasion fails, and U.S.-Cuban relations worsen.

1962 The Cuban Missile Crisis, a conflict between the United States, the Soviet Union, and Cuba, brings the world to the brink of nuclear war.

1963 U.S. President John F. Kennedy is assassinated on November 22, 1963. Vice President Lyndon B. Johnson is inaugurated.

1965 The United States begins officially sending troops to Vietnam to aid South Vietnam in its civil war with North Vietnam.

1967 The Six-Day War breaks out between Israel and neighboring Arab nations Egypt, Syria, and Jordan. Israel seizes the Golan Heights, the Gaza Strip, the Sinai Peninsula, and part of the west bank of the Jordan River.

1973 The Paris Peace Accords end the Vietnam War. North Vietnam later violates the terms of the treaty and, in 1975, takes control of Saigon, the capital of South Vietnam.
• Egypt and Syria launch a surprise attack on Israel, beginning the Yom Kippur War.

1978 U.S. President Jimmy Carter, Israeli President Menachem Begin, and Egyptian President Anwar Sadat sign the Camp David Accords in an attempt to achieve peace in the Middle East.

1979 Religious leader Ayatollah Khomeini declares Iran to be an Islamic republic.

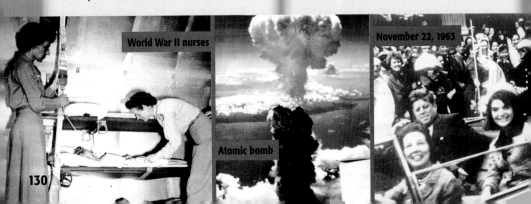

World War II nurses

Atomic bomb

November 22, 1963

1989 The Chinese army crushes a demonstration in Tiananmen Square in Beijing, killing hundreds, possibly thousands, of students and protestors.
• The Berlin Wall is torn down, and the city of Berlin, Germany, is reunified.

1990 Apartheid ends in South Africa. Four years later, Nelson Mandela is elected president in the country's first free, multiracial elections.
• The Persian Gulf War begins when Iraq invades Kuwait.

1991 The Soviet Union dissolves.
• Croatia, Slovenia, and Macedonia declare independence from Yugoslavia. The next year, Bosnia and Herzegovina also declares independence, but war breaks out and does not end until 1995.
• Tim Berners-Lee develops the World Wide Web.

1994 Tensions between the Hutu majority and the Tutsi minority in Rwanda, Africa, lead to a genocide, or systematic killing of a racial or ethnic group. About 800,000 Tutsis are killed.

1999 Honda releases the two-door Insight, the first hybrid car marketed to the masses in the United States. A year later, the Toyota Prius, the first hybrid four-door sedan, is released.

2001 After the September 11 terrorist attacks in New York City and Washington, D.C., the United States declares an international War on Terror, attacking the Taliban government in Afghanistan and searching for Osama bin Laden and al-Qaeda.

2003 With the aid of Britain and other allies, the United States invades Iraq. Though the government falls quickly, resistance and fighting continue. In 2006, Saddam Hussein is executed for crimes against humanity.

• War in the Darfur region of Sudan begins, leading to a humanitarian crisis.

2004 A powerful tsunami kills nearly 300,000 people in Indonesia, Sri Lanka, India, Thailand, and other Asian countries.

2008 A global economic crisis leads to loss of jobs and homes, and to a downturn in trade.

2010 A devastating earthquake hits Haiti.
• An oil rig in the Gulf of Mexico explodes, causing one of the largest oil spills in history.

2011 Protests erupt in the Middle East and North Africa, toppling leaders in Tunisia and Egypt. There is instability throughout the region.
• A massive earthquake strikes Japan, triggering a powerful tsunami.
• After intense fighting in Libya, rebels gain control of most of the country. Libyan President Muammar Gaddafi is killed. The National Transitional Council (NTC) struggles to form a stable government.
• The world population officially exceeds 7 billion on October 31. It continues to rise.

2012 In Syria, demonstrators demand the resignation of President Bashar al-Assad and the overthrow of the government. The government deploys its army to quash the uprising and kills thousands.

MYSTERY PERSON

I was born in France. At age 7, I became the Duke of Normandy. I fought to become King of England. In the Battle of Hastings, in 1066, I ended Anglo-Saxon rule and won the crown.

WHO AM I? _____

Answer on page 243.

Aftermath of Japanese tsunami

The Tribute in Light memorial to September 11

1524 Italian explorer Giovanni da Verrazano is the first European to reach New York Harbor.

1540 In search of gold, Spanish explorer Francisco Vásquez de Coronado travels north from Mexico. One of his lieutenants is the first European to spot the Grand Canyon.

1541 Spaniard Hernando de Soto crosses the Mississippi River.

1579 Sir Francis Drake of England explores California's coastline.

1607 English settlers found Jamestown in Virginia. The colony's leader, John Smith, is captured by Native Americans. According to legend, he is saved by Pocahontas.

1609—1611 Henry Hudson visits the Chesapeake Bay, Delaware Bay, and New York Bay and becomes the first European to sail up the Hudson River.

1620 Pilgrims land at Plymouth, Massachusetts.

1626 Dutchman Peter Minuit buys the island of Manhattan from the Canarsie tribe.

1692 Accusations of witchcraft lead to the Salem witch trials and the executions of 20 people.

1770 Tensions between British soldiers and colonists erupt in the Boston Massacre, when British troops kill five men.

1773 Colonists protest a tax on tea by dressing up as Native Americans, boarding ships, and dumping tea into Boston Harbor. Known as the Boston Tea Party, the protest angers the British, who pass other harsh taxes.

1775 Paul Revere warns the colonists that the British are coming. The Battle of Lexington and Concord is the first fight of the American Revolution. The British surrender at Yorktown, Virginia, in 1781.

1776 Drafted by Thomas Jefferson, the Declaration of Independence is signed, and the United States is formed.

1787 The U.S. Constitution is written and submitted to the states for ratification. By the end of the year, Delaware, Pennsylvania, and New Jersey have accepted it.

1789 George Washington becomes the first President of the United States.

1791 The Bill of Rights, written mostly by James Madison, becomes part of the Constitution.

1803 President Thomas Jefferson buys the Louisiana Territory from France, adding 885,000 square miles (2,292,139 sq km) to the United States.

1804—1806 Meriwether Lewis and William Clark explore the Louisiana Territory. They travel from St. Louis up the Missouri River, then over the Rockies on horseback, reaching the Pacific Ocean in November 1805.

1812 The War of 1812 breaks out between the United States and Britain because of trade and border disputes, as well as disagreements about freedom of the seas. The Treaty of Ghent ends the war in 1814.

1823 President James Monroe issues the Monroe Doctrine, warning that the Americas are not open for colonization.

Boston Tea Party

U.S. Constitution

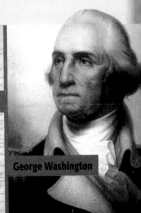

George Washington

1836 Texas declares independence from Mexico. In response, the Mexican army attacks and kills the 189 Texans defending the Alamo.

1838 In what is known as the Trail of Tears, the U.S. government forces 16,000 Cherokees to leave their land in Georgia and relocate to a reservation in Oklahoma. Roughly a quarter of the Cherokees die.

1846 The Mexican-American War begins. At the end of the fighting, in 1848, Mexico gives California and New Mexico (which also includes present-day Arizona, Utah, and Nevada) to the United States. In return, the United States agrees to pay Mexico $15 million.

1848 John Sutter strikes gold in California, kicking off the California gold rush.

1860 Tensions between the North and the South over slavery, taxes, and representation reach a boiling point, and South Carolina secedes from the United States.

1861 Mississippi, Florida, Alabama, Georgia, Louisiana, and Texas secede from the Union, and the Confederate government is formed. The first shots of the American Civil War are fired by Confederate soldiers at Fort Sumter, in Charleston Harbor, in South Carolina. Virginia, Arkansas, Tennessee, and North Carolina also secede from the Union.

1862 The Homestead Act promises 160 acres of land to anyone who remains on the land for five years. This law encourages settlers to move west.

Guess what? More than 200,000 African Americans served in the Union Army during the Civil War. More than 38,000 lost their lives for their country, and 22 won the Medal of Honor.

1863 President Abraham Lincoln issues the Emancipation Proclamation, which frees all slaves in the Confederate states. The Battle of Gettysburg is fought. It is the bloodiest battle of the Civil War.

1865 General Robert E. Lee of the Confederacy surrenders to Union General Ulysses S. Grant at Appomattox Court House, in Virginia, ending the Civil War.
• President Lincoln is assassinated at Ford's Theater by John Wilkes Booth, and Andrew Johnson becomes President.
• The 13th Amendment, which puts an end to slavery, is ratified.

1867 The United States buys Alaska from Russia for $7.2 million.

1869 The transcontinental railroad is completed when the Central Pacific and Union Pacific Railroads are joined at Promontory, Utah.

1890 The Battle of Wounded Knee is the last major defeat for Native American tribes.

1898 The Spanish-American War is fought. At the end of the war, Cuba is independent, and Puerto Rico, Guam, and the Philippines become territories of the United States.

1903 Wilbur and Orville Wright complete their first airplane flight at Kitty Hawk, North Carolina.

1908 Henry Ford, founder of the Ford Motor Company, builds the Model T and sells it for $825, making automobiles much more affordable than ever before.

1917 The United States enters World War I.

1920 With the passage of the 19th Amendment, women get the right to vote.

Gold rush

Civil War soldiers

UPHOLD OUR HONOR

World War I poster

FIGHT FOR

History

133

1929 The U.S. stock market crashes, and the Great Depression begins.

1941 In a surprise attack, Japan bombs the U.S. fleet at Pearl Harbor, in Hawaii. The United States declares war on Japan. Germany and Italy declare war on the United States.

1945 Germany surrenders on May 7, ending the war in Europe. In August, the U.S. aircraft *Enola Gay* drops an atomic bomb on Hiroshima, Japan. Three days later, a U.S. plane drops an atomic bomb on the city of Nagasaki. The effects are devastating. Six days later, Japan surrenders, ending World War II.

1946 The first bank-issued credit card is developed by John Biggins for the Flatbush National Bank of Brooklyn, in New York City.

1950 North Korean communist forces invade South Korea. U.S. forces enter the Korean War to defend South Korea. Despite three years of bitter fighting, little land changes hands.

1954 In *Brown v. Board of Education of Topeka, Kansas,* the U.S. Supreme Court declares that segregated schools are unconstitutional.

1955 Rosa Parks is arrested for refusing to give up her bus seat to a white person, leading to a boycott of the entire bus system in Montgomery, Alabama.

1962 The United States discovers that the Soviet Union has installed missiles capable of reaching the United States on the island of Cuba. Known as the Cuban Missile Crisis, this event brings the United States and the Soviet Union to the brink of nuclear war. After two weeks of extremely tense negotiations, the crisis comes peacefully to an end.

1963 Martin Luther King Jr. delivers his famous "I Have a Dream" speech to a crowd of more than 250,000 people in Washington, D.C.
• President John F. Kennedy is assassinated.

1965 Civil rights advocate and black militant leader Malcolm X is killed.
• A race riot in the Watts section of Los Angeles, California, is one of the worst in history.
• President Lyndon B. Johnson authorizes air raids over North Vietnam.

1968 James Earl Ray shoots and kills Martin Luther King Jr. in Memphis, Tennessee. Riots break out across the country.

1973 The Vietnam War ends when peace accords are signed. Two years later, North Vietnam takes over Saigon (now Ho Chi Minh City), the capital of South Vietnam.

1974 Due to his involvement in the Watergate scandal, President Richard Nixon resigns. Gerald Ford becomes President.

1979 Islamic militants storm the U.S. embassy in Tehran, Iran, and 52 Americans are held hostage for 444 days.

1986 The *Challenger* space shuttle explodes, killing seven crew members, including teacher Christa McAuliffe.

1991 After Iraq invades Kuwait, the United States begins bombing raids. The first Persian Gulf War ends quickly as Iraqi forces are driven from Kuwait.

ENOLA GAY
82
Enola Gay pilot

Martin Luther King Jr. and Malcolm X

President Johnson in Vietnam

1999 President Bill Clinton is acquitted of impeachment charges.

2000 In the extremely close election between Democrat Al Gore and Republican George W. Bush, allegations of voter fraud lead to an election recount. The U.S. Supreme Court determines the outcome, and Bush is declared the winner.

2001 On September 11, two passenger planes are hijacked and flown into the World Trade Center, in New York City, causing the buildings to collapse. Another plane is flown into the Pentagon, near Washington, D.C. A fourth hijacked plane is crashed into a field in Pennsylvania by the passengers on board before it can reach its target. The United States and Britain respond by attacking the Taliban government in Afghanistan for harboring Osama bin Laden, the alleged mastermind of the attacks. The U.S. government declares the War on Terror.

2003 The space shuttle *Columbia* breaks apart during reentry into Earth's atmosphere, killing all seven crew members.
• Along with its allies—Britain and other countries—the United States goes to war in Iraq. Saddam Hussein's government falls quickly, but resistance and fighting continue.

2005 Hurricane Katrina hits the Gulf Coast, destroying parts of Mississippi and Louisiana, and areas along the coast of the southeastern United States. About 80% of New Orleans, Louisiana, is flooded.

2008 A global economic crisis causes a sharp rise in unemployment. Many U.S. homeowners lose their homes.

2009 Barack Obama becomes America's first African-American President.

2010 A controversial federal law is enacted to overhaul the U.S. health care system and extend health insurance to the 32 million Americans who did not have it before.
• An oil rig in the Gulf of Mexico explodes, causing one of the largest oil spills in history.

2011 The U.S. Secretary of Defense announces that the war in Iraq is officially over and that all remaining U.S. troops will leave Iraq by the end of 2011. During the conflict, nearly 4,500 U.S. troops lost their lives in Iraq, and about 30,000 were wounded.

U.S. troops return home from Iraq.

MYSTERY PERSON

I was born in Massachusetts in 1821. During the U.S. Civil War, I was committed to bringing supplies and aid to soldiers on the war front. I soon became known as the "Angel of the Battlefield." At age 60, I founded the American Red Cross. I led the organization for 23 years.

WHO AM I? _____

Answer on page 243.

Columbia

President Clinton

President Obama

Inventions

FROM TIME FOR KIDS MAGAZINE

Edison's Lessons

By Brenda Iasevoli with Time Reporting

Did you turn on a light today? The great inventor Thomas Alva Edison made that possible. He still inspires us today.

Menlo Park, New Jersey, glowed with light on New Year's Eve in 1879. Thomas Alva Edison had accomplished what no other inventor had been able to do. He figured out how to make a practical, long-lasting lightbulb. He didn't stop there. He also created the socket to screw the bulb into. He made the light switch to turn it on with. He even thought of the company that would supply the electricity to the bulb. Edison invented a whole system of electrical power.

In the 1870s, Edison created an "invention factory" in Menlo Park. He

Edison with an electric generator he invented

brought together a team of scientists and engineers. Edison said his team could come up with "a minor invention every 10 days and a big thing every six months or so." Today, companies such as Ford, Google, and Intel follow Edison's example.

Edison expert Paul Israel says Americans have much to learn from Edison. The top lesson the great inventor offers young scientists is to never give up. "Edison never let failure stop him," Israel told TFK. "He knew he had to struggle to find answers and create something new."

A FEW OF EDISON'S INVENTIONS

1868 The automatic vote recorder allowed Congress to keep track of their votes on bills.

Edison's phonograph

1874 The quadruplex telegraph sent coded messages over a wire.

1877 The phonograph was a machine for recorded sound.

1879 His first lightbulb burned for 13 hours.

1892 The kinetoscope allowed people to see moving pictures.

WHAT'S A PATENT?

To prevent people from copying the inventions of others, the government issues patents. A patent is a government license that gives a person the sole right to manufacture and sell an invention. Patents last for up to 20 years. After that, other people can make and sell their own versions of the patented product.

To get a patent, inventors submit a form to the U.S. Patent Office, along with a detailed description and illustrations of the invention. There is also a hefty fee. The Patent Office investigates to make sure no one else has already registered the idea. During this investigation, inventors use the words "patent pending" on their inventions.

Guess what? Thomas Edison filed for 1,093 patents. When he died in 1931, 714 were still active.

COOLEST INVENTIONS OF 2011

Inventors find ways to make our lives easier, greener, and sometimes more fun. Check out the results of their creativity.

POWER PLANT

Enough solar energy strikes the Earth's surface every hour to power the world for an entire year. What if that energy could be stored for later use? A professor at the Massachusetts Institute of Technology has found a way to do just that. He has invented an **ARTIFICIAL LEAF.** Much like a real leaf, it can convert energy from the sun into energy that can be stored.

HELP AT HAND

Need to find the best nearby burger? Just ask SIRI, the latest feature on Apple's new iPhone. Siri can also remind you to take out the garbage or do your homework. And it's better than past digital assistants that operate on voice recognition. You can speak naturally to Siri. There's no need to use special words in order to be understood. Ask away! Siri is ready to serve.

IT'S A BOAT! IT'S A PLANE!

For people who like to travel in style on both land and water, French designer Yelken Octuri has crafted the FLYING YACHT. This gorgeous boat boasts four 133-foot-tall (41 m) masts. When it's time to take to the sky, the masts become wings. The yacht's dual propellers pull it through the air at 240 miles (386 km) per hour.

THE WORLD'S FASTEST CAR

In 1997, Andy Green set a land-speed record of 763 miles (1,228 km) per hour. Now he's out to break that record with the **BLOODHOUND SSC.** He is shooting for 1,000 miles (1,609 km) per hour. This car is powered by both jet and rocket engines. The Bloodhound project is about more than speed. Green and his teammates hope to inspire a generation of scientists and engineers. Start your engines!

A BIRD'S-EYE VIEW

It looks and flies like a hummingbird. But don't be fooled. This tiny aircraft, called the **NANO AIR VEHICLE (NAV)**, is a spying device. The remote-controlled, $4 million NAV has a built-in video camera. Because it is so small, it can go where humans can't. It can scout out safe spots in combat zones, search for earthquake survivors, and even locate a chemical spill.

POP-UP MAP

You don't need 3-D glasses to see this three-dimensional image. The URBAN PHOTONIC SANDTABLE DISPLAY is a full-color holographic map. To create the map, a laser sweeps across a landscape. Software creates the map. Buildings and land features can be displayed at heights of up to 1 foot (30.5 cm). The Department of Defense hopes to use the map for battlefield planning.

THE SWITCH IS ON!

The energy-wasting incandescent bulb will be outlawed by 2014. But many of the newer bulbs give off a harsh white light. So the race is on to create an energy-efficient bulb with a soft glow. The SWITCH BULB may be the answer. It gives off a yellow light and uses only a fraction of the energy that incandescents do. Each bulb costs $20 but lasts 20 years.

EASY ENERGY

Solar power is plentiful. But it takes a lot of solar panels—and space—to collect a usable amount of energy from the sun. That's where Ascent Solar's **THIN-FILM SOLAR PANELS** come in handy. The flexible sheets roll and unroll, and can be used in building materials. A roof or a wall can be made entirely of the thin-film panels, making it easier to soak up the power of the sun.

MILK DUDS

Moo-ve over, cotton. Now there's a fabric made from milk. Biologist and fashion designer Anke Domaske discovered a way to create clothes using sour milk. First, she extracts protein from the milk. Then she spins the protein into yarn. The result is a flexible fabric called QMILCH. It feels similar to silk. A dress or shirt can be made from about 1.5 gallons (5.7 L) of milk. The clothes range in price from $200 to $270.

DRUM PORTAL

UNICEF's (United Nations Children's Fund) **DIGITAL DRUM** is a solar-powered computer center preloaded with educational content. It helps get information about health, education, and other issues to rural communities in Uganda, in Africa, where access to resources is limited. It is made from low-cost metal oil drums, and can hold up against the weather. The first Digital Drum was set up in March at a youth center in the Ugandan city of Gulu.

SOCCER BOT

Goal! The **CHARLI-2** robot was the humanoid—or humanlike—winner at RoboCup 2011, a worldwide soccer competition for robots. The aim is to create robots by 2050 that show advanced competitive behaviors and can defeat human opponents. At 5 feet (1.5 m) tall, CHARLI-2 is stiff and slow. The bot was created at Virginia Tech, by Dennis Hong.

EAR EMOTIONS

Ever wish you could tell how people are feeling just by looking at them? Now you can, with this new product from Japanese company Neurowear. The **NECOMIMI** headband has a sensor on it. The sensor sends brain waves to the band's catlike ears. The ears drop when the wearer is relaxed. They stand straight up when she is concentrating. And when she is both? Then the ears perk up and wiggle wildly.

MYSTERY PERSON

In 1876, when I was just 29 years old, I invented a device that made a whole new form of communication possible. With my invention, voices are carried over wires so that people can talk to other people who are far away. I never guessed that my invention would eventually go cellular and that the wires would not be needed.

WHO AM I? _____

Answer on page 243.

TOP 5 OUTDATED INVENTIONS

According to a survey of 500 teens, these inventions are headed for the scrap heap.

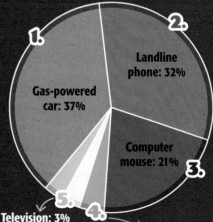

1. Gas-powered car: 37%
2. Landline phone: 32%
3. Computer mouse: 21%
4. Other (books, DVDs, VCRs, radios, and more): 4%
5. Television: 3% / I don't know: 3% (tie)

Inventions

Language and Literature

There's a Word for That

Do you like learning cool new words? If so, you are probably a logophile, or word lover. *Logo* means "word," and *phile* means "lover." Learning new words can be a lot of fun. Just be careful that you don't develop logorrhea. A person with logorrhea talks too much.

NO PB&J FOR ME; I HAVE ARACHIBUTYROPHOBIA!

*Whenever I turn on my electric toothbrush, I hear the most annoying **bombilation**.*

BOMBILATION
(bahm-bi-*lay*-shun)
Loud and continuous buzzing or humming

MUMPSIMUS
(*mump*-si-mus)
A stubborn person who won't try new things
*Stop being such a **mumpsimus**—you're the only one in the world who doesn't use e-mail.*

ARACHIBUTYROPHOBIA
(uh-*rack*-uh-byoo-tuh-ruh-*fo*-bee-yuh)
Fear of peanut butter sticking to the roof of one's mouth

*Please excuse Ryan for being late today. He suffers from **dysania**.*

DYSANIA
(dis-*say*-nee-uh)
Having difficulty getting out of bed in the morning.

QUIDNUNC
(*kwid*-nunk)
A busybody or gossip; someone who always wants to know everyone else's business
*Don't tell Brad about the surprise party, because he's a **quidnunc**.*

BORBORYGMIC
(bore-bo-*rig*-mik)
An adjective describing the noises your stomach makes
*Have a sandwich. The **borborygmic** sounds you're making are driving me crazy.*

*There's a smudge on your **glabella**.*

GLABELLA
(glah-*bell*-uh)
The space between the eyebrows

I CAN'T EAT ANOTHER THING. I'M FARCTATE.

FARCTATE
(*fahrk*-tayt)
Stuffed or filled until solid; an adjective that could be used for someone who has eaten too much

UPDATING THE DICTIONARY

In 2011, the editors of the *Merriam-Webster Dictionary* added more than 150 words and phrases to the dictionary. Here are a few of them.

bromance: a close friendship between two men

fist bump: a hand gesture, almost like a "high five," in which two people curl a hand into a fist and touch their knuckles together

social media: forms of electronic communication where people can post content and share messages, like the computer sites Facebook and YouTube

tweet: a short message posted on Twitter. *Tweet* is also the verb meaning to post a message on Twitter.

Scripps Spelling Bee Winner

Sukanya Roy, an Indian-American 14-year-old girl, won the 84th Scripps Spelling Bee on June 2, 2011. She beat 274 other great spellers and won by spelling the word *cymotrichous* correctly (the word means to have wavy hair). "I went through the dictionary once or twice, and I guess some of the words really stuck," said Sukanya.

LANGUAGES AROUND THE WORLD

There are 6,909 languages spoken in the world. Of these, 473 are almost extinct, which means that only a few people still speak them.

The language with the most speakers is Mandarin Chinese. More than 845 million people speak Mandarin.

In Papua New Guinea, 820 different languages are spoken.

The consonant sounds that are most common in the world's languages are p, t, k, m, and n.

Taki-Taki, a language spoken in Suriname, has only 340 words. This is the smallest number of words in a written language.

English has about 250,000 words. This is the largest number of words in a language.

Award-Winning Books

2012 Newbery Medal
Dead End in Norvelt, by Jack Gantos

2012 Caldecott Medal
A Ball for Daisy, written and illustrated by Chris Raschka

2012 Coretta Scott King Author Award
Heart and Soul: The Story of America and African Americans, written and illustrated by Kadir Nelson

2012 Robert F. Sibert Informational Book Medal
Balloons over Broadway: The True Story of the Puppeteer of Macy's Parade, by Melissa Sweet

2012 Scott O'Dell Award for Historical Fiction
Dead End in Norvelt, by Jack Gantos

2012 Pura Belpré Award
Under the Mesquite, by Guadalupe Garcia McCall

2012 Margaret A. Edwards Award
The Dark Is Rising Sequence, by Susan Cooper

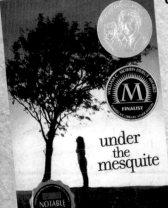

2012 YALSA Award for Excellence in Nonfiction

The Notorious Benedict Arnold: A True Story of Adventure, Heroism & Treachery, by Steve Sheinkin

2011 National Book Award for Young People's Literature

Inside Out & Back Again, by Thanhha Lai

2011 Indies Choice Award for Young Adult Book of the Year

Revolution, by Jennifer Donnelly

2011 Edgar Allan Poe Award, Best Juvenile

The Buddy Files: The Case of the Lost Boy, by Dori Hillestad Butler

2011 *Boston Globe*–Horn Book Award for Nonfiction

The Notorious Benedict Arnold: A True Story of Adventure, Heroism & Treachery, by Steve Sheinkin

BEST-SELLING CHILDREN'S BOOKS OF 2011

1. *The Hunger Games*
   By Suzanne Collins
2. *Diary of a Wimpy Kid: Cabin Fever*
   By Jeff Kinney
3. *Catching Fire*
   By Suzanne Collins
4. *Inheritance*
   By Christopher Paolini
5. *Mockingjay*
   By Suzanne Collins
6. *The Son of Neptune*
   By Rick Riordan
7. *The Throne of Fire*
   By Rick Riordan
8. *Diary of a Wimpy Kid: The Ugly Truth*
   By Jeff Kinney
9. *The Wimpy Kid Do-It-Yourself Book*
   By Jeff Kinney
10. *Elf on the Shelf*
    By Carol V. Aebersold

Some Books to Love

Do you like to read about dragons and magic? How about Greek myths or space travel? Perhaps you prefer to read about events that really took place? Or maybe you'd like to stay up all night cracking a good mystery or unraveling a spooky tale. There are countless books to choose from, and here are a few that you might want to check out. When you read a book you like, tell your friends, teachers, and librarians about it.

A Wrinkle in Time
By Madeleine L'Engle
Meg Murry's search for her father takes her and her friends on a journey through space and time. They meet three zany characters who help Meg battle an evil being who wants to turn all people into robots.

Dave the Potter: Artist, Poet, Slave
By Laban Carrick Hill
Illustrated by Bryan Collier
A talented artist living in South Carolina in the 1800s, Dave was also a slave. But his hardships did not stop him from creating beautiful pottery, some of which survives today.

The Phantom Tollbooth
By Norton Juster
Illustrated by Jules Feiffer
Join Milo as he travels in his magic tollbooth through the Kingdom of Wisdom and the Lands Beyond to save the Princesses Rhyme and Reason.

Interstellar Pig
By William Sleator
Barney's beach vacation is pretty tame, until his out-of-this-world neighbors introduce him to a game called Interstellar Pig. The game ends up being a real-life battle to save the planet.

The House with a Clock in Its Walls
(Lewis Barnavelt Series #1)
By John Bellairs
Join Lewis Barnavelt as he explores his Uncle Jonathan's spooky mansion and uncovers the truth about the hundreds of clocks in the house and the house's mysterious former owner.

The Giver
By Lois Lowry
Jonas lives in a perfect society. But he soon learns that he has a very important role as "Receiver of the Memories"—and that much has been lost to keep the image of perfection going.

Lincoln: A Photobiography
By Russell Freedman
Packed with photos and illustrations, this biography gives us a many-sided picture of our 16th President. The reader will learn more about Lincoln's role in freeing U.S. slaves, get to know his sense of humor, and find out some details of the President's everyday life. This is a serious book but also a fun read.

The True Meaning of Smekday
By Adam Rex
When the Boovs invade Earth, Gratuity Tucci grabs her cat and a friendly alien and drives to Florida to find her mother. Her outrageous adventures are more fun than frightening.

MYSTERY PERSON

I was born March 2, 1904, in Springfield, Massachusetts. I wrote and illustrated many now-famous rhyming children's books under a pen name. Since 1997, schools have celebrated reading on my birthday with Read Across America.

WHO AM I? _____

Answer on page 243.

Chasing Vermeer
By Blue Balliett
Sixth graders Petra and Calder find themselves smack in the middle of an international art heist. Follow the clues as they help to track down a stolen piece of art by famous painter Johannes Vermeer.

Eragon
By Christopher Paolini
When Eragon realizes that he is a Dragon Rider, he takes advice from an old storyteller and uses his sword and dragon to save the empire. The dangers he encounters along the way could end in glory—or total destruction.

The Diary of a Young Girl
By Anne Frank
When she was 16 years old, Anne Frank and her family were forced to hide from the Nazis, who wanted to kill all the Jews in Holland. This book tells of her everyday life in a cramped attic, as well as her hopes and fears.

Boy: Tales of Childhood
By Roald Dahl
Some of the ideas that Roald Dahl wrote in his fantasy books came from his zany real-life adventures. This autobiography is often laugh-out-loud funny.

The Lightning Thief
(Percy Jackson and the Olympians Series #1)
By Rick Riordan
This best-selling novel tells the story of 12-year-old Percy Jackson, who discovers that his father was the Greek god Poseidon. He enlists his mortal friends to prevent a war between the Greek gods Zeus, Poseidon, and Hades.

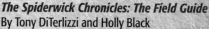

The Spiderwick Chronicles: The Field Guide
By Tony DiTerlizzi and Holly Black
The Grace children—Mallory and her younger twin brothers, Simon and Jared—move into the Spiderwick Estate and find a book that tells them about fairies and other fantastic creatures that live nearby. Their adventures fill this book and several sequels.

The Dreamer
By Pam Muños Ryan
Illustrated by Peter Sís
As a boy, the Nobel prize–winning poet Pablo Neruda lived in fear of his harsh father. Author Pam Muños Ryan imagines what Neruda was like as a boy. In the book, he escapes his difficult home life by daydreaming, creating stories in his head, and finding beauty in nature. This fictional biography tells of his artistic and physical journey to independence.

Language and Literature

Math and Money

WHAT IS MATHEMATICS?

Mathematics is the study of figures and numbers. It deals with shapes, sizes, amounts, and patterns. Its focus is on measuring numeric relationships, analyzing data, and predicting outcomes. Nearly all sciences use mathematics.

ARITHMETIC uses only numbers to solve problems.

ALGEBRA uses both numbers and unknown variables in the form of letters. Algebra helps you to solve problems even when you have very little information.

GEOMETRY is the study of two- and three-dimensional shapes. Geometry will teach you how to figure out the volume of any container.

CALCULUS involves the computation of problems that contain constantly changing measurements.

A two-dimensional shape is flat. It is has two measurements: height and width. A triangle is two-dimensional.

A three-dimensional shape has depth, too. A pyramid is three-dimensional. It has three measurements: height, width, and depth.

EVERYDAY MATH

Ever wonder why you have to memorize multiplication tables or work out those tough long-division problems? Here are just a few times when your mathematical knowledge can come in handy.

- When you need to make a double-size batch of brownies
- After a meal, when it is time to calculate a tip at a restaurant
- Before you buy something, when you must make sure you have enough money for the item you want plus the sales tax
- In order to find the best shopping bargain based on price and quantity
- When you need to know what time it is in a different time zone
- During sporting events, to determine and predict athletes' statistics
- After the pizza delivery person has arrived, and you need to know how much to contribute for each slice you plan to eat
- When you're buying seeds for your garden and want to know how many you'll need to plant a row
- During holiday shopping season, when you want to buy all your gifts without running out of money

There are also countless jobs that make regular use of arithmetic, algebra, geometry, calculus, statistics, and more. Here are just a few: farmer, architect, accountant, carpenter, geologist, bridge engineer, construction manager, computer programmer, doctor, handyman, meteorologist, and, of course, math teacher.

COMMON FORMULAS

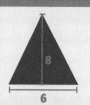

TO FIND THE AREA OF A TRIANGLE:
Multiply the base of the triangle by the height of the triangle. Divide by 2.

area = (base x height) ÷ 2

EXAMPLE: **area = (6 x 8) ÷ 2, or 24 square units**

TO FIND THE AREA OF A RECTANGLE:
Multiply the base of the rectangle by its height.

area = base x height

EXAMPLE: **area = 6 x 3, or 18 square units**

TO FIND THE AREA OF A SQUARE:
Multiply the length of one side of the square by itself.

area = side x side

EXAMPLE: **area = 4 x 4, or 16 square units**

The **radius** of a circle is the length of a straight line from the center of the circle to any point on the perimeter of the circle.

TO FIND THE AREA OF A CIRCLE:
Multiply the radius by itself. Then multiply the product by 3.14 (which is also known as π, or **pi**).

area = radius x radius x 3.14
(or area = πr^2)

EXAMPLE: **area = 5 x 5 x 3.14, or 78.5 square units**

The **diameter** of a circle is the length of a straight line beginning on the perimeter of the circle, passing through the center and ending on the perimeter of the circle. The diameter is twice as long as the radius. The **circumference** of a circle is the distance around the entire circle.

TO FIND THE CIRCUMFERENCE OF A CIRCLE:
Multiply the diameter by 3.14.

circumference = diameter x 3.14
(or circumference = diameter x π)

EXAMPLE: **circumference = 10 x 3.14, or 31.4 units**

MYSTERY PERSON

I was born in England in 1642 and made many advances in mathematics, optics, and acoustics. I am known as the Father of Calculus. I am most famous for developing the laws of gravity. Some people say that I discovered gravity when an apple fell on my head, but that's not exactly how it happened.

WHO AM I? _____

Answer on page 243.

Math and Money

147

Get Down to Business!

By Andrea Delbanco

Becoming an entrepreneur is a great way to make money, even though it's hard work. If you're dedicated and have excellent organizational skills, it can be rewarding: Sometimes, a small business can grow into a multimillion-dollar company! Neale S. Godfrey, author of *Ultimate Kids' Money Book*, shares these tips for starting a successful business.

STEP 1: HAVE AN INNOVATIVE IDEA.

Suppose you like dogs and have free time and compassion for people with busy schedules. Why not start a dog-walking service?

STEP 2: FIND OUT IF YOUR BUSINESS HAS A CHANCE OF SUCCEEDING.

Come up with questions and do a market survey. Ask prospective clients about their likes and needs. Find out how much they would be willing to pay for your services. The responses to your questionnaire will help you decide if you should move forward with your plan. Also, check out the competition. If there's another dog-walking service in your neighborhood, your business has a smaller chance at success.

STEP 3: COMPILE A BUSINESS PLAN AND A BUDGET.

A detailed business plan says what product will be sold, how it will be sold, who the customers will be, and how much it will cost to start. A budget outlines your finances in detail.

STEP 4: CONTACT POTENTIAL CUSTOMERS.

Reach out to anyone who might need you. Then, set a work schedule for yourself. Finally, you have to actually start walking dogs!

STEP 5: KEEP TABS ON YOUR BUSINESS.

Once your business is up and running, look at how it's doing. If you have money left over after your business expenses are paid, you've made a profit. You can consider yourself a successful entrepreneur!

Handing out business cards is one great way to spread the word about your new company.

Thomas Bryant
Dog Walkers, Inc.
555-7734

guess what? Money is printed at the Bureau of Engraving and Printing. They have two manufacturing facilities, in Washington, D.C., and Fort Worth, Texas. They produce 23.5 million bills a day and use about 8.5 tons of ink. In total, these notes are worth about $453 million. Bills usually last about two years before they have to be replaced.

going green Some green businesses are perfect for young entrepreneurs. Kids can make money by collecting and returning recyclables, by selling crafts made from recycled materials, or by growing organic vegetables and setting up a roadside stand.

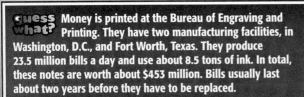

THE KIDS VEGETABLE STAND

INCOMES AROUND THE WORLD

The average annual income of residents of different countries varies greatly. The average annual income of a person in the United States is $47,140. How does that compare with other countries?

Australia	$46,710
China	$4,260
Ethiopia	$380
Germany	$43,330
Jamaica	$4,750
Japan	$42,150
Hungary	$12,990
Mexico	$9,330
Norway	$85,380
Pakistan	$1,050
Peru	$4,710
Rwanda	$540
Serbia	$5,820
South Africa	$6,100
Sri Lanka	$2,290
Uruguay	$10,590

HOW MONEY IS MADE

In the United States, the Bureau of Engraving and Printing goes through a painstaking 65-step process to make paper money. First, the pictures and writing are engraved by hand into pieces of steel. Plastic imprints are made of these steel engravings and are put together to create a template for making 32 bills at the same time. After several steps, a printing plate made from this template is put on a rotary printing press that can print 8,000 sheets in an hour. That's a lot of sheets—and a lot of money!

Coins are made by first stamping blank disks out of a coiled sheet of metal that is 1,500 feet (457 m) long. The blanks are cleaned, shined, and milled to create the raised (and sometimes grooved) edge of the coin. Then the coins are put through a press, which imprints the words and pictures onto them. After inspection, they are counted, bagged, and sent out to Federal Reserve Banks, which pass them on to local banks.

THE FACES OF MONEY

In the United States, the people featured on money are chosen by Congress. Most U.S. currency features a picture of a former President. Here are some exceptions.

» Alexander Hamilton, the first Secretary of the Treasury, is on the $10 bill.

» Benjamin Franklin appears on the $100 bill.

» Salmon P. Chase is on the $10,000 bill. He was Secretary of the Treasury when the first paper bills were designed.

ONE PRICEY COIN!

The highest price ever paid for a U.S. coin was $7.59 million for a 1933 double eagle $20 gold coin on December 8, 2009. What's so special about this coin? Although 445,000 of these coins were made in 1933, none were officially circulated, because 1933 was the last year that gold was used for coins in the United States. Most of the double eagles were melted down. Two are in the U.S. Mint. About 20 others were stolen. When the stolen coins showed up at auctions, federal agents confiscated them. Eventually, the statute of limitations ran out (which means that the crime happened so long ago that the thieves could no longer be brought to trial). Now, the rare coins belong to the collectors who have them.

> **guess what?** "Eagle" was a popular nickname for the $10 coin that was used in the United States between 1795 and 1933. That's why the $20 coin is called the double eagle.

Math and Money

FROM
TIME
FOR KIDS
MAGAZINE

Return of the Muppets!

By TFK Kid Reporter Jack Wetzel

After more than 10 years away, the lovable, fuzzy characters of *The Muppets* finally returned to the big screen. The film's story follows Muppets fan Gary (played by Jason Segel), his girlfriend Mary (*Enchanted* star Amy Adams), and his brother and best friend Walter, as they try to save Muppet Theater from the evil oil baron Tex Richman (Chris Cooper). The movie reunites the entire Muppets gang, including fan favorites Miss Piggy and Kermit the Frog.

TFK Kid Reporter Jack Wetzel sat down with Jason Segel in 2011 in Beverly Hills, California, to talk about the Muppets and what its like to be an actor. In addition to starring in the film, Segel cowrote the screenplay with Nicholas Stoller.

TFK: Growing up, you said you watched *The Muppets*. Do you have any memories you can share?

JASON SEGEL: I just remember being a kid and watching it with my family and seeing that my parents were enjoying it the same way I was enjoying it. It wasn't just a show for kids, sort of like *The Simpsons* today or the Pixar movies. It was a perfect mix [for] adults and kids.

TFK: What was it like performing with the Muppets? Who is your favorite Muppet?

SEGEL: It was really cool. I'm much taller than all of those Muppets, so I had to do a lot of sitting so they could kind of be the same height as me. It was really fun to see these guys do their thing after such a long time. Fozzie was my favorite.

TFK: Did you do anything special to prepare for your role as Gary?

SEGEL: I just tried to remind myself of what I was like when I was a kid, because Gary is very kidlike. We just had to be Muppety.

TFK: What advice do you have for kids that want to go into acting and writing?

SEGEL: It's all about hard work. Some people think, "I'll just become an actor so I don't have to have a real job! It'll be fun and easy!" But you have to work hard at anything you want to do if you want to succeed. So just be prepared for a lot of hard work.

Actor Jason Segel introduces Walter, the new Muppet.

going green

Some movie producers are trying to be gentle on the environment. *The Muppets* was a green set. An environmental steward made sure that everyone reduced, reused, and recycled as much as possible, especially at mealtimes.

TOP 5

HIGHEST-GROSSING FILMS OF 2011

1. *Harry Potter and the Deathly Hallows: Part 2*	$1.3 billion
2. *Transformers: Dark of the Moon*	$1.1 billion
3. *Pirates of the Caribbean: On Stranger Tides*	$1 billion
4. *Kung Fu Panda 2*	$663 million
5. *The Twilight Saga: Breaking Dawn, Part 1*	$648 million

Harry Potter and the Deathly Hallows: Part 1, Glee, and American Idol all triumphed at the Teen Choice Awards. Here are a few of the night's big winners.

Alex Pettyfer

MOVIES

CHOICE SCI-FI/FANTASY MOVIE: *Harry Potter and the Deathly Hallows: Part 1*

CHOICE ACTOR, SCI-FI/FANTASY: Taylor Lautner, *The Twilight Saga: Eclipse*

CHOICE ACTRESS, SCI-FI/FANTASY: Emma Watson, *Harry Potter and the Deathly Hallows: Part 1*

CHOICE ANIMATED MOVIE VOICE: Johnny Depp, *Rango*

CHOICE VILLAIN: Tom Felton, *Harry Potter and the Deathly Hallows: Part 1*

CHOICE BREAKOUT MALE: Alex Pettyfer, *I Am Number Four/Beastly*

CHOICE SUMMER MOVIE STAR, MALE: Daniel Radcliffe, *Harry Potter and the Deathly Hallows: Part 2*

CHOICE SUMMER MOVIE STAR, FEMALE: Emma Watson, *Harry Potter and the Deathly Hallows: Part 2*

The stars of Harry Potter

Cory Monteith

TELEVISION

CHOICE TV SHOW, DRAMA: *Gossip Girl*

CHOICE TV SHOW, COMEDY: *Glee*

CHOICE TV ACTOR, COMEDY: Cory Monteith, *Glee*

CHOICE TV ACTRESS, COMEDY: Selena Gomez, *Wizards of Waverly Place*

CHOICE TV SHOW, ANIMATED: *The Simpsons*

CHOICE TV PERSONALITY: Jennifer Lopez, *American Idol*

CHOICE TV REALITY COMPETITION SHOW: *American Idol*

CHOICE BREAKOUT STAR: Darren Criss, *Glee*

CHOICE BREAKOUT SHOW: *The Voice*

CHOICE VILLAIN: Justin Bieber, *CSI*

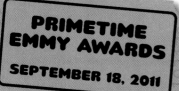

The judges of *American Idol*

Darren Criss

PRIMETIME EMMY AWARDS
SEPTEMBER 18, 2011

OUTSTANDING COMEDY SERIES: *Modern Family*

OUTSTANDING LEAD ACTOR IN A COMEDY: Jim Parsons, *The Big Bang Theory*

OUTSTANDING LEAD ACTRESS IN A COMEDY: Melissa McCarthy, *Mike & Molly*

OUTSTANDING SUPPORTING ACTOR IN A COMEDY: Ty Burrell, *Modern Family*

OUTSTANDING SUPPORTING ACTRESS IN A COMEDY: Julie Bowen, *Modern Family*

OUTSTANDING REALITY COMPETITION PROGRAM: *The Amazing Race*

Jim Parsons

Movies and TV

Set in the late 1920s, **The Artist** tells the story of George Valentin, who gained fame and fortune as a star of silent movies. When "talkies," or motion pictures with sound, come onto the scene, he worries that he will lose everything. George meets a young woman named Peppy, who wants to make her big break in the movies. The story includes glitzy dance numbers, sword fights, car chases, beautiful music, and one very loyal dog. But what makes this story even more unique is that it is both a silent movie and a black-and-white film. Audiences loved it, and it won the Golden Globe for Best Comedy or Musical. Actor Jean Dujardin also won a Golden Globe for his portrayal of George.

Two kids' movies took home awards. Martin Scorsese won the directing award for **Hugo,** and *The Adventures of Tintin* won the animated film category, beating out *Arthur Christmas, Cars 2, Puss in Boots,* and *Rango.*

The Artist

Hugo

PEOPLE'S CHOICE AWARDS
JANUARY 11, 2012

Lea Michele

TELEVISION

FAVORITE NETWORK DRAMA SHOW: *Supernatural*
FAVORITE NETWORK DRAMA ACTOR: Nathan Fillion
FAVORITE NETWORK DRAMA ACTRESS: Nina Dobrev
FAVORITE NETWORK COMEDY ACTOR: Neil Patrick Harris
FAVORITE NETWORK COMEDY ACTRESS: Lea Michele
FAVORITE TV COMPETITION SHOW: *American Idol*
FAVORITE DAYTIME TV HOST: Ellen DeGeneres, *The Ellen DeGeneres Show*

MOVIES

FAVORITE MOVIE: *Harry Potter and the Deathly Hallows: Part 2*
FAVORITE MOVIE ACTOR: Johnny Depp
FAVORITE MOVIE ACTRESS: Emma Stone
FAVORITE MOVIE ICON: Morgan Freeman
FAVORITE ACTION MOVIE STAR: Hugh Jackman
FAVORITE COMEDIC MOVIE ACTRESS: Emma Stone
FAVORITE COMEDIC MOVIE ACTOR: Adam Sandler
FAVORITE MOVIE STAR UNDER 25: Chloë Grace Moretz
FAVORITE ANIMATED MOVIE VOICE: Johnny Depp as *Rango*
FAVORITE MOVIE SUPERHERO: Ryan Reynolds as Green Lantern

Emma Stone

Chloë Grace Moretz

ACADEMY AWARDS
FEBRUARY 26, 2012

At the 84th Annual Academy Awards, or Oscars, *The Artist* was the big winner, picking up five awards, including Best Picture and Best Actor (Jean Dujardin). *Hugo* also won five Oscars (Visual Effects, Sound Mixing, Sound Editing, Cinematography, and Art Direction). The award for Best Animated Feature went to *Rango*, the tale of a chameleon who finds himself in Dirt, a lawless Wild West town. "Man or Muppet," from *The Muppets,* won the Oscar for Best Original Song.

NICKELODEON KIDS' CHOICE AWARDS
APRIL 2, 2011

FAVORITE TV SHOW: *iCarly*
FAVORITE REALITY SHOW: *American Idol*
FAVORITE CARTOON: *SpongeBob SquarePants*
FAVORITE TV ACTOR: Dylan Sprouse
FAVORITE TV ACTRESS: Selena Gomez
FAVORITE TV SIDEKICK: Jennette McCurdy
FAVORITE MOVIE: *The Karate Kid*
FAVORITE MOVIE ACTOR: Johnny Depp
FAVORITE MOVIE ACTRESS: Miley Cyrus
FAVORITE ANIMATED MOVIE: *Despicable Me*

Selena Gomez

going green
GREAT GREEN MOVIES

You can learn a lot about animal habitats and the environment simply by watching movies.

Born to Be Wild 3D takes audiences from the rugged savanna in Kenya, in Africa, to the lush rain forest of Borneo, in Indonesia. This documentary features a pair of extraordinary women who have devoted their lives to saving endangered animals.

Rio is a 3-D animated film, in which you'll meet Blu, a rare Spix's macaw. Blu's life has been so sheltered that he never even learned to fly! Blu is brought to Rio de Janeiro, Brazil, where he meets another Spix's macaw—a female named Jewel. When the pair are captured by smugglers, they must rely on each other and some wacky new friends to escape.

African Cats is a documentary that follows the true stories of the families of lions and cheetahs that live along a river at the Masai Mara National Reserve in Kenya, Africa. The protected park, established in 1961, is one of the wildest places on Earth.

MYSTERY PERSON

I was born in 1965 in England and grew up in Chepstow, Wales. I started writing a novel during a train journey. In the next five years, I outlined five books and wrote the first one. It was published in 1997. The highest-grossing movie series of all time is based on my books.

WHO AM I? _____

Answer on page 243.

Movies and TV

Music

GRAMMY AWARDS
February 12, 2012

RECORD OF THE YEAR: "Rolling in the Deep," Adele

ALBUM OF THE YEAR: *21,* Adele

SONG OF THE YEAR: "Rolling in the Deep," Adele

BEST NEW ARTIST: Bon Iver

BEST POP SOLO PERFORMANCE: "Someone Like You," Adele

BEST POP PERFORMANCE BY A DUO OR GROUP: "Body and Soul," Tony Bennett & Amy Winehouse

BEST POP VOCAL ALBUM: *21,* Adele

BEST TRADITIONAL POP VOCAL ALBUM: *Duets II,* Tony Bennett & Various Artists

BEST ROCK VOCAL PERFORMANCE: "Walk," Foo Fighters

BEST ROCK SONG: "Walk," Foo Fighters

BEST ROCK ALBUM: *Wasting Light,* Foo Fighters

BEST R&B PERFORMANCE: "Is This Love," Corinne Bailey Rae

BEST R&B SONG: "Fool for You," Cee Lo Green

BEST COUNTRY SOLO PERFORMANCE: "Mean," Taylor Swift

BEST COUNTRY PERFORMANCE BY A DUO OR GROUP: "Barton Hollow," The Civil Wars

BEST COUNTRY SONG: "Mean," Taylor Swift

BEST COUNTRY ALBUM: *Own The Night,* Lady Antebellum

BEST CHILDREN'S ALBUM: *All About Bullies . . . Big and Small,* Various Artists

Adele

Foo Fighters

guess what? You may think of him as an actor, but did you know that, in 1989, Will Smith won the first Grammy award for Best Rap Performance? He took home the award for DJ Jazzy Jeff and the Fresh Prince's hit single "Parents Just Don't Understand."

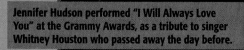

Jennifer Hudson performed "I Will Always Love You" at the Grammy Awards, as a tribute to singer Whitney Houston who passed away the day before.

AMERICAN MUSIC AWARDS
November 20, 2011

Maroon 5

ARTIST OF THE YEAR: Taylor Swift

FAVORITE COUNTRY FEMALE ARTIST: Taylor Swift

FAVORITE COUNTRY MALE ARTIST: Blake Shelton

FAVORITE COUNTRY BAND, DUO, OR GROUP: Lady Antebellum

FAVORITE COUNTRY ALBUM: *Speak Now,* Taylor Swift

FAVORITE POP/ROCK MALE ARTIST: Bruno Mars

FAVORITE POP/ROCK FEMALE ARTIST: Adele

FAVORITE POP/ROCK BAND, DUO, OR GROUP: Maroon 5

FAVORITE POP/ROCK ALBUM: *21,* Adele

FAVORITE LATIN MUSIC ARTIST: Jennifer Lopez

FAVORITE SOUL/R&B FEMALE ARTIST: Beyoncé

FAVORITE SOUL/R&B MALE ARTIST: Usher

During his acceptance speech, Bruno Mars said he'd like to share his award with the other nominees, Pitbull and Justin Bieber.

Jennifer Lopez

guess what? Bruno Mars is a stage name. When the singer was born in Honolulu, Hawaii, his parents named him Peter Gene Hernandez.

MTV VIDEO MUSIC AWARDS
August 28, 2011

VIDEO OF THE YEAR: "Firework," Katy Perry

BEST FEMALE VIDEO: "Born This Way," Lady Gaga

BEST MALE VIDEO: "U Smile," Justin Bieber

BEST COLLABORATION: "E.T.," Katy Perry and Kanye West

BEST ROCK VIDEO: "Walk," Foo Fighters

BEST ART DIRECTION: "Rolling in the Deep," Adele, Art Direction by Nathan Parker

Justin Bieber

Katy Perry

Music

TEEN CHOICE AWARDS
August 7, 2011

Taylor Swift

CHOICE MALE ARTIST: Justin Bieber

CHOICE FEMALE ARTIST: Taylor Swift

CHOICE GROUP: Selena Gomez & the Scene

CHOICE R&B/HIP-HOP TRACK: "Run the World (Girls)," Beyoncé

CHOICE SINGLE: "Who Says," Selena Gomez & the Scene

CHOICE MALE COUNTRY ARTIST: Keith Urban

CHOICE FEMALE COUNTRY ARTIST: Taylor Swift

CHOICE COUNTRY SINGLE: "Mean," Taylor Swift

CHOICE COUNTRY GROUP: Lady Antebellum

CHOICE BREAKOUT ARTIST: Bruno Mars

CHOICE BREAKUP SONG: "Back to December," Taylor Swift

CHOICE LOVE SONG: "Love You like a Love Song," Selena Gomez & the Scene

Selena Gomez & the Scene

guess what? In 2009, Selena Gomez became the youngest-ever ambassador for UNICEF (the United Nations Children's Fund), which works to improve the lives and health of kids worldwide. In 2012, she traveled to the Democratic Republic of the Congo for humanitarian work.

MYSTERY PERSON

My birth name is Eleanora Fagan, and I grew up in Baltimore in the 1920s. I changed my name when I started singing in Harlem nightclubs. Although I had no musical training and did not know how to read music, my voice and my ability to interpret songs made me one of the greatest jazz singers of all time. I died when I was just 44 years old. *Lady Sings the Blues,* a movie about my life, was released in 1972.

WHO AM I? _____

Answer on page 243.

COUNTRY MUSIC AWARDS
November 9, 2011

ENTERTAINER OF THE YEAR: Taylor Swift

Blake Shelton

FEMALE VOCALIST OF THE YEAR: Miranda Lambert

MALE VOCALIST OF THE YEAR: Blake Shelton

ALBUM OF THE YEAR: *My Kinda Party,* Jason Aldean

SINGLE OF THE YEAR: "If I Die Young," The Band Perry

NEW ARTIST OF THE YEAR: The Band Perry

VOCAL GROUP OF THE YEAR: Lady Antebellum

VOCAL DUO OF THE YEAR: Sugarland

Lady Antebellum

PEOPLE'S CHOICE AWARDS
January 11, 2012

FAVORITE MALE ARTIST: Bruno Mars

FAVORITE FEMALE ARTIST: Katy Perry

FAVORITE BAND: Maroon 5

FAVORITE POP ARTIST: Demi Lovato

Demi Lovato

FAVORITE COUNTRY ARTIST: Taylor Swift

FAVORITE SONG OF THE YEAR: "E.T.," Katy Perry featuring Kanye West

FAVORITE ALBUM OF THE YEAR: *Born This Way,* Lady Gaga

guess what? During an interview for a literacy campaign called Read Every Day, Lead a Better Life, Taylor Swift talked about how reading helped her to become the songwriter she is today. "I discovered writing when I discovered poetry. . . . I love poetry because if you get it right, put the right rhymes at the right ends of the sentences, you can almost make words bounce off a page. I think my love of poetry fed into songwriting."

Music

Just about every country, every culture, and every generation has its own musical style. Some overlap—but there are unique qualities to each genre, or type.

BLUEGRASS mixes country and folk music, with some Irish and Scottish overtones and a bit of jazz. Banjos and fiddles are often used in bluegrass.

BLUES came out of the Deep South of the United States. It had its roots in slave songs, spirituals, and country ballads. Blues music uses specific chords to create very expressive music. It greatly influenced jazz, rock, and rhythm and blues (R&B) music.

CLASSICAL music is a formal style, based on European traditions and following standard rules for structure and instruments. It's often played by full orchestras, though there are pieces for piano and other single instruments. **OPERA** is a classical form that is sung, usually with very elaborate lyrics called a libretto.

There are many kinds of classical music.

COUNTRY music is from the southern United States. Early on, it was the music that cowboys listened to. Usually folksy and twangy, it has expanded to include rock rhythms.

GOSPEL, one of several types of Christian music, is usually sung by energetic, passionate choirs. It includes elements of the blues, African spirituals, and folk music (especially songs of enslaved African Americans).

JAZZ started in African-American communities in New Orleans and spread across the country. It's known for its strong, complicated rhythms and the use of trumpets and horns. Jazz soloists are known for their distinct voices.

Operas often tell very dramatic stories.

POP is short for "popular," and it refers to music that is loved by a large group—usually young people. Pop music has easy-to-follow melodies. Many countries have their own forms—but U.S. pop sells best.

RAP music came out of black communities in New York City in the 1970s. It uses spoken lyrics and rhymes set to a beat. Rap often features slang and improvised lyrics, and pieces of music sampled from earlier tunes.

Country singer Carrie Underwood

Guess what? In case the 1977 *Voyager* spacecraft (see page 238) encountered any alien life in space, scientists put an album on board. A committee chose songs from all over the world that they thought represented the sounds on Earth. In addition to the sounds of waves, thunder, and animal calls, they included "Johnny B. Goode" by Chuck Berry, "Melancholy Blues" by Louis Armstrong, a Navajo chant, Beethoven's Fifth Symphony, Stravinsky's "Rite of Spring," and songs from Mexico, China, Senegal, and Zaire.

REGGAE, from Jamaica, uses a special beat (actually an offbeat) and lots of percussion instruments like steel drums and maracas, as well as guitars and cowbells.

RHYTHM AND BLUES, or R&B, is often a mixture of the blues, jazz, and gospel. Some R&B is also called **SOUL** music. **CONTEMPORARY R&B** is very different from the original R&B produced in the 1940s and 1950s.

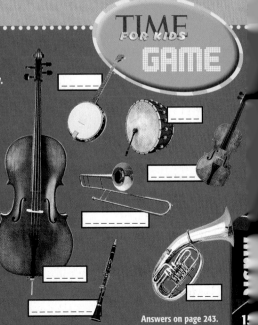

ROCK started out in the 1950s as rock 'n' roll. It emphasizes the beat and is usually played on electric guitars, bass guitars, and drums.

Reggae singer Bob Marley

HEAVY METAL is a type of rock music that does not focus on the melody. It emphasizes the electric guitar, often distorts guitar sounds, and is played very loud. **ROCKABILLY** has country and southern influences.

TEJANO, from Texas, is sung in Spanish and includes elements of Latino music. Latino styles are often dance music, such as salsa, bossa nova, and merengue.

Keith Richards and Mick Jagger of the rock band the Rolling Stones

RECORD BREAKER The world's largest orchestra, with more than 6,400 musicians, was assembled on May 15, 2000. The members of the Vancouver Symphony Orchestra were joined by band students from all over British Columbia in playing Beethoven's Ninth Symphony for 9 minutes and 44 seconds. Maestro Bramwell Tovey conducted.

MUSICAL WORD SEARCH

TIME FOR KIDS GAME

Write the name of each instrument next to its picture. Then, circle the names in the puzzle below.

A	O	E	N	O	B	M	O	R	T
X	K	L	C	N	A	B	E	J	G
I	T	U	L	A	F	Z	M	Q	B
V	E	N	B	E	I	K	U	A	A
G	N	K	V	Z	C	H	R	Z	N
P	I	J	I	D	H	C	D	P	J
E	R	L	O	O	I	T	D	E	O
F	A	R	L	A	N	R	U	M	G
S	L	O	I	K	Y	U	T	B	W
T	C	H	N	Y	L	B	E	U	A

_ _ _ _ _

_ _ _ _

_ _ _ _ _ _ _ _

_ _ _ _ _ _ _ _

_ _ _ _ _

_ _ _ _ _ _

Answers on page 243.

15

Presidents

The Road to the White House

Before the disputed election of 2000, many Americans forgot that our Presidents are not chosen by majority vote. Instead, members of the electoral college cast the final votes. Here's how the election process works in the United States.

START

1.

Candidates announce that they are running for President.

To be eligible, a person must be a natural-born U.S. citizen and at least 35 years of age. He or she must have been a U.S. resident for at least 14 years.

THIS WAY

Mitt Romney campaigns before the primary elections.

2.

Let the campaigns begin!

The first part of a presidential run is known as the **nomination campaign.** This is when several Democratic candidates and several Republican candidates compete against one another for votes within their party. Candidates crisscross the country giving speeches, raising money, and trying to win the trust of the voters. They are also fighting for the support of the delegates. Delegates are members of the Democratic and Republican parties who attend the national party conventions in the summer before each presidential election. By pledging their support for a candidate, they choose which candidate gets nominated by each party.

4.

Each party holds a national nominating convention.

In the summer of a presidential election year, both parties gather their members for a **national convention.** Thousands of members of each party flock to the conventions, where they attempt to whip up excitement for the party and the upcoming election. The delegates from each party cast their ballots for their nominee. With rousing speeches, the nominee from each party is formally announced. Each nominee also introduces his or her running mate, who will become Vice President if the nominee is elected. In 2012, the site of the Democratic National Convention is Charlotte, North Carolina. The site of the Republican National Convention is Tampa, Florida.

THIS WAY

3.

Primary elections and caucuses take place.

To help decide which candidate from each party will win that party's nomination, states hold gatherings to hear from potential voters. Some states hold **primary elections**. These are similar to the general election except people may vote only for candidates or delegates from their own political party. Some states hold a **caucus**, at which party leaders and citizens get together, discuss the issues, debate the candidates, and then cast their votes. Caucuses vary from state to state and are different for both political parties.

THIS WAY

Barack Obama and Hillary Rodham Clinton debate in 2007.

guess what? When it comes to presidential campaigns, Iowa is known as "first in the nation." That is because its caucus is the first to take place in the nominating process for both presidential candidates.

5.
The nominees campaign and campaign . . . and campaign.

During this part of the process, the nominees from both major parties compete against one another for votes all around the country. Representatives from third parties (such as the Independence Party, the Green Party, or the Libertarian Party) try to win over voters as well.

Gerald Ford campaigning in 1976

6.
Citizens vote in the general election.

Every election year, votes are cast on the Tuesday following the first Monday in November.

THIS WAY

7.
The Electoral College votes for President.

The Electoral College came about as a compromise. When the Constitution was being written in 1787, some of the Founding Fathers wanted Congress to be in charge of electing the President. Others felt that the citizens should be allowed to elect their leader by popular vote. So our early leaders put the Electoral College in place. With this system, a group of electors from each state actually choose the President.

When voters cast their ballots for a candidate on election day, it is as if they are voting for the group of electors rather than a particular candidate. Each state has a number of electors equal to the number of its senators and representatives. Washington, D.C., also has three electors. Usually, all of the electors vote for the party that won the most votes in their state. Maine and Nebraska divide their electoral votes among the candidates. To win the presidency, a candidate must receive at least 270 of the 538 possible electoral votes. If this majority is not reached, the House of Representatives chooses the President.

Lyndon B. Johnson casts his ballot in 1964.

THIS WAY

8.
The new President takes the oath of office.

On January 20, the country's new leader is inaugurated. He or she states the presidential oath:

"I do solemnly swear (or affirm) that I will faithfully execute the office of President of the United States, and will to the best of my ability, preserve, protect, and defend the Constitution of the United States."

Abraham Lincoln's inauguration

FINISH

Presidents

U.S. PRESIDENTS

GEORGE WASHINGTON

Born: February 22, 1732, in Virginia **Died:** December 14, 1799
Political Party: None (first term), Federalist (second term)
Vice President: John Adams **First Lady:** Martha Dandridge Custis

 George and Martha Washington had no children of their own, but George helped to raise Martha's two children from an earlier marriage.

SERVED 1789–1797

2 JOHN ADAMS

Born: October 30, 1735, in Massachusetts **Died:** July 4, 1826
Political Party: Federalist
Vice President: Thomas Jefferson **First Lady:** Abigail Smith

 John Adams and Thomas Jefferson were close friends when Adams was inaugurated. By the end of his presidency, the two had such serious political differences that Adams did not attend Jefferson's swearing-in ceremony when he was elected President.

SERVED 1797–1801

THOMAS JEFFERSON 3

Born: April 13, 1743, in Virginia **Died:** July 4, 1826
Political Party: Democratic-Republican
Vice Presidents: Aaron Burr, George Clinton
First Lady: Martha Wayles Skelton (d. 1782)

 Thomas Jefferson founded and designed the University of Virginia.

SERVED 1801–1809

4 JAMES MADISON

Born: March 16, 1751, in Virginia **Died:** June 28, 1836
Political Party: Democratic-Republican
Vice Presidents: George Clinton, Elbridge Gerry
First Lady: Dorothy "Dolley" Payne Todd

 The British burned down the White House while James Madison was President, in 1814.

SERVED 1809–1817

JAMES MONROE 5

Born: April 28, 1758, in Virginia **Died:** July 4, 1831
Political Party: Democratic-Republican
Vice President: Daniel D. Tompkins **First Lady:** Elizabeth "Eliza" Kortright

 James Monroe was one of three Presidents to die on the Fourth of July. Thomas Jefferson and John Adams were the others.

SERVED 1817–1825

6 JOHN QUINCY ADAMS

Born: July 11, 1767, in Massachusetts **Died:** February 23, 1848
Political Party: Democratic-Republican
Vice President: John C. Calhoun **First Lady:** Louisa Catherine Johnson

John Quincy Adams did not place his hand on the Bible when he took his oath of office. Instead, he used a book of laws.

SERVED 1825–1829

ANDREW JACKSON

Born: March 15, 1767, in South Carolina Died: June 8, 1845
Political Party: Democratic
Vice Presidents: John C. Calhoun, Martin Van Buren
First Lady: Rachel Donelson Robards (d. 1828)

 In 1806, Andrew Jackson dueled with a man who had insulted his wife. Jackson was shot, yet he managed to shoot and kill the other man. Jackson had a bullet in his chest for the rest of his life.

SERVED 1829–1837

MARTIN VAN BUREN

 Born: December 5, 1782, in New York Died: July 24, 1862
Political Party: Democratic
Vice President: Richard M. Johnson First Lady: Hannah Hoes (d. 1819)

 The sultan of the Middle Eastern country Oman gave Martin Van Buren a pair of tiger cubs. Members of Congress insisted the animals belonged to the people, so the President sent them to a zoo.

SERVED 1837–1841

WILLIAM HENRY HARRISON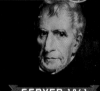

Born: February 9, 1773, in Virginia Died: April 4, 1841
Political Party: Whig
Vice President: John Tyler First Lady: Anna Tuthill Symmes

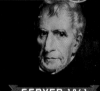 *William Henry Harrison died of pneumonia one month after his inauguration. Many believed he fell ill because he gave his long inaugural address outside, in the cold, without wearing a coat.*

SERVED 1841

JOHN TYLER

 Born: March 29, 1790, in Virginia Died: January 18, 1862
Political Party: Whig
Vice President: None First Ladies: Letitia Christian (d. 1842), Julia Gardiner

 After the presidency, John Tyler moved into a home that he named Sherwood Forest, after the legendary woods Robin Hood and his merry band used as a hideout. Tyler saw himself as a political outlaw, like Robin Hood.

SERVED 1841–1845

JAMES K. POLK

Born: November 2, 1795, in North Carolina Died: June 15, 1849
Political Party: Democratic
Vice President: George M. Dallas First Lady: Sarah Childress

 James K. Polk was President when the first gas lights were installed in the White House.

SERVED 1845–1849

ZACHARY TAYLOR

Born: November 24, 1784, in Virginia Died: July 9, 1850
Political Party: Whig
Vice President: Millard Fillmore First Lady: Margaret Mackall Smith

 Zachary Taylor's second daughter, Sarah Knox, married Jefferson Davis. Davis later became the President of the Confederacy, which was made up of the states that seceded from the United States in 1860 and 1861.

SERVED 1849–1850

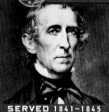

Presidents

MILLARD FILLMORE  13

Born: January 7, 1800, in New York **Died:** March 8, 1874
Political Party: Whig
Vice President: None **First Lady:** Abigail Powers

 Millard Fillmore was Vice President from 1849 to 1850. When President Zachary Taylor died, Fillmore became President. The only time he ran for the presidency, in 1856, he lost.

SERVED 1850-1853

14 FRANKLIN PIERCE

Born: November 23, 1804, in New Hampshire **Died:** October 8, 1869
Political Party: Democratic
Vice President: William R. King **First Lady:** Jane Means Appleton

 Franklin Pierce never worked with a Vice President. William Rufus DeVane King had been elected, but was too ill to attend Pierce's inauguration and died a few weeks later.

SERVED 1853-1857

JAMES BUCHANAN  15

Born: April 23, 1791, in Pennsylvania **Died:** June 1, 1868
Political Party: Democratic
Vice President: John C. Breckinridge **First Lady:** None

 James Buchanan did not enjoy being President. After his first term, he refused to run again.

SERVED 1857-1861

16 ABRAHAM LINCOLN

Born: February 12, 1809, in Kentucky **Died:** April 15, 1865
Political Party: Republican
Vice Presidents: Hannibal Hamlin, Andrew Johnson **First Lady:** Mary Todd

 Abraham Lincoln grew a beard because 11-year-old Grace Bedell said he would look better with one. She wrote to him, suggesting a beard would make his face look less thin.

SERVED 1861-1865

ANDREW JOHNSON  17

Born: December 29, 1808, in North Carolina **Died:** July 31, 1875
Political Parties: Union, Democratic
Vice President: None **First Lady:** Eliza McCardle

 Though Andrew Johnson owned slaves and felt that slavery should not be controlled by Congress, he more strongly believed secession was illegal, and fought for the Union during the Civil War.

SERVED 1865-1869

18 ULYSSES S. GRANT

Born: April 27, 1822, in Ohio **Died:** July 23, 1885
Political Party: Republican
Vice Presidents: Schuyler Colfax, Henry Wilson **First Lady:** Julia Boggs Dent

 Days before his death, Ulysses S. Grant completed his memoirs. His book is considered by many to be an impressive military history of the U.S. Civil War.

SERVED 1869-1877

RUTHERFORD B. HAYES

Born: October 4, 1822, in Ohio **Died:** January 17, 1893
Political Party: Republican
Vice President: William A. Wheeler **First Lady:** Lucy Ware Webb

Guess What? *Rutherford B. Hayes was the first President to have a typewriter and a telephone in the White House.*

SERVED 1877–1881

JAMES A. GARFIELD

Born: November 19, 1831, in Ohio **Died:** September 19, 1881
Political Party: Republican
Vice President: Chester A. Arthur **First Lady:** Lucretia Rudolph

Guess What? *James Garfield was the last President to be born in a log cabin.*

SERVED 1881

CHESTER A. ARTHUR

Born: October 5, 1829, in Vermont **Died:** November 18, 1886
Political Party: Republican
Vice President: None **First Lady:** Ellen Lewis Herndon (d. 1880)

Guess What? *Chester Arthur was nicknamed "Elegant Arthur" because he dressed stylishly.*

SERVED 1881–1885

GROVER CLEVELAND

Born: March 18, 1837, in New Jersey **Died:** June 24, 1908
Political Party: Democratic
Vice President: Thomas A. Hendricks **First Lady:** Frances Folsom

Guess What? *In 1886, Grover Cleveland married Frances Folsom in the White House's Blue Room. He was the only President to be married inside the White House.*

SERVED 1885–1889

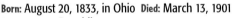

BENJAMIN HARRISON

Born: August 20, 1833, in Ohio **Died:** March 13, 1901
Political Party: Republican
Vice President: Levi P. Morton **First Lady:** Caroline Lavina Scott (d. 1892)

Guess What? *Benjamin Harrison is the only grandchild of a President to be elected President. William Henry Harrison was his grandfather.*

SERVED 1889–1893

GROVER CLEVELAND

Born: March 18, 1837, in New Jersey **Died:** June 24, 1908
Political Party: Democratic
Vice President: Adlai E. Stevenson **First Lady:** Frances Folsom

Guess What? *Grover Cleveland is the only President to have served two nonconsecutive terms. That means that his terms were not back to back.*

SERVED 1893–1897

Presidents

WILLIAM McKINLEY  25

Born: January 29, 1843, in Ohio **Died:** September 14, 1901
Political Party: Republican
Vice Presidents: Garret A. Hobart, Theodore Roosevelt
First Lady: Ida Saxton

 William McKinley's wife, Ida, suffered from epilepsy. Whenever she had a seizure in public, McKinley would cover her face with a handkerchief.

SERVED 1897–1901

26 THEODORE ROOSEVELT

Born: October 27, 1858, in New York **Died:** January 6, 1919
Political Party: Republican
Vice President: Charles W. Fairbanks **First Lady:** Edith Kermit Carow

 Teddy Roosevelt was a student at Columbia University's School of Law when he was elected to the New York State Assembly in 1881. He left law school to go into politics instead.

SERVED 1901–1909

WILLIAM H. TAFT  27

Born: September 15, 1857, in Ohio **Died:** March 8, 1930
Political Party: Republican
Vice President: James S. Sherman **First Lady:** Helen Herron

 William H. Taft was a big eater. The cow that supplied milk for the First Family could not keep up. So a cow named Pauline Wayne was shipped in from Wisconsin. Pauline became quite famous and was often seen grazing on the White House lawn.

SERVED 1909–1913

28 WOODROW WILSON

Born: December 28, 1856, in Virginia **Died:** February 3, 1924
Political Party: Democratic
Vice President: Thomas R. Marshall
First Ladies: Ellen Louise Axson (d. 1914), Edith Bolling Galt

Woodrow Wilson is the first President to have been president of a major university—Princeton University.

SERVED 1913–1921

WARREN G. HARDING  29

Born: November 2, 1865, in Ohio **Died:** August 2, 1923
Political Party: Republican
Vice President: Calvin Coolidge **First Lady:** Florence Kling

 Warren G. Harding was a newspaper editor before he went into politics.

SERVED 1921–1923

30 CALVIN COOLIDGE

Born: July 4, 1872, in Vermont **Died:** January 5, 1933
Political Party: Republican
Vice President: Charles G. Dawes **First Lady:** Grace Anna Goodhue

 In 1924, President Coolidge signed the Indian Citizenship Act, which granted U.S. citizenship to all Native Americans born in the country.

SERVED 1923–1929

HERBERT C. HOOVER

Born: August 10, 1874, in Iowa **Died:** October 20, 1964
Political Party: Republican
Vice President: Charles Curtis **First Lady:** Lou Henry

 Herbert C. Hoover was the first President who was a millionaire.

SERVED 1929-1933

FRANKLIN D. ROOSEVELT

Born: January 30, 1882, in New York **Died:** April 12, 1945
Political Party: Democratic
Vice Presidents: John Garner, Henry Wallace, Harry S Truman
First Lady: Anna Eleanor Roosevelt

 *Franklin Roosevelt was the only President to be elected for four terms.*

SERVED 1933-1945

HARRY S TRUMAN

Born: May 8, 1884, in Missouri **Died:** December 26, 1972
Political Party: Democratic
Vice President: Alben W. Barkley
First Lady: Elizabeth "Bess" Virginia Wallace

The S used as Harry Truman's middle initial does not stand for anything. It was a compromise to honor both of his grandfathers, Anderson Shipp Truman, whose middle name began with an S, and Solomon Young, who first name began with an S.

SERVED 1945-1953

DWIGHT D. EISENHOWER

Born: October 14, 1890, in Texas **Died:** March 28, 1969
Political Party: Republican
Vice President: Richard M. Nixon **First Lady:** Mamie Geneva Doud

Dwight D. Eisenhower suffered from a heart attack while in office but recovered after only seven weeks.

SERVED 1953-1961

JOHN F. KENNEDY

Born: May 29, 1917, in Massachusetts **Died:** November 22, 1963
Political Party: Democratic
Vice President: Lyndon B. Johnson **First Lady:** Jacqueline Lee Bouvier

John F. Kennedy won a Pulitzer Prize for his book Profiles in Courage. *The prizes honor excellence in journalism and the arts. He was the first President to win a Pulitzer.*

SERVED 1961-1963

LYNDON B. JOHNSON

Born: August 27, 1908, in Texas **Died:** January 22, 1973
Political Party: Democratic
Vice President: Hubert H. Humphrey
First Lady: Claudia Alta "Lady Bird" Taylor

District judge Sarah T. Hughes administered the oath of office to Lyndon B. Johnson aboard Air Force One after President Kennedy was assassinated. It was the first time a woman gave the oath.

SERVED 1963-1969

Presidents

RICHARD M. NIXON  37

Born: January 9, 1913, in California **Died:** April 22, 1994
Political Party: Republican
Vice Presidents: Spiro T. Agnew, Gerald R. Ford
First Lady: Thelma Catherine "Pat" Ryan

 Richard Nixon was the only President to resign, or step down, from the presidency. He resigned after a scandal known as Watergate.

SERVED 1969–1974

38 GERALD R. FORD

Born: July 14, 1913, in Nebraska **Died:** December 26, 2006
Political Party: Republican
Vice President: Nelson A. Rockefeller
First Lady: Elizabeth "Betty" Anne Bloomer Warren

 *Born in 1913, Gerald R. Ford was named Leslie L. King Jr. after his father. When his mother remarried in 1916, the family began calling him Gerald Ford Jr. after his stepfather. He did not legally change his name until 1935.*

SERVED 1974–1977

JIMMY CARTER 39

Born: October 1, 1924, in Georgia
Political Party: Democratic
Vice President: Walter F. Mondale **First Lady:** Rosalynn Smith

 Jimmy Carter and his wife, Rosalynn, volunteer one week a year for Habitat for Humanity, an organization that helps poor people renovate and build housing for themselves.

SERVED 1977–1981

40 RONALD REAGAN

Born: February 6, 1911, in Illinois **Died:** June 5, 2004
Political Party: Republican
Vice President: George H.W. Bush **First Lady:** Nancy Davis

Ronald Reagan was 73 when he was elected the second time, making him the oldest person ever elected President.

SERVED 1981–1989

GEORGE H.W. BUSH  41

Born: June 12, 1924, in Massachusetts
Political Party: Republican
Vice President: J. Danforth Quayle **First Lady:** Barbara Pierce

 Millie's Book is a book about the day-to-day life of President Bush's dog, Millie, and her time in the White House. Both Millie and First Lady Barbara Bush are listed as the authors of the book.

SERVED 1989–1993

42 BILL CLINTON

Born: August 19, 1946, in Arkansas
Political Party: Democratic
Vice President: Albert Gore Jr. **First Lady:** Hillary Rodham

 President Clinton's inauguration ceremony was the first to be broadcast live over the Internet.

SERVED 1993–2001

GEORGE W. BUSH  43

Born: July 6, 1946, in Connecticut
Political Party: Republican
Vice President: Dick Cheney   **First Lady:** Laura Welch

Guess what? *In 1993, George W. Bush ran a marathon. He completed the 26.2 miles (42.2 km) in 3 hours, 44 minutes, and 52 seconds. He was the first marathon runner to become President.*

SERVED 2001–2009

44 ## BARACK OBAMA

Born: August 4, 1961, in Hawaii
Political Party: Democratic
Vice President: Joe Biden   **First Lady:** Michelle Robinson

Guess what? *Obama was known as "Barry" until he entered college.*

SERVED 2009–

SQUEAKERS: The Closest Elections in U.S. History

Bush vs. Gore (2000) When the electoral votes for every state except Florida were counted, Republican George W. Bush had 246 electoral votes, and Democrat Al Gore had 266. To win, a candidate must receive at least 270 of the 538 possible electoral votes. So, Florida's 25 electoral votes would decide the election. But the race in Florida was too close to call, with many ballots in dispute because they were not clearly marked. Votes were counted and recounted, with each candidate coming out on top on different days. Finally, the Supreme Court decided in favor of Bush, and he became President.

Hayes vs. Tilden (1876) Democrat Samuel Tilden won the popular vote, but there was no clear winner in the electoral college. Tilden won 184 electoral votes. Republican Rutherford B. Hayes had 165. But there were 20 electoral votes outstanding. These votes—from Louisiana, Florida, Oregon, and South Carolina—were disputed because each state submitted two sets of election returns, showing different results. Congress appointed an Electoral Commission and, after much heated debate and some deal-making, Rutherford B. Hayes was elected.

HAYES   TILDEN

Thomas Jefferson

Jefferson vs. Burr (1800) This dispute was not between the candidates of two parties. Instead, it was between two candidates from the same political party. At the time, the person who became President was the person who received the most electoral votes. The vice presidency went to the candidate with the second-highest number of votes. But Thomas Jefferson and Aaron Burr, both Democratic-Republicans, ended up with the same number of electoral votes. The election was turned over to the House of Representatives, which, after voting 36 times, elected Thomas Jefferson as President. The Constitution was later amended to prevent a tie from happening again.

Presidents

169

FROM TIME FOR KIDS MAGAZINE

A World of Mummies

By Jaime Joyce

Ancient Egypt is famous for mummies. But did you know that Egypt isn't the only place where mummies have been found? Or that Egyptian mummification isn't the only way to preserve the dead? The *Mummies of the World* exhibit, which is traveling throughout 2012 and 2013, showcases more than 40 human and animal mummies. These preserved bodies are from countries all over the world, including Egypt, Germany, and Argentina. A highlight of the exhibit is a 6,420-year-old figure from Peru.

One of the exhibit's most unusual mummies is a howler monkey from Argentina. It is dressed in a feathered skirt and collar. Another unusual mummy, from Peru, is known as the Tattooed Woman. Three oval markings can still be seen on her chest and one at the corner of her mouth. When the woman died, her body was placed in a crouched position in the desert. It was naturally mummified by hot, dry air. Other mummies in the show have also been naturally mummified, in caves, in sand, and in wet muddy areas called bogs.

A LOOK INTO THE PAST

Mummies help us better understand the past. Researchers start with simple observations. Clothing, jewelry, and other objects left with a mummy can offer clues about a person's lifestyle and culture. Researchers also use technology such as CT scans to look inside mummies. They can tell how long a person lived, what foods he or she ate, and what diseases he or she might have suffered from. "One of the most important things we can learn from this exhibition is what kinds of lives people led," Derrick Pitts of the Franklin Institute told TFK. Danielle Romanuski, 11, visited the exhibit with her family. "The people were just like us," she said about the mummies.

To learn more about the exhibit, go to *mummiesoftheworld.com*.

Ancient Egyptian mummy skull

A Hungarian mummy from 1806

Mummified howler monkey

guess what? Ancient Egyptians did not consider the brain to be as important as the heart. During the process of mummification, the brain was removed and thrown away, but the heart was usually left inside the body.

BRANCHES OF SCIENCE

Science is the field of knowledge that studies and organizes information and draws conclusions based on measurable results. Science includes many different fields of study. Some are included here.

Oceanographer

Earth sciences focus on the Earth and study its composition and structure. **Geology** is the study of the Earth's inner rock formations. **Geography** is concerned with the study and mapping of the Earth's terrain. **Oceanography** is the study of oceans and their currents and habitats. **Meteorology** is the study of weather.

Archaeologists

Life sciences explore the nature of living things. **Biology** covers the study of how living things evolve, reproduce, thrive, and relate to one another. **Botany** focuses on plants, **zoology** on animals, **entomology** on insects, and **microbiology** on microscopic organisms.

Entomologist

Physical sciences study the properties of energy and matter and their relationship to each other. **Physics** seeks to explain how the universe behaves through the workings of matter, energy, and time. **Chemistry** is the study of chemical elements and how they interact on an atomic level. **Astronomy** is the study of space and its galaxies.

Social sciences investigate how humans behave and live together. **Psychology** explores individual human behavior, while **sociology** analyzes human behavior in groups. **Anthropology** studies human physical traits as well as cultures and languages. **Archaeology** studies society by looking at artifacts and other records. **Economics** focuses on how money, goods, and businesses affect society. **Law** concerns the rules of society, and **political science** studies government.

Technology, which is about finding practical solutions through science in fields such as **computer science, engineering,** and **biotechnology,** is sometimes included as a branch of science. **Mathematics** differs from other branches of science because it deals with concepts rather than physical evidence.

Engineer

Albert Einstein (1879–1955) was a physicist who proposed the theory of relativity. This complicated theory states (among other things) that every person's perception depends on when and where he or she is in place and time. Einstein worked on complicated math and physics formulas but also loved music and nature.

BIG NAMES IN SCIENCE

Some people call **Galileo** the Father of Astronomy, because he helped develop the telescope and proposed theories about the universe. He lived from 1564 to 1642, and promoted the theory that the world is round, not flat.

Charles Darwin wrote *On the Origin of Species* (published in 1859), which explained his theory of evolution. He stated that certain mutations enable some species to better survive their habitats. These mutations are then passed down to their offspring. As a result, species evolve, or develop new characteristics, over time.

Nobel Prize winner **Marie Curie** is another famous scientist. A physicist, she and her husband (also a physicist) discovered the properties of two new chemical elements, radium and polonium, in 1898. Modern medical cancer treatments are based on her discoveries. In 1952, **Jonas Salk** created a vaccine against the polio virus, which can cause paralysis. Salk's discovery saved the lives of hundreds of thousands of people and has prevented the disability of many more.

SCIENTISTS AT WORK TODAY

There are countless scientists working today. Some are exploring how plants can be better used in medicines. Some are developing new energy sources to replace fossil fuels. Others travel to remote places to find new species of animals. Check out what these cool scientists are up to.

Nick Toberg and Till Wagner, Polar-Ice Physicists

Toberg and Wagner have done sea-ice fieldwork aboard the Greenpeace ship *Arctic Sun* in the waters north of Norway. "There is plentiful data to suggest that the ice is thinning as well as shrinking in area. It's a downward spiral," they wrote. The changes happening in the Arctic are a warning for the entire world.

Nick Toberg

Robin Moore, Herpetologist

Moore and his team went to Haiti in October 2011 to search for lost amphibians. His goal was to find the La Selle grass frog, last seen in 1985. Moore and the team strapped on headlamps and made their way through the forest, inching slowly forward toward the sounds of the frogs. They never found the La Selle frog, but they did find six other long-lost species. One of the frogs they found is the Mozart's frog, named after classical music composer Wolfgang Amadeus Mozart. They also found a species that can make its voice sound as if it's coming from elsewhere. "It took hours to find that frog," says Moore.

A **herpetologist** is a scientist who studies amphibians and reptiles.

Robin Moore

A **volcanologist** is a geologist who studies volcanoes.

Nina Fascione, Conservationist

Fascione is the head of Bat Conservation International (BCI). She is working to find a cure for a mysterious sickness that has killed more than a million bats in Canada and the United States. The disease is called white-nose syndrome (*sin*-drome). Fascione says more money is needed to study the disease. It is important to find a cure. Bats are helpful for many reasons. They spread the seeds of tropical plants, and they eat tons of insects, which is a big help to farmers. "But maybe the most important reason to protect bats is that we need to conserve wildlife species so future generations can appreciate the wonders of nature just as we can," says Fascione.

Nina Fascione

Michael Rampino, Geologist

Michael Rampino travels to areas where volcanoes have erupted in the past and will probably erupt again. He studies ash and other materials from the eruptions. "Being a volcanologist is fun," he says. "It's cool traveling the world studying volcanoes. When I talk to students, I tell them that my inspiration is to understand the events that shaped Earth's history."

Michael Rampino

Michael Pittman, Paleontologist

Dinosaur expert Michael Pittman was part of an international team of scientists working near the China-Mongolia border. The team discovered a new species of dinosaur that had only one finger on each hand. It is the only known single-digit dino and was part of a family called theropods. The new dinosaur was small, about the size of a parrot, and lived as far back as 84 million years ago. Researchers say it used its fingers to dig up bugs.

Michael Pittman sits in the Gobi desert, next to a tail bone from a long-tailed, long-necked sauropod dinosaur.

Joseph Hahn, Neurosurgeon

Dr. Joseph Hahn was a neurosurgeon (a doctor who operates on the brain) for 33 years. Now he is in charge of all the doctors at his hospital. "Surgery is rewarding," Hahn Says. "Former patients come back and tell me how grateful they are that I operated on them. Now I get to pass on what I've learned to a new generation of doctors. It's been fun. It's still fun, and I still love coming to work."

Piotr Naskrecki, Entomologist

Harvard University entomologist Piotr Naskrecki hikes through the world's oldest habitats to find organisms, or living things, that have remained nearly unchanged for millions of years. "Ancient organisms often possess characteristics that make them the ultimate survivors," says Naskrecki. These plants and creatures offer clues about how life existed on Earth before humans were a part of its history.

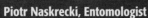
Piotr Naskrecki in Papua New Guinea

Science

173

TRACKING DOWN KILLER BACTERIA

When a health problem is detected, the Centers for Disease Control (CDC) springs into action, investigating causes and determining how to eliminate the danger. Sometimes, CDC agents need to act like detectives, using science and other skills to unravel mysterious causes of illness.

On September 2, 2011, the Colorado Department of Public Health and Environment notified the CDC that seven people had become ill with listeriosis since August 28. Listeriosis is a serious bacterial infection that's usually caused by eating food contaminated with *Listeria monocytogenes* bacteria. In most people, it causes flulike symptoms, but in elderly, newborn, pregnant, and already ill people, it can be deadly. Over the next few days, more people in several states became sick.

To get to the bottom of the outbreak, CDC workers interviewed all of the victims and found that they had eaten cantaloupes. The health workers discovered that the fruits the victims ate were all grown in the Rocky Ford area of southeastern Colorado. By September 5, CDC members had collected leftover cantaloupes from a victim's home and from several supermarkets for testing.

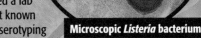

Microscopic *Listeria* bacterium

Scientists used a lab test known as serotyping to look at the markers on the surface of the bacteria and identify the specific strain of bacteria found in the cantaloupes. Investigators found that all the victims had the same strain of bacteria, which made them believe that all the infections had the same source. Then, they conducted DNA fingerprinting, which identified the bacteria's specific genetic pattern, and checked it against the PulseNet database to see where the disease had spread.

The agents traced the cantaloupes to their source and found that they all came from Jensen Farms, which had shipped cantaloupes to at least 24 states from July 29 to September 10, 2011. After testing cantaloupes in Jensen Farms' field, as well as the equipment in their packing facilities, the scientists were confident that they knew the exact cause of the contamination. On September 12, the CDC issued a warning about the Rocky Ford cantaloupes and told people nationwide not to eat them.

By November 2, 2011, the outbreak was under control. But, 139 people had been infected, and 29 had died. It was a terrible outbreak. Luckily, the CDC and local public health officers were able to use science to find the source of the bacteria and stop more people from getting sick.

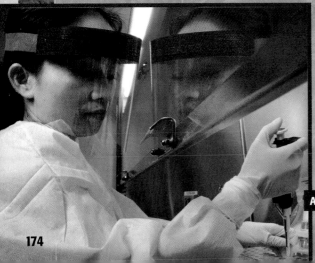

Farmer Eric Jensen inspects fields of rotting cantaloupes.

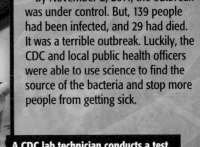

A CDC lab technician conducts a test.

THE BUILDING BLOCKS OF NATURE

Everything on Earth is made up of **atoms**. An atom consists of two parts:

✳ A nucleus that contains one or more **protons** and **neutrons**

✳ One or more **electrons** that circle around the nucleus. The number of electrons will always be equal to the number of protons in an atom.

Protons are particles that have a positive electrical charge. Electrons are particles that have a negative electrical charge. Neutrons have no electrical charge. The opposite charges of protons and electrons cause an attraction between these particles. This attraction keeps the electrons spinning around the nucleus.

Atoms combine to form **elements,** such as hydrogen, oxygen, nitrogen, carbon, and sodium. **Molecules** are formed when two or more different kinds of atoms are joined in a chemical reaction. What results is a substance that has different chemical properties than the atoms that form it.

✳ Water is made up of molecules that contain two hydrogen atoms and one oxygen atom. Water is very different from either pure oxygen or pure hydrogen.

✳ Table salt is made up of molecules that contain one sodium atom and one chlorine atom.

✳ Carbon dioxide is made up of molecules that include one carbon atom and two oxygen atoms.

Mixtures are combinations of molecules that are not chemically joined. The molecules can be separated out of the mixture at any time. Salt water is a mixture of the molecules of salt and water. The salt can be separated from the water if the water evaporates.

MICROSCOPES AND WHAT WE SEE WITH THEM

One of the most important tasks that a scientist performs is close observation. Microscopes help scientists to see tiny things in great detail. They magnify, or enlarge, the image of an item placed beneath a lens. Some microscopes use light for magnification. With a light microscope, we can see things that are 200 times smaller than the thickness of a human hair. But that is nothing compared with what the world's most powerful microscope can see! There are microscopes that can see things that are smaller than one ten-billionth of a meter.

MICROSCOPIC MATCHUP

Here are some extreme close-ups. Can you match each photo to one of the words below?

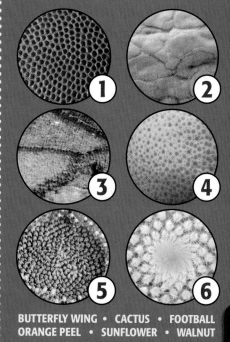

BUTTERFLY WING • CACTUS • FOOTBALL
ORANGE PEEL • SUNFLOWER • WALNUT

Answers on page 243.

TIME
FOR KIDS
GAME

Science

175

Next Stop: Mars

By Elizabeth Winchester

An artist's rendering of Curiosity at work

NASA launched Curiosity, a mobile robot, or rover, to Mars on November 26, 2011. The U.S. space agency estimated that the 64-million-mile (103 million km) journey from Cape Canaveral, Florida, to the Red Planet would take almost nine months. Upon arrival, Curiosity is expected to explore the planet for at least one Martian year, which is 687 Earth days. It will scoop soil and drill rocks, producing samples. Instruments inside the rover will study the samples. Curiosity's cameras will take pictures. NASA scientists will interpret the information.

"We are very excited about Curiosity going to Mars and not only telling us about present-day conditions but also telling us about the past," Pamela Conrad told TFK. She is a mission scientist. The main goal of the mission, called the Mars Science Laboratory (MSL), is to determine if Mars could ever have supported life and if clues in the rocks there can prove it.

MISSION POSSIBLE

Curiosity is much bigger and more powerful than any other spacecraft NASA has sent to Mars. The rover is about the size of a car. Curiosity is twice as long as Spirit or Opportunity, two rovers that landed on Mars in 2004. Curiosity can travel longer than earlier

Building Curiosity

rovers. Its battery allows it to function year-round. Previous rovers ran on solar power and were forced to hibernate in the winter. Curiosity can roll over bigger obstacles, and is equipped with powerful tools, including a drill. Past Mars missions have found evidence of water, which all living things need to survive. Curiosity will use its tools to search for other requirements for life, such as carbon and other minerals.

WE ARE CURIOUS

When she was in sixth grade, Clara Ma won NASA's essay contest to name the rover. "Curiosity is the passion that drives us through our everyday lives," she wrote.

Mars missions from 1976 to the present have helped shed light on the Red Planet. Why are we still curious? "Mars is one of our nearest neighbor planets," says Conrad. "It's a good place to figure out what makes a planet livable and learn if planets like our own are very rare or possibly common."

NASA's Mars Science Laboratory (MSL) spacecraft, which carries Curiosity—began its mission aboard a United Launch Alliance Atlas V rocket on November 26, 2011.

guess what?

Curiosity travels aboard a spacecraft that uses the stars to navigate. A star scanner keeps the spacecraft on track by constantly monitoring the rocket's position in relation to different stars.

THE SOLAR SYSTEM

The sun is at the center of our solar system. It consists mostly of ionized gas and supports life on Earth. Planets rotate around the sun. Early astronomers were able to see the six closest planets to the sun simply by looking up, but Uranus, Neptune, and Pluto (which is now considered a dwarf planet) can be seen only by telescope. Mercury, Venus, Earth, and Mars are called the terrestrial planets because they have solid, rocky bodies. The outer four planets do not have surfaces because they are made up of gases.

MERCURY
At the closest point in its orbit, Mercury is about 29 million miles (47 million km) from the sun. Because it's so close, Mercury can be seen only within an hour or so of the rising or setting of the sun.

VENUS
Venus is similar in size to Earth but has no oceans. It's covered by a layer of thick clouds, which trap heat in its atmosphere. Its average surface temperature is 847°F (463°C).

EARTH
About 70% of Earth is covered with water. Nearly all of Earth's water is found in the oceans, which are salty. Only 3% is drinkable freshwater. Earth has a diameter of 7,926.2 miles (12,756 km), and its average surface temperature is 59°F (15°C).

MARS
Mars is prone to dust storms that engulf the entire planet. It has two moons and is about 141.71 million miles (227.9 million km) from the sun.

JUPITER
Jupiter is the biggest planet in the solar system. Four of its many moons are planet-size themselves. Its diameter is 11 times bigger than Earth's.

SATURN
Known as the ringed planet, Saturn spins very quickly. It only takes 11 hours for the planet to rotate fully on its axis. Saturn's famous rings are made up of ice and rock.

URANUS
Uranus was discovered by William Herschel in 1781. With a diameter of 31,763 miles (51,118 km), it is about four times the size of Earth.

NEPTUNE
Neptune was the first planet located by mathematical predictions instead of observation. With an average surface temperature of –353°F (–214°C), it is extremely cold on Neptune.

Space

WHAT'S IN SPACE?

STARS

The center of our solar system is a star that we call the sun. It is made up of a hot ball of gases that are constantly exploding. There would be no life on Earth without the sun, because its heat and energy are what cause the chemical reactions that give us oxygen, water, and food. There are billions of stars throughout the galaxies. We have not yet learned whether any of these suns support life the way our sun does.

The sun

GALAXIES

The universe consists of billions of trillions of stars. Scientists aren't sure if every star has planets or other bodies orbiting it, because many stars are simply too far away to observe with today's tools. A group of millions of stars (along with dust, gas, and debris) bound together by gravity is known as a galaxy. (Galaxies are like the enormous neighborhoods that make up the universe.)

Our sun and its planets exist in a part of the universe called the Milky Way galaxy. The Milky Way is huge. If it were possible to travel at the speed of light—186,282 miles per second (299,792 km per second)—it would still take 100,000 years to go from one end of the Milky Way to the other.

Messier 101 is a galaxy about twice as large as the Milky Way.

DWARF PLANETS

In 2006, the International Astronomical Union created a new system of classification to describe worlds that are more developed than asteroids (which are rocky bodies orbiting the sun), but not as complicated as planets. Pluto (which had previously been called a planet), Eris, and the asteroid Ceres became the first dwarf planets.

All objects have gravity. That means that they pull objects toward them. But, the more massive an object is, the greater its gravitational pull. Earth's gravitational pull tugs people and objects downward and keeps us from floating away. The sun's gravitational pull keeps eight planets and lots of other objects in space orbiting around it. Dwarf planets orbit the sun but do not have a gravitational pull that is as strong as a planet has.

MOONS

A moon is a natural satellite made of rock or ice that orbits a planet or other solar body. Mercury and Venus have no moons. Mars has two. Neptune has 13. Uranus has 27, and Jupiter has 62! Some moons orbit dwarf planets that are large enough to have a field of gravity to hold them in an orbit. Earth has just one moon, which is about 240,000 miles (386,243 km) away.

Mimas, one of Saturn's moons

COMETS

A comet is made up of frozen gas, rocks, dust, and ice. It's like a cosmic snowball, orbiting in space. When a comet gets near the sun, it heats up and parts of it begin to melt. Its dust and gases spread out into a formation that can be a few miles long, a few hundred miles, or even a few hundred million miles in length.

This comet was spotted in 2001.

An artist's comparison of the sizes of Earth, dwarf planets, and their moons.

Earth's moon

Eris

Earth

Ceres

Pluto

Charon (Pluto's moon)

People have been studying space since ancient times. Until the 1950s, however, all of this activity took place on the ground. Then, on October 4, 1957, Russian scientists launched Sputnik, an unmanned satellite, into space. On January 31, 1958, the National Aeronautics and Space Administration (NASA), which runs the U.S. space program, launched its own satellite, Explorer 1. NASA sent its first spaceman, Alan Shepard, into space later that year, and on February 20, 1962, another American astronaut, John Glenn, became the first human to orbit Earth in a spaceship.

Space exploration took a giant leap forward on July 20, 1969, when U.S. astronaut Neil Armstrong stepped onto the surface of the moon. Here are some other dates to remember.

Hubble

1971 The Russians launch *Salyut I,* the first space station.

1976 NASA's Viking I lands on Mars.

Viking I

1978 NASA's Pioneer 1 and Pioneer 2 reach Venus's atmosphere.

1979–81 NASA's Voyager spacecrafts pass Jupiter and Saturn, taking the first close-up pictures of these planets.

1981 The first space shuttle, *Columbia,* is launched by NASA.

1983 America's first woman astronaut, Sally Ride, travels into space.

1990 The Hubble space telescope is launched.

1998 Construction begins on the International Space Station.

2003 China lauches *Shenzhou 5,* its first manned space mission.

2004 *SpaceShipOne*, the first privately launched spacecraft, lifts off from Mojave, California.

2008 India launches its first unmanned moon mission.

2011 Space shuttle *Atlantis* takes off on a final mission. NASA retires its shuttles.

Atlantis

MYSTERY PERSON

I was born on March 9, 1934, in the Soviet Union. After joining the air force, I trained to be a cosmonaut. On April 12, 1961, I became the first human in space. I orbited Earth one time during a 108-minute flight on *Vostok 1.* My flight paved the way for space exploration.

WHO AM I? _____

Answer on page 243.

SPACE SUITS

An astronaut's space suit is like a traveling home, containing all the things needed to sustain and protect life. Space suits provide oxygen to breathe and pressurization to keep the astronaut's blood from boiling in space. Designing a space suit is a big challenge. It needs to protect the person inside, but still be mobile enough that the astronaut can move around and conduct repairs.

Space

TFK Talks to Shaun White

The star snowboarder (and skateboarder) chats with TFK's Vickie An about his many jobs and about his plans for the 2014 Winter Olympics in Sochi, Russia.

TFK: You've got two Olympic gold medals in snowboarding. Are you itching for a third in Sochi, Russia?

SHAUN WHITE: I'd love to [compete in the Games again]. Nothing compares to the feeling you get when you're up there. It's this world stage. You're no longer you—you're Team America. It's amazing.

TFK: Is it hard to come up with new tricks?

WHITE: It's tough! But I find taking time away makes me a better boarder.

TFK: How do you feel about skateboarding possibly becoming an Olympic sport?

WHITE: I support it. It gives credit to the guys who are out there every day on the ramps doing dangerous tricks and pushing the envelope.

TFK: Is it true you're into rally racing too?

WHITE: I'm still in my learning phase. It's my favorite style of race-car driving. It's extremely fast, and there's dirt flying in the air. It's really cool.

TFK: You helped create a new flavor of gum. What was that like?

WHITE: It's Stride Whitemint. My friends and I sat down for a few hours and just tested different gums.

TFK: I bet your jaw hurt after that!

WHITE: I know! We weren't allowed to share which flavor we liked, but we all chose the same one. It's tasty!

TFK: You are also designing home goods for kids. What will they look like?

WHITE: Our blue monster is on the sheets, and there is a skateboard lamp. We never thought about doing anything for the home before.

CROSS-COUNTRY SKIING

The 2012 U.S. Cross-Country Championships took place in Rumford, Maine, from January 2 to 8.

Women's Freestyle Sprint	Jessica Diggins
Men's Freestyle Sprint	Torin Koos
Women's Classical Sprint	Daria Gaiazova
Men's Classical Sprint	Tyler Kornfield
Women's 10K Freestyle	Jessica Diggins
Men's 15K Freestyle	Tad Elliott
Women's 20K Classical	Jessica Diggins
Men's 30K Classical	Noah Hoffman

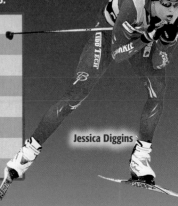

Jessica Diggins

||||||||||||||||||||||||||||||||||||||||||| FIGURE SKATING

Patrick Chan

The World Figure Skating Championships were originally scheduled for Tokyo, but after Japan was hit by a devastating earthquake and tsunami in March 2011, Moscow stepped in to host. Skating fans around the world were treated to some thrilling performances. Japan's Miki Ando became a national heroine with her stirring gold medal win in the women's competition. Ando defeated silver medalist Yuna Kim by only 1.29 points. Canada's Patrick Chan set a world record with his score in the men's short program, finished first in the men's free skating competition, and went on to easily win the gold. Americans Meryl Davis and Charlie White made history by being the first couple from the United States to take home the gold in the ice dancing competition.

Miki Ando

The 2011 World Figure Skating Championships were held April 25 to May 1 in Moscow, Russia. Here are the winners.

Men	Patrick Chan	Canada
Women	Miki Ando	Japan
Pairs	Aliona Savchenko and Robin Szolkowy	Germany
Ice Dance	Meryl Davis and Charlie White	United States

The 2012 U.S. Figure Skating Championships were held in San Jose, California, January 22 to 29. Here are the winners.

Men	Jeremy Abbott
Women	Ashley Wagner
Pairs	Caydee Denney and John Coughlin
Ice Dance	Meryl Davis and Charlie White

Meryl Davis and Charlie White

FOOTBALL

SUPER BOWL XLVI

Lucas Oil Stadium, Indianapolis, Indiana | February 5, 2012
Final score: New York Giants 21, New England Patriots 17

Manningham's spectacular catch

Eli Manning was named Super Bowl MVP.

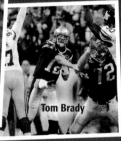

Tom Brady

Super Bowl XLVI was a low-scoring game where both teams showed off their tough defense along with the skill of their quarterbacks. Patriots quarterback Tom Brady threw a touchdown pass at the end of the first half and another one to start the second half. But that was the last time the Patriots scored. The Giants could not score a touchdown for most of the second half and had to settle for two field goals. But with just a few minutes left in the game and the Giants down by two points, Giants quarterback Eli Manning threw a 38-yard pass to wide receiver Mario Manningham. Manningham struggled to stay inbounds and hold onto the football, but managed to do both. That set up the Giants for the touchdown that put them ahead. Brady got the ball back with less than a minute left, but the Patriots could not score. The Giants won their second Super Bowl in five years.

> **Guess what?** New York Giants receiver Victor Cruz celebrates each touchdown with a salsa dance. He turned down an offer to be on *Dancing with the Stars*.

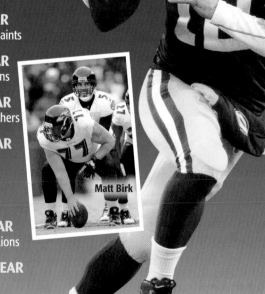

Aaron Rodgers

Matt Birk

2011–2012 NFL AWARD WINNERS

MOST VALUABLE PLAYER
Aaron Rodgers, quarterback, Green Bay Packers

OFFENSIVE PLAYER OF THE YEAR
Drew Brees, quarterback, New Orleans Saints

DEFENSIVE PLAYER OF THE YEAR
Terrell Suggs, linebacker, Baltimore Ravens

OFFENSIVE ROOKIE OF THE YEAR
Cam Newton, quarterback, Carolina Panthers

DEFENSIVE ROOKIE OF THE YEAR
Von Miller, linebacker, Denver Broncos

COACH OF THE YEAR
Jim Harbaugh, San Francisco 49ers

COMEBACK PLAYER OF THE YEAR
Matthew Stafford, quarterback, Detroit Lions

WALTER PAYTON MAN OF THE YEAR
Matt Birk, center, Baltimore Ravens

|||||||| COLLEGE FOOTBALL

BOWL CHAMPIONSHIP SERIES FINAL

Superdome, New Orleans | January 9, 2012
Final score: University of Alabama Crimson Tide 21,
Louisiana State University (LSU) Tigers 0
This showdown was characterized by strong defense on both sides. Alabama kept LSU from scoring, but scored only one touchdown itself. Alabama kicker Jeremy Shelley tied a bowl record with five field goals.

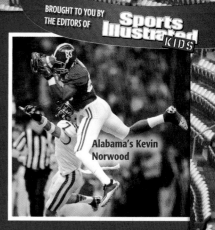
Alabama's Kevin Norwood

OTHER 2012 BCS GAMES

ROSE BOWL	FIESTA BOWL	SUGAR BOWL	ORANGE BOWL
(Pasadena, California)	(Glendale, Arizona)	(New Orleans, Louisiana)	(Miami, Florida)
January 2, 2012	January 2, 2012	January 3, 2012	January 4, 2012
Oregon 45	Oklahoma State 41	Michigan 23	West Virginia 70
Wisconsin 38	Stanford 38	Virginia Tech 20	Clemson 33

HEISMAN TROPHY

Every year, the Heisman Trophy, named after legendary coach John Heisman, is given to the most outstanding player in college football "whose performance best exhibits the pursuit of excellence with integrity." The winner of this important award is chosen by a panel of sportswriters from around the country.

The 2011 award went to Baylor University quarterback Robert Griffin III. Griffin, a junior, is the first player from Baylor to win the Heisman. He led his team to one of its best seasons ever. He passed for 3,998 yards, threw for 36 touchdowns, and had 644 rushing yards and 9 rushing touchdowns.

Robert Griffin III

RECORD BREAKER

University of Wisconsin quarterback Russell Wilson set a record for most consecutive games with a touchdown pass, in December 2011, during the first quarter of the Big Ten championship game against Michigan State. The three-yard completion extended Wilson's streak to 37 consecutive games, passing former Texas Tech star Graham Harrell's NCAA record. Wilson's streak began while he was playing for North Carolina State.

BASEBALL

Game 1 of the World Series

2011 WORLD SERIES

The St. Louis Cardinals and the Texas Rangers met in one of the greatest World Series ever. The Rangers and Cardinals are two power-hitting teams, but the first two matches were low-scoring, one-run games. Game 3 was a 16–7 Cardinals victory in which St. Louis superstar Albert Pujols blasted three homers, tying Babe Ruth and Reggie Jackson for the single-game home run record. The Rangers were on the brink of their first World Series championship when they were one strike away from winning Game 6. But the Cardinals battled back to tie up the game in the 9th inning. Then the Rangers were ahead by two runs in the 10th inning, and the Cardinals fought back again to tie the game. The Cardinals eventually won the game in the 11th inning on David Freese's walk-off home run. Many fans called the game the greatest in baseball history. The Cardinals easily won Game 7, 6–2, giving them their 11th World Series title.

guess what? With their Game 6 victory, the Cardinals became the first team to come back in the 9th and 10th innings of a World Series game. They were also the first team to score runs in the 8th, 9th, 10th, and 11th innings.

2011 MLB LEAGUE LEADERS

BATTING

Home Runs
American League: Jose Bautista, Toronto Blue Jays, 43
National League: Matt Kemp, Los Angeles Dodgers, 39

Batting Average
American League: Miguel Cabrera, Detroit Tigers, .344
National League: Jose Reyes, New York Mets, .337

PITCHING

Earned Run Average
American League: Justin Verlander, Detroit Tigers, 2.40
National League: Clayton Kershaw, Los Angeles Dodgers, 2.28

Strikeouts
American League: Justin Verlander, Detroit Tigers, 250
National League: Clayton Kershaw, Los Angeles Dodgers, 248

Jose Reyes

RECORD BREAKER St. Louis's hometown hero, third baseman David Freese, was named the series MVP for his clutch hitting. Freese drove in a record-setting 21 RBIs during the postseason, including a two-run double in Game 7.

2011 LITTLE LEAGUE WORLD SERIES

The 65th annual Little League World Series featured eight teams from the United States and eight teams from around the world. It was a grueling tournament that ended with the championship matchup of Ocean View Little League of Huntington, California, versus Hamamatsu Minami Little League of Hamamatsu City, Japan. In a tightly fought contest, the Huntington team's first baseman, Nick Pratto, hit a two-out bases-loaded walk-off single to give his team a 2–1 win.

guess what? Former hockey star Chris Drury has the rare honor of winning a Little League World Series and the NHL Stanley Cup.

Bye-Bye, Bats!

Batters like composite bats (made of aluminum and graphite) for their light swings and spring action. The bats get better with use, while wood and metal bats generally get worse. For these reasons, composite bats are a big hit with Little Leaguers. But for these same reasons, composite bats have been benched. This season, for the first time, Little League has banned most of them. Little League officials passed the ban in December due to safety concerns: Balls were flying off of the bats too fast, hard, and far, putting players at risk for injury. Many players—and parents—are upset about the ban, because their expensive equipment is no longer allowed. And some sluggers are confused about exactly which bats are banned. Visit *littleleague.org* for details before your next game.

Craig Kimbrel

Justin Verlander

2011 MLB AWARD WINNERS

MOST VALUABLE PLAYER
American League: Justin Verlander, Detroit Tigers
National League: Ryan Braun, Milwaukee Brewers

CY YOUNG AWARD (BEST PITCHER)
American League: Justin Verlander, Detroit Tigers
National League: Clayton Kershaw, Los Angeles Dodgers

ROOKIE OF THE YEAR
American League: Jeremy Hellickson, Tampa Bay Rays
National League: Craig Kimbrel, Milwaukee Brewers

MANAGER OF THE YEAR
American League: Joe Maddon, Tampa Bay Rays
National League: Kirk Gibson, Arizona Diamondbacks

guess what? Justin Verlander of the Detroit Tigers is the 10th player to win the Cy Young Award and be named MVP in the same year. The last time that happened was in 1992, when Dennis Eckersley of the Oakland As won both honors.

Sports

BASKETBALL

||||||||||||||||||||||||||||||||||||||||||||||||

2011 NBA FINALS

The 2011 NBA Finals featured the Eastern Conference champion Miami Heat against the Western Conference champion Dallas Mavericks. The Heat looked tough to beat, with superstars LeBron James, Chris Bosh, and Dwyane Wade leading the way. The series was close, with five of the six games determined by differences of less than 10 points. The Mavericks came back from a 15-point deficit in Game 2. The series went back and forth, with Miami taking the lead twice and Dallas tying it twice. In the tie-breaking Game 5, Dallas sunk 13 three-point shots and came from behind to win, taking the series lead with three wins to two. Dallas fell behind early in Game 6, but then scored a spectacular 21 points to Miami's 4. Dallas held on and won their first NBA championship.

Dirk Nowitzki

LeBron James

guess what? German-born Dirk Nowitzki was Dallas's top scorer in five of the six games of the NBA finals. The Mavericks veteran played most of the series with a splint on his finger protecting a torn tendon. His scoring and gutsy leadership earned him the series MVP award.

RECORD BREAKER In February 2011, Boston Celtics guard Ray Allen passed Reggie Miller for the all-time NBA lead in three-point field goals. Miller had held the record for more than 13 years and was at the game to see his record fall.

TOP SCORER
Kevin Durant
(Oklahoma City Thunder)
played 78 games and averaged 27.7 points per game.

MOST ASSISTS
Steve Nash
(Phoenix Suns)
played 75 games and averaged 11.4 assists per game.

MOST REBOUNDS
Kevin Love
(Minnesota Timberwolves)
played 73 games and averaged 15.2 rebounds per game.

2011 WNBA CHAMPIONSHIP

The Eastern Conference champion Atlanta Dream went up against the Western Conference Minnesota Lynx in the 2011 WNBA Finals. The Atlanta Dream came into the finals led by their top scorer, Angel McCoughtry, and rebounder Erika de Souza. The Lynx were a strong team with offensive superstar Seimone Augustus and rebounding powerhouse Rebekkah Brunson. Despite McCoughtry's record-setting 38 points in Game 1, the Lynx proved to be too strong an opponent. The Lynx swept the Dream in three games to capture the WNBA championship.

Augustus played hard in the 2011 WNBA finals, leading her Minnesota Lynx to the league championship. For her tough play and timely scoring, she was awarded the MVP trophy.

COLLEGE BASKETBALL |||||

2011 NCAA MEN'S DIVISION 1 CHAMPIONSHIP

The 2011 NCAA men's basketball final, held April 4, 2011, in Houston, Texas, pitted the Connecticut Huskies against the Butler Bulldogs. The Huskies were the third-ranked team in the NCAA, while the Bulldogs were ranked eighth. Surprisingly, the match was a defensive battle that saw Connecticut trailing 22–19 at halftime. Led by Bob Cousy Award–winning point guard Kemba Walker, the Huskies went on a massive offensive run that clinched the championship for them. The final score was Connecticut Huskies 53, Butler Bulldogs 41. Kemba Walker took home the Most Outstanding Player award.

2011 NCAA WOMEN'S DIVISION 1 CHAMPIONSHIP

The 2011 NCAA women's basketball final featuring the Notre Dame Fighting Irish and the Texas A&M Aggies was held April 6, 2011, in Indianapolis, Indiana. It was a wild contest. Both teams swapped the lead several times during the matchup. Notre Dame was ahead at halftime, but the Aggies clawed their way back into the match. Outstanding forward Danielle Adams took command and led the Aggies to their first NCAA crown with a 76–70 victory.

Adams was a powerhouse in the tournament, scoring 30 points and pulling down nine rebounds in the final game. She was named tournament MVP.

Seimone Augustus

TOP SCORER
Diana Taurasi
(Phoenix Mercury)
played 32 games and averaged 21.6 points per game.

MOST ASSISTS
Lindsay Whalen
(Minnesota Lynx)
played 34 games and averaged 5.9 assists per game.

MOST REBOUNDS
Tina Charles
(Connecticut Sun)
played 34 games and averaged 11 rebounds per game.

HOCKEY

Tim Thomas

2011 STANLEY CUP

The Vancouver Canucks ended the regular season with the best record in the NHL, so it was no surprise that they ended up in the Stanley Cup playoffs. But the Boston Bruins finished third in their division and hadn't gone to the finals since 1990. In the first six games, each team won on their home ice. In the first game in Boston, the Bruins' sensational young forward, Nathan Horton, was knocked unconscious in the first period by the Canucks' Aaron Rome. Rome was ejected from the game. In the second period, the Bruins scored four goals, added four more in the third, and beat the Canucks 8–1.

The Stanley Cup championship was decided in Game 7 in Vancouver. Horton couldn't play, but he did accompany his teammates to Canada. Bruins goalie Tim Thomas turned aside all of the Canucks' 37 shots for a shutout, and the Bruins were Stanley Cup champions.

2011 NHL AWARD WINNERS

AWARD	GIVEN TO ...	2011 WINNER (TEAM)
Conn Smythe Trophy	Stanley Cup playoffs MVP	Tim Thomas (Boston Bruins)
Hart Memorial Trophy	Most valuable player	Corey Perry (Anaheim Ducks)
Ted Lindsay Award	Best player as voted by fellow NHL players	Daniel Sedin (Vancouver Canucks)
Vezina Trophy	Best goaltender	Tim Thomas (Boston Bruins)
James Norris Memorial Trophy	Best defenseman	Nicklas Lidstrom (Detroit Red Wings)
Calder Memorial Trophy	Best rookie	Jeff Skinner (Carolina Hurricanes)
Art Ross Trophy	Top point scorer	Daniel Sedin (Vancouver Canucks)
Frank J. Selke Trophy	Best defensive forward	Ryan Kesler (Vancouver Canucks)
Jack Adams Award	Best coach	Dan Bylsma (Pittsburgh Penguins)

SOCCER

MAJOR LEAGUE SOCCER

In 2011, Major League Soccer's Los Angeles Galaxy beat the Houston Dynam to win the MLS Cup. Landon Donovan scored the only goal in the 1–0 game assisted by Robbie Keane and his famous teammate David Beckham.

Landon Donovan

2011 FIFA WOMEN'S WORLD CUP

The FIFA Women's World Cup is held every four years. In 2011, it was played in Germany, and it was one of the most thrilling Women's World Cups in history. The matches were played in overflowing stadiums, and the competition was filled with drama and surprises. The United States and Japan met in the final match, and it was a nailbiter. In the end, a shoot-out would determine the winner. It was Japan's Saki Kumagai who kicked home the game-winner, giving Japan their first championship.

AUTO RACING

||||||||||||||||||||||||||||||||||||||||||||||||

BROUGHT TO YOU BY THE EDITORS OF **Sports Illustrated KIDS**

2011 INDIANAPOLIS 500

The 95th Indianapolis 500 was held on May 29, 2011, and after almost three hours of racing, it was decided in the final seconds. Rookie J.R. Hildebrand was leading in the last seven laps and looked like the winner, but then he hit the wall on the final turn of the last lap. He lost one wheel and the car's steering, but skidded toward the finish line anyway. Dan Wheldon, who was in second place, slipped around Hildebrand in the last 1,000 feet (305 m), winning his second Indy 500. Hildebrand came in second. Sadly, it would be Wheldon's last win. Four months later, he was killed in a crash during the Izod IndyCar World Championship at Las Vegas Motor Speedway.

The final moments of the Indianapolis 500

Tony Stewart passes Jimmie Johnson at the Martinsville Speedway in October 2011.

2011 CHASE FOR THE SPRINT CUP

The Sprint Cup Series is considered the top racing series of the National Association for Stock Car Auto Racing (NASCAR). It consists of 36 races. The first 26 races make up the regular season, as drivers rack up points for their finishes. After that, the 12 drivers with the most points compete in the Chase, the final 10 races of the series. The driver with the most points after those 10 races is awarded the Sprint Cup, NASCAR's greatest prize. In 2011, the Chase ended with the Ford 400 on November 20, 2011. The 2011 Sprint Cup Series title came down to Carl Edwards versus Tony Stewart in the last race of the season. Stewart won the race and Edwards came in second, but they were tied on points. The number of total wins served as the tiebreaker to decide which driver came in first and which came in second. Stewart had five wins, and Edwards had just one.

guess what? NASCAR's biggest event is the Daytona 500. Unlike the Super Bowl or the World Series, this race comes at the beginning of the season, not the end.

Tony Stewart

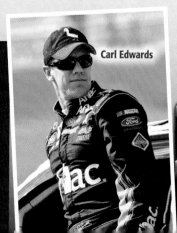

Carl Edwards

THE FINAL STANDINGS OF THE TOP THREE WINNERS OF THE CHASE:

1. Tony Stewart	2,403
2. Carl Edwards	2,403
3. Kevin Harvick	2,330

Sports

TENNIS

Li Na

2011 TENNIS CHAMPIONS

Australian Open
Men's Singles: Novak Djokovic
Women's Singles: Kim Clijsters
Men's Doubles: Bob Bryan and Mike Bryan
Women's Doubles: Gisela Dulko and Flavia Pennetta
Mixed Doubles: Katarina Srebotnik and Daniel Nestor

French Open
Men's Singles: Rafael Nadal
Women's Singles: Li Na
Men's Doubles: Max Mirnyi and Daniel Nestor
Women's Doubles: Lucie Hradecka and Andrea Hlavackova
Mixed Doubles: Casey Dellacqua and Scott Lipsky

Wimbledon
Men's Singles: Novak Djokovic
Women's Singles: Petra Kvitova
Men's Doubles: Bob Bryan and Mike Bryan
Women's Doubles: Kveta Peschke and Katarina Srebotnik
Mixed Doubles: Jurgen Melzer and Iveta Benesova

U.S. Open
Men's Singles: Novak Djokovic
Women's Singles: Samantha Stosur
Men's Doubles: Jurgen Melzer and Philipp Petzschner
Women's Doubles: Liezel Huber and Lisa Raymond
Mixed Doubles: Melanie Oudin and Jack Sock

Davis Cup (Men's International Team Tennis):
Spain defeated Argentina, three matches to one.

Fed Cup (Women's International Team Tennis):
Czech Republic defeated Russia, three matches to two.

Novak Djokovic

SURFING

Kelly Slater

2011 WORLD SURFING CHAMPIONSHIPS

Four champions are recognized every year by the Association of Surfing Professionals (ASP). The titles for best male, female, and longboard surfers are awarded based on points surfers receive in competitions on the ASP World Tour. In 2011, Americans made a clean sweep of the major titles. Kelly Slater was the men's champion for a record 11th time, while Hawaii native Carissa Moore was the women's champion. On the women's longboard, Lindsay Steinriede took top honors, and Taylor Jensen was the men's longboard champ.

CYCLING

2011 TOUR DE FRANCE

The Tour de France is an exhausting bike race that takes place every summer. The 2011 race began on the Passage du Gois and ended in Paris, and covered 2,162 miles (3,479 km). Here are the top five finishers.

NAME	COUNTRY	RACE TIME
1. Cadel Evans	Australia	86:12:22
2. Andy Schleck	Luxembourg	86:13:56
3. Frank Schleck	Luxembourg	86:14:52
4. Thomas Voeckler	France	86:15:42
5. Alberto Contador	Spain	86:16:19

Cadel Evans

GOLF

Rory McIlroy

Yani Tseng

MEN

Masters: Charl Schwartzel
U.S. Open: Rory McIlroy
British Open: Darren Clarke
PGA Championship: Keegan Bradley
U.S. Amateur Championship: Kelly Kraft

WOMEN

Kraft Nabisco Championship: Stacy Lewis
LPGA Championship: Yani Tseng
U.S. Women's Open: So Yeon Ryu
Women's British Open: Yani Tseng
U.S. Amateur Championship: Danielle Kang

RECORD BREAKER At 22, Rory McIlroy from Northern Ireland was the youngest U.S. Open champion since 1923. He posted a record low score, too, and ended up winning by eight shots.

going green
There are more than 16,000 golf courses in the United States, and the average American golf course uses more than 300,000 gallons (1,135,624 L) of water a day to keep its greens healthy. To save on water, some golf course managers have started growing native plant species on some areas of their courses. These native species need little to no watering. Other conservation efforts include computer-controlled irrigation systems that conserve water by tracking local weather conditions and watering only when needed.

GYMNASTICS

2011 WORLD CHAMPIONSHIPS

The Artistic Gymnastics World Championships were held in Tokyo, Japan, from October 7 to 16.

Jordyn Wieber

EVENT	GOLD MEDAL	COUNTRY
Men's Team All-Around		China
Men's Individual All-Around	Kohei Uchimura	Japan
Men's Floor	Kohei Uchimura	Japan
Men's Pommel Horse	Krisztian Berki	Hungary
Men's Rings	Chen Yibing	China
Men's Vault	Yang Hak Seon	South Korea
Men's Parallel Bars	Danell Leyva	United States
Men's Horizontal Bar	Zou Kai	China
Women's Team All-Around		United States
Women's Individual All-Around	Jordyn Wieber	United States
Women's Vault	McKayla Maroney	United States
Women's Uneven Bars	Viktoria Komova	Russia
Women's Balance Beam	Sui Lu	China
Women's Floor	Ksenia Afanaseva	Russia

Kohei Uchimura

2011 COLLEGE GYMNASTICS

The University of Alabama won its fifth NCAA Women's Gymnastics Championship, edging out defending champion UCLA (University of California, Los Angeles). On the men's side, Stanford took the title for the second time in three years.

Alabama's Geralen Stack-Eaton

DOGSLEDDING

IDITAROD

The Iditarod is an annual sled dog race covering more than 1,150 miles (1,917 km) across the mountain ranges, frozen rivers, and forests of Alaska, from Anchorage to Nome. It's been called the Last Great Race on Earth. On March 15, 2011, Alaska native John Baker and his team of 10 dogs rode into Nome in a record time of 8 days, 18 hours, 46 minutes, and 39 seconds, breaking the previous Iditarod record time by almost four hours. Baker's lead dogs were Velvet and Snickers. As Baker and his team ran through the streets of Nome, a spectator yelled, "Good dogs! Good dogs!" "I think so," Baker replied.

Playing It Cool

By Cameron Keady

In 2011, the American Academy of Pediatrics, a medical association made up of children's doctors, issued new guidelines to young athletes about playing sports outside.

Between 2001 and 2009, more than 3,000 U.S. children under the age of 20 received emergency-room treatment for heat-related illness due to playing sports or exercising in high heat. Sports like football are especially dangerous because of players' uniforms and heavy padding, and the fact that the football season often begins in late summer when temperatures are still high.

The doctors' report recommends that every young athlete be evaluated to play in the heat. With solid training, plenty of drinking water, time-outs, and emergency treatment available on the sidelines, young athletes can play even in high heat and humidity—within reason.

GUIDELINES FOR THE SIDELINES

Whether you're on the field or in the swimming pool, it's important to follow the new guidelines for the last weeks of summer—and whenever it's very hot and humid.

- Make sure staff trained in heat safety and treatment is available at all times.
- Allow yourself time to slowly get used to the heat when playing sports.
- Hydrate! Drink anywhere from three to six cups of water an hour.
- Look out for your teammates. If someone seems to be struggling or feeling dizzy, get help right away.
- Give yourself a break. Take at least one rest period for every two hours of physical activity.

HORSE RACING

The three biggest horse races in the United States are the Kentucky Derby, at Churchill Downs in Louisville, Kentucky; the Preakness Stakes, at Pimlico Race Course in Baltimore, Maryland; and the Belmont Stakes, at Belmont Park in Elmont, New York. These three races take place within a five-week period from early May to early June, and make up the Triple Crown of Thoroughbred Racing, or Triple Crown for short.

2011 TRIPLE CROWN RACE RESULTS

Here are the horses that finished in the top three for each of the races that make up the Triple Crown.

Kentucky Derby
1. Animal Kingdom
2. Nehro
3. Mucho Macho Man

Belmont Stakes
1. Ruler on Ice
2. Stay Thirsty
3. Brilliant Speed

Preakness Stakes
1. Shackleford
2. Animal Kingdom
3. Astrology

Ruler on Ice

guess what? Winning all three races in the Triple Crown is considered an amazing feat and currently comes with a bonus of $5 million. The last horse to do it was Affirmed in 1978, ridden by jockey Steve Cauthen.

Sports

193

X GAMES

The X Games, held every winter and summer, showcase the best in extreme sports. Athletes from all over the world participate, showing off their skills with a skateboard, snowboard, bike, motorcycle, rally car, snowmobile, or pair of skis. Some events are based on pure speed, while others reward competitors for style and amazing tricks.

Nate Adams

2011 SUMMER X GAMES
JULY 28–31, LOS ANGELES, CALIFORNIA

Skateboard
Bob Burnquist (Big Air), **Shaun White** (Vert), **Nyjah Huston** (Men's Street), **Marisa Dal Santo** (Women's Street), **Raven Tershy** (Park), **Julian Christianson** (Hometown Heroes Amateur Street), **Ryan Decenzo** (Game of SK8)

Moto X
Nate Adams (Freestyle), **Nate Adams** (Speed and Style), **Vicki Golden** (Women's Racing), **Taddy Blazusiak** (Men's Enduro), **Maria Forsberg** (Women's Enduro), **Matt Buyten** (Step Up), **Jackson Strong** (Best Trick), **Jeremy Stenberg** (Best Whip)

BMX
Steve McCann (Freestyle Big Air), **Jamie Bestwick** (Vert), **Daniel Dhers** (Park), **Garrett Reynolds** (Street)

Nyjah Huston

Rally Car
Liam Doran (Racing), **Brian Deegan** (RallyCross)

David Wise

2012 WINTER X GAMES
JANUARY 26–29, ASPEN, COLORADO

Skiing
Samson Danniels (Mono Skier X), **Bobby Brown** (Big Air), **Chris Del Bosco** (Men's Skier X), **Marte Gjefsen** (Women's Skier X), **Tom Wallisch** (Men's Slopestyle), **Kaya Turski** (Women's Slopestyle), **David Wise** (Men's SuperPipe), **Roz Groenewoud** (Women's SuperPipe)

Snowboard
Mark McMorris (Big Air), **Nate Holland** (Men's Snowboarder X), **Dominique Maltais** (Women's Snowboarder X), **Mark McMorris** (Men's Slopestyle), **Jamie Anderson** (Women's Slopestyle), **Shaun White** (Men's SuperPipe), **Kelly Clark** (Women's SuperPipe), **Forest Bailey** (Street)

Snowmobile
Colten Moore (Freestyle), **Heath Frisby** (Best Trick)

going green

The organizers and athletes of the X Games are very concerned about the environment and do all they can to make the games sustainable. All trash is sorted and recycled. Pipes and courses at the winter games are made out of dirt that is then sprayed with water to make an icy surface—rather than using tons of water to make tons of snow. At the summer games, wooden ramps and platforms are made of wood from responsibly managed forests and are recycled after the games.

Dominique Maltais

194

TIME FOR KIDS GAME

LOST LOCKER!

Jimmy can't remember which gym locker is his. Follow the clues to help him find his uniform in time for the game!

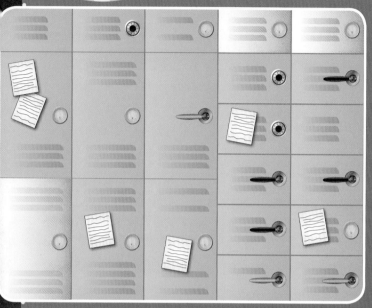

1. The locker is green.
2. The locker does not have a black handle.
3. The locker has exactly three vents.
4. He will need a key to unlock the locker.
5. There is only one note on the locker.

Answer on page 243.

MYSTERY PERSON

I was born on September 12, 1913, in Alabama. I became a world-famous track-and-field star. At Ohio University, I broke three world records. I won four gold medals at the 1936 Olympics in Berlin, Germany. It was a victory over Adolph Hitler, who wanted to showcase his country's white athletes.

WHO AM I? _____

Answer on page 243.

UPCOMING OLYMPICS

The Olympics are held every two years. They alternate between winter sports such as ice hockey, figure skating, speed skating, skiing, luge, snowboarding, and bobsledding, and summer events such as swimming, soccer, basketball, gymnastics, volleyball, archery, wrestling, and weight lifting. The next Winter Games will be held in Sochi, Russia, in 2014. After that, the Winter Games will be in Pyeongchang, South Korea, in 2018. London, England, is hosting the 2012 Summer Olympics. In 2016, the Summer Games will be held in Rio de Janeiro, Brazil.

2008 Summer Olympics

Sports

The Future of Ford

By TFK Kid Reporter Gabrielle Healy

TFK Kid Reporter Gabrielle Healy spoke to Alan Mulally, the head of the Ford Motor Company, in his office at Ford headquarters in Dearborn, Michigan, about the key to his business success and what cars will be like in the future.

TFK: What are your responsibilities as the CEO [chief executive officer] and president of Ford?

ALAN MULALLY: The most important thing is to ensure that everyone associated with Ford has a good business plan. We have a long-term plan to create products and services that people really want and value.

TFK: What will cars be like in the future?

MULALLY: In a couple of years, we'll be able to have regular conversations with our cars. You'll be able to say, "I would like to go to Pizza Hut. Could you give me the shortest route and tell me if there's traffic?"

TFK: How does Ford decide what kinds of vehicles kids my age will want?

MULALLY: We decide by anticipating the needs of all the people who are buying vehicles. We decide which features are important to them. For example, today quality is very important. Safety is very important. Fuel efficiency is very important, and so is being connected to the Internet.

TFK: What kinds of jobs will be available for my generation when I graduate from college in 12 to 15 years?

MULALLY: Almost every occupation you can think of, we need that kind of talent. We treasure engineers, artists, writers, manufacturing folks, and lawyers. So everything you can imagine that you study in school, we need those skills at Ford. We need those skills to manufacture the vehicles, communicate what people want in them, as well as tell people what's available.

The Ford Focus is an electric car. The newer models of the Focus feature special computer applications that allow owners to check up on their vehicles or even charge them remotely.

Focus RS

The Model T

Henry Ford and the Ford Motor Company did not invent the car, but they did change the industry hugely. Ford's car was the first one that was affordable to the general public. It was manufactured on an assembly line that was efficient because each person on the assembly did just one thing and did not spend time moving from one task to another. The Model T cost just $825, about half as much as other cars on the market. By 1918, half of all the cars in the United States were Model Ts.

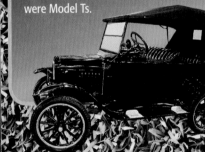

Guess what? There were many designs for automobiles before Henry Ford designed the Model T. One of the first was made in 1335 by Italian Guido da Vigevano, who used a windmill to drive gears that made wheels turn.

WHAT KEEPS AN AIRPLANE IN THE SKY?

How can great big airplanes, filled with hundreds of people and lots of heavy luggage, stay in the sky? Four factors come into play: weight, lift, drag, and thrust.

is what pulls something down and causes it to fall. Weight is closely related to gravity. On Earth, gravity refers to the force that pulls all objects toward the ground. To cancel out weight, airplanes use their wings to get lift. Wings are designed to be the right shape and to move around in the air in a way that keeps the plane in the air. The wings are flat on the top and curved on the bottom so that there is less air pressure on the bottom of the wing. This lower pressure makes the wing go up—and the plane that is attached to the wing goes up also. Airplanes are built so that their weight is carefully balanced.

Drag slows down a plane. It's the force of friction that makes it hard to move through the air, just as it is hard for you to walk through a strong wind. But planes have engines to give them thrust and allow them to move forward. Sometimes the engine moves a propeller to create thrust. On a jet plane, strong gusts of air are forced out the back of the plane to push it forward. If the plane has more thrust than drag, it will move forward.

> **AERODYNAMICS** is the study of how things move around in the air.

LIFT

DRAG

THRUST

WEIGHT

CARS OF THE FUTURE

More than 30,000 people die every year in traffic accidents, and many more suffer injuries. The good news is that since 1990, the number of people who die in car accidents has fallen by more than 20%. This is partly due to child safety seats, air bags, seat-belt laws, and laws against talking on cell phones while driving. And new electronic innovations will make cars safer. Some car designers even talk about crashless cars. Here are a few new additions to cars that show how technology is making cars safer.

> Safety belts that can absorb the energy of a crash and both tighten and release a little to secure a person during an impact, without inflicting injuries

> Sensors that detect other cars ahead and let the driver know if a collision is about to happen

> Side air bags that protect a passenger's head, neck, chest, and pelvis in a crash

> Lane departure warnings (LDWs) that check the lane markings painted on the road and let the driver know if the car is drifting out of its lane

Milestones in Transportation History

In 1860, it could take half a year to travel from the East Coast to the West Coast of the United States. Now, passengers can fly across the country in six or seven hours. In 1950, putting a human on the moon was the stuff of science fiction films. But in 1969, a space vehicle made it happen for real. Here are just a few of the major inventions and events in the history of transportation.

1783 The Montgolfier brothers create the first hot air balloons.

1787 The first successful steam-powered ship is introduced in the United States. By 1807, there is regular steamboat service along the Hudson River in New York and along the Mississippi River. In 1822, the SS *Robert Fulton* completes the first steamboat trip from New York City, New York, to New Orleans, Louisiana.

1803 The first steam-powered locomotive (an early type of train) is invented by Richard Trevithick.

1830 The first passenger railroad in the United States opens. Part of the Baltimore & Ohio Railroad, this 13-mile (21 km) line connects Baltimore and Ellicott City, Maryland.

1832 People begin traveling through New York City aboard horse-drawn streetcars.

1863 The world's first subway opens in London, England.

1869 The transcontinental railroad in the United States is complete. The Central Pacific and Union Pacific Railroads are connected at Promontory Point, Utah. Using the transcontinental railroad, it only takes six days for a person to travel from Omaha, Nebraska, to Sacramento, California.

1871 The cable car is invented by Andrew Hallidie. A cable car system is introduced in San Francisco, California, in 1873. Later, Hallidie's inventions are used to set up cable cars in Chicago, Illinois; Los Angeles, California; Cincinnati, Ohio; and other cities.

1885 German engineer Gottlieb Daimler invents the first car with an internal combustion engine in Germany. It is considered a forerunner of the type of gasoline-powered car that many people drive today.

1897 *Argonaut I*, a gasoline-powered vehicle, is the first successful submarine to operate in the open sea.

1903 Wilbur and Orville Wright design and build the first engine-powered airplane. Over a period of four days, they complete several successful but short flights in Kitty Hawk, North Carolina. The longest one lasts 59 seconds. The plane travels 852 feet (260 m).

1908 On October 1, 1908, the Ford Motor Company introduces the Model T., which it produces until 1927.

1927 Charles Lindbergh is the first person to fly by himself nonstop across the Atlantic Ocean from New York to France. It takes him 33.5 hours to fly 3,610 miles (5,810 km). Five years later, Amelia Earhart becomes the first woman to make a solo flight across the Atlantic Ocean.

1970 Pan Am operates the first commercial jumbo jet, the Boeing 747.

1981 NASA launches the space shuttle *Columbia*. For more information on space firsts, see page 179.

2000 Amtrak launches the Acela, a high-speed train. It can travel at speeds up to 150 miles (241 km) per hour.

2005 The super-jumbo Airbus A380 makes its first flight. The world's largest passenger plane, it can seat 853 people.

2010 Trains on a railway line between Shanghai and Hangzhou, China, travel at an average of 217 miles (350 km) per hour. These high-speed trains set records for going faster than 258 miles (416 km) per hour.

2011 Electric cars become widely available throughout the United States, with many models able to travel 50 miles (80.5 km) on a single charge. Charging stations are installed in many cities.

MYSTERY PERSON

I enlisted in the U.S. Air Force in 1941 when I was 18 years old and worked as an airplane mechanic until I went overseas to fight in World War II. When I came back, I entered test pilot school and was selected to fly the new supersonic plane called the X-1. On October 14, 1947, I broke the sound barrier over the town of Victorville, California.

WHO AM I? _____

Answer on page 243.

Eco-Friendly and Efficient Travel

What's the most efficient way to get around? It depends whether you're more interested in how fast you get there or in how much carbon dioxide you send into the atmosphere (see page 85).

These figures are for a trip from New York City to San Francisco. That's about 2,900 miles (4,667 km).

Type of vehicle	How long it takes	How much CO_2/person
Average U.S. car (23 mpg; 9.4 L/100km) with 1 passenger*	58 hours	2,400 pounds (1,089 kg)
Prius (46 mpg; 4.7 L/100km) with 4 passengers*	58 hours	306 pounds (140 kg)
Bus 	3–5 days, with 4 transfers	520 pounds (236 kg)
Train	3 days	1,220 pounds (553 kg)
Plane	about 5 hours, 30 minutes	2,446 pounds (1,109 kg)

*At an average of 50 miles (80.5 km) per hour

Transportation

United States

STATE BREAKDOWN

As of January 2012, the population of the United States was 312,805,865. Between 2000 and 2010, the population increased by 9.7%. Check out each individual state for information about its population, mottos, state symbols, and more.

ALABAMA

CAPITAL: Montgomery

LARGEST CITY: Birmingham

POSTAL CODE: AL

LAND AREA: 50,750 square miles (131,443 sq km)

POPULATION (2011): 4,802,740

ENTERED UNION (RANK): December 14, 1819 (22)

MOTTO: *Audemus jura nostra defendere.* (We dare maintain our rights.)

TREE: Southern longleaf pine

FLOWER: Camellia

BIRD: Yellowhammer

NICKNAMES: Yellowhammer State, Cotton State, Heart of Dixie

FAMOUS ALABAMIAN: Rosa Parks, civil rights activist

 Helen Keller, the famous deaf and blind author and activist, grew up in Tuscumbia, Alabama. Her childhood home, Ivy Green, is open for visitors.

Birmingham

Montgomery

ALASKA

CAPITAL: Juneau

LARGEST CITY: Anchorage

POSTAL CODE: AK

LAND AREA: 570,374 square miles (1,477,267 sq km)

POPULATION (2011): 722,718

ENTERED UNION (RANK): January 3, 1959 (49)

MOTTO: North to the future

TREE: Sitka spruce

FLOWER: Forget-me-not

BIRD: Willow ptarmigan

NICKNAMES: The Last Frontier, Land of the Midnight Sun

FAMOUS ALASKAN: Scott Gomez, hockey player

 Many active volcanoes can be found in the Cook Inlet in southern Alaska, including Iliamna Volcano, Augustine Volcano, and Redoubt Volcano, which erupted most recently in 2009.

CANADA

Anchorage

Juneau

ARIZONA

CAPITAL: Phoenix

LARGEST CITY: Phoenix

POSTAL CODE: AZ

LAND AREA:
113,642 square miles (296,400 sq km)

POPULATION (2011): 6,482,505

ENTERED UNION (RANK):
February 14, 1912 (48)

MOTTO: *Ditat deus.* (God enriches.)

TREE: Palo verde

FLOWER: Saguaro cactus blossom

BIRD: Cactus wren

NICKNAME: Grand Canyon State

FAMOUS ARIZONAN: Joan Ganz Cooney, founder of *Sesame Street*

 In 1962, engineers discovered that London Bridge in the United Kingdom was, in fact, falling down. The British built a replacement bridge, and American businessman Robert McCulloch bought the old bridge for $2,460,000. Since 1971, a perfectly rebuilt London Bridge has stood in Lake Havasu City, Arizona.

Phoenix

ARKANSAS

CAPITAL: Little Rock

LARGEST CITY:
Little Rock

POSTAL CODE: AR

LAND AREA: 52,075 square miles (134,874 sq km)

POPULATION (2011): 2,937,979

ENTERED UNION (RANK):
June 15, 1836 (25)

MOTTO: *Regnat populus.* (The people rule.)

TREE: Pine

FLOWER: Apple blossom

BIRD: Mockingbird

NICKNAME: Natural State

FAMOUS ARKANSAN: Johnny Cash, singer and songwriter

 The foot bones of a dinosaur were found near Lockesburg, Arkansas, in 1972. A professor who examined the bones gave the birdlike, meat-eating dinosaur a fitting name: the Arkansaurus.

Little Rock

CALIFORNIA

CAPITAL: Sacramento

LARGEST CITY: Los Angeles

POSTAL CODE: CA

LAND AREA: 155,973 square miles (403,970 sq km)

POPULATION (2011): 37,691,912

ENTERED UNION (RANK): September 9, 1850 (31)

MOTTO: *Eureka!* (I have found it!)

TREE: California redwood

FLOWER: Golden poppy

BIRD: California valley quail

NICKNAME: Golden State

FAMOUS CALIFORNIAN: Zac Efron, actor

Guess what? *The La Brea tar pit is one of the most famous fossil sites in the world. More than 3 million fossils, including mammoths, saber-toothed cats, and giant ground sloths, have been found there. These animals were preserved in sticky tar for 40,000 years.*

Sacramento

Los Angeles

COLORADO

CAPITAL: Denver

LARGEST CITY: Denver

POSTAL CODE: CO

LAND AREA: 103,730 square miles (268,660 sq km)

POPULATION (2011): 5,116,796

ENTERED UNION (RANK): August 1, 1876 (38)

MOTTO: *Nil sine numine* (Nothing without the deity)

TREE: Colorado blue spruce

FLOWER: Rocky Mountain columbine

BIRD: Lark bunting

NICKNAME: Centennial State

FAMOUS COLORADAN: AnnaSophia Robb, Actress

Guess what? *In 1996, the government of Colorado made the Colorado hairstreak butterfly the state insect.*

Denver

CONNECTICUT

CAPITAL: Hartford

LARGEST CITY: Bridgeport

POSTAL CODE: CT

LAND AREA: 5,018 square miles (12,997 sq km)

POPULATION (2011): 3,580,709

ENTERED UNION (RANK): January 9, 1788 (5)

MOTTO: *Qui transtulit sustinet.* (He who transplanted sustains.)

TREE: White oak

FLOWER: Mountain laurel

BIRD: American robin

NICKNAMES: Constitution State, Nutmeg State

FAMOUS NUTMEGGER: Marcus Camby, basketball player

Guess What? *Nobel Prize–winning playwright Eugene O'Neill spent summers at the Monte Cristo Cottage in New London, Connecticut. His childhood in the cottage helped to inspire his most famous play,* **Long Day's Journey into Night.**

Hartford

Bridgeport

DELAWARE

CAPITAL: Dover

LARGEST CITY: Wilmington

POSTAL CODE: DE

LAND AREA: 1,955 square miles (5,063 sq km)

POPULATION (2011): 907,135

ENTERED UNION (RANK): December 7, 1787 (1)

MOTTO: Liberty and independence

TREE: American holly

FLOWER: Peach blossom

BIRD: Blue hen chicken

NICKNAMES: Diamond State, First State, Small Wonder

FAMOUS DELAWAREAN: Ryan Phillippe, actor

Guess What? *Delaware has a state star. The Delaware Diamond, named by 12-year-old Amy Nerlinger in a contest held by the Delaware Museum of Natural History, is located in the Big Dipper constellation.*

Wilmington

Dover

Colorado

United States

FLORIDA

CAPITAL: Tallahassee

LARGEST CITY: Jacksonville

POSTAL CODE: FL

LAND AREA: 53,927 square miles (139,670 sq km)

POPULATION (2011): 19,057,542

ENTERED UNION (RANK): March 3, 1845 (27)

MOTTO: In God we trust.

TREE: Sabal palm (cabbage palmetto)

FLOWER: Orange blossom

BIRD: Mockingbird

NICKNAME: Sunshine State

FAMOUS FLORIDIAN: Janet Reno, first female Attorney General

 Established by President Theodore Roosevelt in 1903, Pelican Island National Wildlife Refuge was the first federal land set aside for the protection of wildlife in the United States.

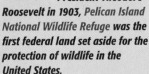

GEORGIA

CAPITAL: Atlanta

LARGEST CITY: Atlanta

POSTAL CODE: GA

LAND AREA: 57,919 square miles (150,010 sq km)

POPULATION (2011): 9,815,210

ENTERED UNION (RANK): January 2, 1788 (4)

MOTTO: Wisdom, justice, and moderation

TREE: Live oak

FLOWER: Cherokee rose

BIRD: Brown thrasher

NICKNAMES: Peach State, Empire State of the South

FAMOUS GEORGIAN: Dakota Fanning, actress

 Coca-Cola was invented by John Pemberton of Atlanta, Georgia, in 1886. It was first sold at soda fountains for five cents per glass.

IDAHO

CAPITAL: Boise

LARGEST CITY: Boise

POSTAL CODE: ID

LAND AREA:
82,751 square miles (214,325 sq km)

POPULATION (2011): 1,584,985

ENTERED UNION (RANK):
July 3, 1890 (43)

MOTTO: *Esto perpetua.*
(Let it be perpetual.)

TREE: Western white pine

FLOWER: Syringa

BIRD: Mountain bluebird

NICKNAME: Gem State

FAMOUS IDAHOAN: Gutzon Borglum, Mount Rushmore sculptor

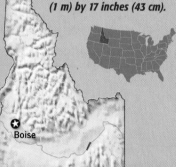

guess what? *The Balanced Rock, in central Idaho, is more than 48 feet (15 m) tall and weighs about 40 tons (36,287 kg). This large rock sits on top of a much smaller rock, which is only about 3 feet (1 m) by 17 inches (43 cm).*

Boise

HAWAII

CAPITAL: Honolulu (on the island of Oahu)

LARGEST CITY: Honolulu

POSTAL CODE: HI

LAND AREA: 6,423 square miles (16,636 sq km)

POPULATION (2011): 1,374,810

ENTERED UNION (RANK):
August 21, 1959 (50)

MOTTO: *Ua mau ke ea o ka aina i ka pono.* (The life of the land is perpetuated in righteousness.)

TREE: Kuku'i (candlenut)

FLOWER: Yellow hibiscus

BIRD: Nene (Hawaiian goose)

NICKNAME: Aloha State

FAMOUS HAWAIIAN: Bette Midler, singer and actress

guess what? *Pineapples are not native to Hawaii. They weren't grown on the tropical islands until the late 1700s or early 1800s. The Hawaiian word for pineapple,* hala kahiki, *means "foreign hala." Hala is a traditional Hawaiian fruit.*

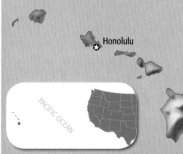

Honolulu

PACIFIC OCEAN

ILLINOIS

CAPITAL: Springfield

LARGEST CITY: Chicago

POSTAL CODE: IL

LAND AREA:
55,593 square miles (143,986 sq km)

POPULATION (2011): 12,869,257

ENTERED UNION (RANK):
December 3, 1818 (21)

MOTTO: State sovereignty, national union

TREE: White oak

FLOWER: Purple violet

BIRD: Cardinal

NICKNAMES: Prairie State, Land of Lincoln

FAMOUS ILLINOISAN: Ronald Reagan,
40th U.S. President

guess what? *The Adler Planetarium in Chicago, opened in 1930, was the first planetarium to be built in the United States. In fact, it was the first planetarium in the Western Hemisphere.*

INDIANA

CAPITAL: Indianapolis

LARGEST CITY:
Indianapolis

POSTAL CODE: IN

LAND AREA: 35,870 square miles
(92,903 sq km)

POPULATION (2011): 6,516,922

ENTERED UNION (RANK):
December 11, 1816 (19)

MOTTO: The crossroads of America

TREE: Tulip tree (yellow poplar)

FLOWER: Peony

BIRD: Cardinal

NICKNAMES: Hoosier State,
Crossroads of America

FAMOUS INDIANAN, OR HOOSIER:
Michael Jackson, musician

guess what? *Abraham Lincoln lived in Illinois when he was elected President, but he grew up in Indiana. Lincoln lived in Indiana with his family from the age of 7 to the age of 21.*

IOWA

CAPITAL: Des Moines

LARGEST CITY: Des Moines

POSTAL CODE: IA

LAND AREA: 55,875 square miles (144,716 sq km)

POPULATION (2011): 3,062,309

ENTERED UNION (RANK): December 28, 1846 (29)

MOTTO: Our liberties we prize, and our rights we will maintain.

TREE: Oak

FLOWER: Wild prairie rose

BIRD: Eastern goldfinch (American goldfinch)

NICKNAME: Hawkeye State

FAMOUS IOWAN: William "Buffalo Bill" Cody, scout and entertainer

Guess what? *Since 1973, the Des Moines Register has hosted RAGBRAI (The Register's Annual Great Bicycle Ride Across Iowa). More than 275,650 people have participated in the seven-day, 472-mile (760 km) ride across the state.*

Des Moines ★

KANSAS

CAPITAL: Topeka

LARGEST CITY: Wichita

POSTAL CODE: KS

LAND AREA: 81,823 square miles (211,922 sq km)

POPULATION (2011): 2,871,238

ENTERED UNION (RANK): January 29, 1861 (34)

MOTTO: *Ad astra per aspera* (To the stars through difficulties)

TREE: Cottonwood

FLOWER: Sunflower

BIRD: Western meadowlark

NICKNAMES: Sunflower State, Jayhawk State, Wheat State

FAMOUS KANSAN: Amelia Earhart, first woman to fly solo across the Atlantic Ocean

Guess what? *The Santa Fe Trail stretched from Independence, Missouri, to Santa Fe, New Mexico. It was used by the U.S. military and by settlers and traders, mostly between 1821 and 1880. An important route for western expansion, the trail crossed the entire length of Kansas. Miles of trail ruts—some 300 to 400 feet (91 m to 122 m) wide—can still be seen.*

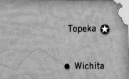
Topeka ★
● Wichita

United States

207

KENTUCKY

CAPITAL: Frankfort

LARGEST CITY: Louisville

POSTAL CODE: KY

LAND AREA:
39,732 square miles (102,906 sq km)

POPULATION (2011): 4,369,356

ENTERED UNION (RANK):
June 1, 1792 (15)

MOTTO: United we stand, divided we fall.

TREE: Tulip poplar

FLOWER: Goldenrod

BIRD: Cardinal

NICKNAME: Bluegrass State

FAMOUS KENTUCKIAN: Diane Sawyer, news anchor and journalist

guess what? *When it was built in 1866, the 1,057-foot-long (322 m) Covington and Cincinnati Suspension Bridge, between Kentucky and Ohio, was the longest suspension bridge in the world. It held the honor for a few years, until the Niagara Clifton Bridge, between New York and Ontario, Canada, surpassed it in 1869.*

Louisville • ★ Frankfort

LOUISIANA

CAPITAL: Baton Rouge

LARGEST CITY:
New Orleans

POSTAL CODE: LA

LAND AREA: 43,566 square miles (112,836 sq km)

POPULATION (2011): 4,574,836

ENTERED UNION (RANK):
April 30, 1812 (18)

MOTTO: Union, justice, and confidence

TREE: Bald cypress

FLOWER: Magnolia

BIRD: Eastern brown pelican

NICKNAME: Pelican State

FAMOUS LOUISIANAN: Harry Connick Jr., actor and singer

guess what? *The city of New Orleans has a rich heritage, influenced by Spanish, French, Creole, and American culture. This heritage is reflected in the architecture of the Vieux Carré, which means "Old Square" in French. This area is often referred to as the French Quarter.*

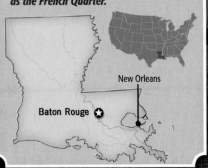

New Orleans

Baton Rouge ★

MAINE

CAPITAL: Augusta

LARGEST CITY: Portland

POSTAL CODE: ME

LAND AREA:
30,865 square miles (79,940 sq km)

POPULATION (2011): 1,328,188

ENTERED UNION (RANK):
March 15, 1820 (23)

MOTTO: *Dirigo.* (I lead.)

TREE: White pine

FLOWER: White pine cone and tassel

BIRD: Black-capped chickadee

NICKNAME: Pine Tree State

FAMOUS MAINER: Olympia
Snowe, U.S. senator

In 1919, Acadia National Park (originally called Lafayette National Park) in Maine became the first National Park east of the Mississippi River. Today the park includes more than 73 square miles (190 sq km) of protected land.

Augusta

Portland

MARYLAND

CAPITAL: Annapolis

LARGEST CITY:
Baltimore

POSTAL CODE: MD

LAND AREA: 9,775 square miles
(25,317 sq km)

POPULATION (2011): 5,828,289

ENTERED UNION (RANK):
April 28, 1788 (7)

MOTTO: *Fatti maschii, parole femine*
(Manly deeds, womanly words)

TREE: White oak

FLOWER: Black-eyed Susan

BIRD: Baltimore oriole

NICKNAMES: Free State,
Old Line State

FAMOUS MARYLANDER:
Harriet Tubman, abolitionist,
Underground Railroad operator

The flag that inspired "The Star Spangled Banner" was sewn in Maryland. It flew over Fort McHenry in Baltimore during the War of 1812. When lawyer Francis Scott Key looked up the morning after the Battle of Baltimore and saw the flag still waving in the wind, he wrote the poem that would become our national anthem. The flag is enormous. Each stripe is 2 feet (61 cm) tall!

Baltimore

Unite

MICHIGAN

CAPITAL: Lansing

LARGEST CITY: Detroit

POSTAL CODE: MI

LAND AREA:
56,809 square miles (147,135 sq km)

POPULATION (2011): 9,876,187

ENTERED UNION (RANK):
January 26, 1837 (26)

MOTTO: *Si quaeris peninsulam amoenam circumspice.* (If you seek a pleasant peninsula, look about you.)

TREE: White pine

FLOWER: Apple blossom

BIRD: American robin

NICKNAMES: Wolverine State, Great Lakes State

FAMOUS MICHIGANDER OR MICHIGANIAN:
Stevie Wonder, singer

Guess what? *The Ford Model T car, introduced in 1908, was invented, designed, and produced at the Ford Piquette Avenue Plant in Detroit, Michigan.*

MASSACHUSETTS

CAPITAL: Boston

LARGEST CITY: Boston

POSTAL CODE: MA

LAND AREA:
7,838 square miles (20,300 sq km)

POPULATION (2011): 6,587,536

ENTERED UNION (RANK):
February 6, 1788 (6)

MOTTO: *Ense petit placidam sub libertate quietem.* (By the sword we seek peace, but peace only under liberty.)

TREE: American elm

FLOWER: Mayflower

BIRD: Black-capped chickadee

NICKNAMES: Bay State, Old Colony State, Baked Bean State

FAMOUS BAY STATER: Alicia Sacramone, gymnast and Olympic medalist

Guess what? *Completed in 1912, Fenway Park is the oldest major league baseball stadium still in use in the United States.*

Boston ✪

Lansing ✪

Detroit •

MINNESOTA

CAPITAL: Saint Paul

LARGEST CITY: Minneapolis

POSTAL CODE: MN

LAND AREA: 79,617 square miles (206,208 sq km)

POPULATION (2011): 5,344,861

ENTERED UNION (RANK): May 11, 1858 (32)

MOTTO: *L'Etoile du nord* (Star of the north)

TREE: Red (or Norway) pine

FLOWER: Pink and white lady's slipper

BIRD: Common loon

NICKNAMES: North Star State, Gopher State, Land of 10,000 Lakes

FAMOUS MINNESOTAN: Charles Schulz, *Peanuts* cartoonist

guess what? *F. Scott Fitzgerald, author of The Great Gatsby, was born in and spent much of his life in Saint Paul, Minnesota. He revised his first book, This Side of Paradise, in his parents' Saint Paul home.*

Minneapolis
St. Paul

MISSISSIPPI

CAPITAL: Jackson

LARGEST CITY: Jackson

POSTAL CODE: MS

LAND AREA: 46,914 square miles (121,507 sq km)

POPULATION (2011): 2,978,512

ENTERED UNION (RANK): December 10, 1817 (20)

MOTTO: *Virtute et armis* (By valor and arms)

TREE: Magnolia

FLOWER: Magnolia

BIRD: Mockingbird

NICKNAME: Magnolia State

FAMOUS MISSISSIPPIAN: Brett Favre, football player

guess what? *Built in 1848, the Biloxi Lighthouse was one of the first cast-iron lighthouses to be built in the South. It is also the only lighthouse in the United States located in the middle of an interstate highway.*

Jackson

MISSOURI

CAPITAL:
Jefferson City

LARGEST CITY:
Kansas City

POSTAL CODE: MO

LAND AREA: 68,898 square miles
(178,446 sq km)

POPULATION (2011): 6,010,688

ENTERED UNION (RANK):
August 10, 1821 (24)

MOTTO: *Salus populi suprema lex esto.*
(The welfare of the people shall be the
supreme law.)

TREE: Flowering dogwood

FLOWER: Hawthorn

BIRD: Bluebird

NICKNAME: Show Me State

FAMOUS MISSOURIAN: Mark Twain, author
of *Huckleberry Finn* and *The
Adventures of Tom Sawyer*

 **At 630 feet
(192 m) tall, the
Gateway Arch in Saint Louis
is the tallest man-made
monument in the United
States. Completed in 1965, this "gateway
to the West" commemorates President
Thomas Jefferson's encouragement of
settlers moving west and increasing the
size of the United States.**

MONTANA

CAPITAL: Helena

LARGEST CITY: Billings

POSTAL CODE: MT

LAND AREA:
145,556 square miles (376,990 sq km)

POPULATION (2011): 998,199

ENTERED UNION (RANK):
November 8, 1889 (41)

MOTTO: *Oro y plata* (Gold and silver)

TREE: Ponderosa pine

FLOWER: Bitterroot

BIRD: Western meadowlark

NICKNAME: Treasure State

FAMOUS MONTANAN: Evel Knievel,
motorcycle daredevil

 **On July 25,
1806,
explorer William Clark
etched his signature into
a rock formation known
as Pompey's Pillar, near Billings,
Montana. This carving is the only
remaining physical evidence of the
historic Lewis and Clark expedition.**

NEVADA

CAPITAL: Carson City

LARGEST CITY: Las Vegas

POSTAL CODE: NV

LAND AREA: 109,806 square miles (284,397 sq km)

POPULATION (2011): 2,723,322

ENTERED UNION (RANK): October 31, 1864 (36)

MOTTO: All for our country

TREE: Single-leaf piñon pine

FLOWER: Sagebrush

BIRD: Mountain bluebird

NICKNAMES: Sagebrush State, Silver State, Battle Born State

FAMOUS NEVADAN: Andre Agassi, tennis player

Guess what? *The Nevada state gemstone is the Virgin Valley Black Fire Opal. Virgin Valley, which is in northern Nevada, is the only place in North America where lots of black fire opals can be found.*

Carson City

Las Vegas

NEBRASKA

CAPITAL: Lincoln

LARGEST CITY: Omaha

POSTAL CODE: NE

LAND AREA: 76,878 square miles (199,114 sq km)

POPULATION (2011): 1,842,641

ENTERED UNION (RANK): March 1, 1867 (37)

MOTTO: Equality before the law

TREE: Eastern cottonwood

FLOWER: Goldenrod

BIRD: Western meadowlark

NICKNAMES: Cornhusker State, Beef State

FAMOUS NEBRASKAN: Standing Bear, Native American civil rights advocate

Guess what? *Carhenge in Alliance, Nebraska, is a replica of Stonehenge, the prehistoric rock formation in England. Instead of being built from stone like Stonehenge, Carhenge is formed by 38 different cars. This wacky sculpture was built in 1987.*

Omaha

Lincoln

NEW HAMPSHIRE

CAPITAL: Concord

LARGEST CITY: Manchester

POSTAL CODE: NH

LAND AREA: 8,969 square miles (23,230 sq km)

POPULATION (2011): 1,318,194

ENTERED UNION (RANK): June 21, 1788 (9)

MOTTO: Live free or die.

TREE: White birch (canoe birch or paper birch)

FLOWER: Purple lilac

BIRD: Purple finch

NICKNAME: Granite State

FAMOUS NEW HAMPSHIRITE: Bode Miller, skier and Olympic medalist

 Tupperware gets its name from Earl Tupper, an inventor from Berlin, New Hampshire.

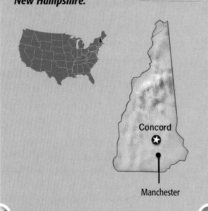

Concord

Manchester

NEW JERSEY

CAPITAL: Trenton

LARGEST CITY: Newark

POSTAL CODE: NJ

LAND AREA: 7,419 square miles (19,215 sq km)

POPULATION (2011): 8,821,155

ENTERED UNION (RANK): December 18, 1787 (3)

MOTTO: Liberty and prosperity

TREE: Red oak

FLOWER: Common meadow violet

BIRD: Eastern (or American) goldfinch

NICKNAME: Garden State

FAMOUS NEW JERSEYITE: Edwin "Buzz" Aldrin, astronaut

Lucy the Elephant is no average elephant. She's the biggest elephant in the world—and she is a building! Built in Margate, New Jersey, in 1881, Lucy's body is divided into rooms that can be accessed by a staircase in her left rear leg.

Newark

Trenton

NEW MEXICO

CAPITAL: Santa Fe

LARGEST CITY: Albuquerque

POSTAL CODE: NM

LAND AREA: 121,365 square miles (314,335 sq km)

POPULATION (2011): 2,082,224

ENTERED UNION (RANK): January 6, 1912 (47)

MOTTO: *Crescit eundo.* (It grows as it goes.)

TREE: Piñon pine

FLOWER: Yucca

BIRD: Roadrunner

NICKNAMES: Land of Enchantment, Cactus State

FAMOUS NEW MEXICAN: William Hanna, animator

Guess What? *The world's first nuclear detonation took place at White Sands Missile Range in New Mexico on July 16, 1945.*

NEW YORK

CAPITAL: Albany

LARGEST CITY: New York City

POSTAL CODE: NY

LAND AREA: 47,224 square miles (122,310 sq km)

POPULATION (2011): 19,465,197

ENTERED UNION (RANK): July 26, 1788 (11)

MOTTO: *Excelsior* (Ever upward)

TREE: Sugar maple

FLOWER: Rose

BIRD: Bluebird

NICKNAME: Empire State

FAMOUS NEW YORKER: Jonas Salk, developer of polio vaccine

Guess What? *The USS* Intrepid *was one of the most active ships in World War II. Now, the huge, newly restored ship is anchored off the west side of Manhattan. It is home to the Intrepid Sea, Air & Space Museum.*

NORTH CAROLINA

CAPITAL: Raleigh

LARGEST CITY: Charlotte

POSTAL CODE: NC

LAND AREA:
48,708 square miles (126,154 sq km)

POPULATION (2011): 9,656,401

ENTERED UNION (RANK):
November 21, 1789 (12)

MOTTO: *Esse quam videri*
(To be rather than to seem)

TREE: Pine

FLOWER: Flowering dogwood

BIRD: Cardinal

NICKNAME: Tar Heel State

FAMOUS NORTH CAROLINIAN:
Dale Earnhardt Jr., NASCAR driver

 The Cape Hatteras Light Station in North Carolina's Outer Banks is the tallest lighthouse in the country. The lighthouse is 207 feet (63 m) tall, though 10 feet (3 m) of the structure are underground.

Raleigh

Charlotte

NORTH DAKOTA

CAPITAL: Bismarck

LARGEST CITY: Fargo

POSTAL CODE: ND

LAND AREA:
68,994 square miles
(178,694 sq km)

POPULATION (2011): 683,932

ENTERED UNION (RANK):
November 2, 1889 (39)

MOTTO: Liberty and union, now and forever, one and inseparable

TREE: American elm

FLOWER: Wild prairie rose

BIRD: Western meadowlark

NICKNAMES: Sioux State, Flickertail State, Peace Garden State, Rough Rider State

FAMOUS NORTH DAKOTAN:
Louis L'Amour, author

 The border between North Dakota and Canada is the longest unfortified international border in the world. Planted on that border is the 3.65-square-mile (9.45 sq km) International Peace Garden. Opened in 1932, the park features 150,000 species of plants, grasses, and flowers.

Fargo

Bismarck

OHIO

CAPITAL: Columbus

LARGEST CITY: Columbus

POSTAL CODE: OH

LAND AREA: 40,953 square miles (106,068 sq km)

POPULATION (2011): 11,544,951

ENTERED UNION (RANK): March 1, 1803 (17)

MOTTO: With God, all things are possible.

TREE: Buckeye

FLOWER: Scarlet carnation

BIRD: Cardinal

NICKNAME: Buckeye State

FAMOUS OHIOAN: Maya Lin, artist and architect; designer of the Vietnam Veterans Memorial

 During World War II, Cincinnati's Union Terminal was a major transfer point for American soldiers. Between 17,000 and 34,000 passengers and 216 trains passed through the station every day.

Columbus ⭐

OKLAHOMA

CAPITAL: Oklahoma City

LARGEST CITY: Oklahoma City

POSTAL CODE: OK

LAND AREA: 68,679 square miles (177,879 sq km)

POPULATION (2011): 3,791,508

ENTERED UNION (RANK): November 16, 1907 (46)

MOTTO: *Labor omnia vincit.* (Labor conquers all things.)

TREE: Eastern redbud

FLOWER: Mistletoe

BIRD: Scissor-tailed flycatcher

NICKNAME: Sooner State

FAMOUS OKLAHOMAN: Carrie Underwood, singer

 Of the approximately 5.2 million Native Americans that live in the United States, more than 480,000 live in Oklahoma. Only California is home to more Native Americans.

Oklahoma City ⭐

OREGON

CAPITAL: Salem

LARGEST CITY: Portland

POSTAL CODE: OR

LAND AREA: 96,003 square miles (248,648 sq km)

POPULATION (2011): 3,871,859

ENTERED UNION (RANK): February 14, 1859 (33)

MOTTO: *Alis volat propriis.* (She flies with her own wings.)

TREE: Douglas fir

FLOWER: Oregon grape

BIRD: Western meadowlark

NICKNAME: Beaver State

FAMOUS OREGONIAN: Beverly Cleary, author

 Every year, the town of Cannon Beach, Oregon, holds an enormous sand castle contest. **Contestants are given about 12 hours—from one high tide to the next—to build sculptures of anything they want: traditional castles, cars, animals . . . you name it!**

PENNSYLVANIA

CAPITAL: Harrisburg

LARGEST CITY: Philadelphia

POSTAL CODE: PA

LAND AREA: 44,820 square miles (116,084 sq km)

POPULATION (2011): 12,742,886

ENTERED UNION (RANK): December 12, 1787 (2)

MOTTO: Virtue, liberty, and independence

TREE: Hemlock

FLOWER: Mountain laurel

BIRD: Ruffed grouse

NICKNAME: Keystone State

FAMOUS PENNSYLVANIAN: Mary Cassatt, painter

 Lakemont Park amusement park in Altoona, Pennsylvania, is home to the world's oldest operating wooden roller coaster. The coaster, named "Leap-the-Dips," was built in 1902.

Harrisburg ✪

Philadelphia

RHODE ISLAND

CAPITAL: Providence

LARGEST CITY: Providence

POSTAL CODE: RI

LAND AREA:
1,045 square miles (2,707 sq km)

POPULATION (2011): 1,051,302

ENTERED UNION (RANK): May 29, 1790 (13)

MOTTO: Hope

TREE: Red maple

FLOWER: Violet

BIRD: Rhode Island red (chicken)

NICKNAME: Ocean State

FAMOUS RHODE ISLANDER:
Gilbert Stuart, artist who painted the portrait of George Washington seen on the $1 bill

 Built in 1828, the Flying Horse Carousel in Westerly, Rhode Island, is the oldest carousel of its kind in the United States. Unlike most carousels operating today, where horses are mounted to the floor, these horses hang from chains attached to the center frame. This makes riders feel like they are flying.

 Providence

SOUTH CAROLINA

CAPITAL: Columbia

LARGEST CITY: Columbia

POSTAL CODE: SC

LAND AREA: 30,111 square miles (77,987 sq km)

POPULATION (2011): 4,679,230

ENTERED UNION (RANK): May 23, 1788 (8)

MOTTOES: *Animis opibusque parati* (Prepared in mind and resources); *Dum spiro spero.* (While I breathe, I hope.)

TREE: Palmetto

FLOWER: Yellow jessamine

BIRD: Carolina wren

NICKNAME: Palmetto State

FAMOUS SOUTH CAROLINIAN:
Marian Wright Edelman, activist, founder of Children's Defense Fund

 The first shots of the American Civil War were fired from Fort Sumter in Charleston, South Carolina, on April 12, 1861.

Columbia

 United States

219

SOUTH DAKOTA

CAPITAL: Pierre

LARGEST CITY: Sioux Falls

POSTAL CODE: SD

LAND AREA: 75,898 square miles (196,575 sq km)

POPULATION (2011): 824,082

ENTERED UNION (RANK): November 2, 1889 (40)

MOTTO: Under God the people rule.

TREE: Black Hills spruce

FLOWER: Pasqueflower

BIRD: Ring-necked pheasant

NICKNAMES: Mount Rushmore State, Coyote State

FAMOUS SOUTH DAKOTAN: Sitting Bull, Sioux chief

Guess what? *Karl E. Mundt National Wildlife Refuge in southern South Dakota is a favorite winter nesting area for bald eagles.*

Pierre Sioux Falls

TENNESSEE

CAPITAL: Nashville

LARGEST CITY: Memphis

POSTAL CODE: TN

LAND AREA: 41,220 square miles (106,760 sq km)

POPULATION (2011): 6,403,353

ENTERED UNION (RANK): June 1, 1796 (16)

MOTTO: Agriculture and commerce

TREE: Tulip poplar

FLOWER: Iris

BIRD: Mockingbird

NICKNAME: Volunteer State

FAMOUS TENNESSEAN: Dolly Parton, musician and actress

Guess what? *The world's largest fish fry takes place every year in Paris, Tennessee. During the six-day festival, visitors eat more than 13,000 pounds (5,897 kg) of catfish.*

Nashville

Memphis

TEXAS

CAPITAL: Austin

LARGEST CITY:
Houston

POSTAL CODE: TX

LAND AREA: 261,914 square miles
(678,357 sq km)

POPULATION (2011): 25,674,681

ENTERED UNION (RANK):
December 29, 1845 (28)

MOTTO: Friendship

TREE: Pecan

FLOWER: Texas bluebonnet

BIRD: Mockingbird

NICKNAME: Lone Star State

FAMOUS TEXAN: Selena Gomez, actress
and singer

guess what? *Bracken Bat Cave near San Antonio, Texas, is home to the largest bat colony in the world. Every summer, more than 20 million Mexican free-tailed bats live there.*

UTAH

CAPITAL:
Salt Lake City

LARGEST CITY:
Salt Lake City

POSTAL CODE: UT

LAND AREA: 82,168 square miles
(212,815 sq km)

POPULATION (2011): 2,817,222

ENTERED UNION (RANK):
January 4, 1896 (45)

MOTTO: Industry

TREE: Blue spruce

FLOWER: Sego lily

BIRD: California gull

NICKNAME: Beehive State

FAMOUS UTAHN: Philo T. Farnsworth,
inventor of the television

guess what? *The Sundance Film Festival—one of the most respected film festivals in the world—is held in Park City, Utah, every winter. Each year, 200 films are chosen from more than 9,000 submissions, and more than 50,000 people make their way to the snowy city to participate in the festivities.*

Austin ⭐   Houston ●

Salt Lake City ⭐

United States

VIRGINIA

CAPITAL: Richmond

LARGEST CITY: Virginia Beach

POSTAL CODE: VA

LAND AREA: 39,598 square miles (102,559 sq km)

POPULATION (2011): 8,096,604

ENTERED UNION (RANK): June 25, 1788 (10)

MOTTO: *Sic semper tyrannis* (Thus always to tyrants)

TREE: Flowering dogwood

FLOWER: American dogwood

BIRD: Cardinal

NICKNAMES: The Old Dominion, Mother of Presidents

FAMOUS VIRGINIAN: Arthur Ashe, tennis player

 Assateague Island, off the coast of Virginia, is home to wild ponies that have lived there for more than 300 years. Once a year, the ponies are herded across the Assateague Channel to Chincoteague Island. There, a public auction is held, and some of the ponies are sold in order to keep the pony population down.

VERMONT

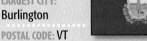

CAPITAL: Montpelier

LARGEST CITY: Burlington

POSTAL CODE: VT

LAND AREA: 9,249 square miles (23,956 sq km)

POPULATION (2011): 626,431

ENTERED UNION (RANK): March 4, 1791 (14)

MOTTO: Freedom and unity

TREE: Sugar maple

FLOWER: Red clover

BIRD: Hermit thrush

NICKNAME: Green Mountain State

FAMOUS VERMONTER: Joseph Smith, founder of the Mormon Church

 There are more than 100 covered bridges in Vermont. In the early 19th century, bridge builders in the Northeast put roofs over bridges to protect the wooden supports from harsh winters.

Burlington

Montpelier

Richmond

Virginia Beach

WASHINGTON

CAPITAL: Olympia

LARGEST CITY: Seattle

POSTAL CODE: WA

LAND AREA: 66,582 square miles (172,447 sq km)

POPULATION (2011): 6,830,038

ENTERED UNION (RANK): November 11, 1889 (42)

MOTTO: *Al-ki* (an Indian word meaning "by and by" or "hope for the future")

TREE: Western hemlock

FLOWER: Coast rhododendron

BIRD: Willow goldfinch

NICKNAME: Evergreen State

FAMOUS WASHINGTONIAN: Apolo Anton Ohno, speed skater and Olympic medalist

Guess what? *Mount Rainier (also known by its Native American name, Mount Tacoma) is a volcano that has been dormant for more than 2,000 years. Part of the Cascade mountain range, Mount Rainier is home to more glaciers than any other place in the continental United States. Roughly 35 square miles (91 sq km) of snow and ice cover its peak.*

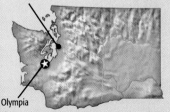

Seattle

Olympia

WEST VIRGINIA

CAPITAL: Charleston

LARGEST CITY: Charleston

POSTAL CODE: WV

LAND AREA: 24,087 square miles (62,385 sq km)

POPULATION (2011): 1,855,364

ENTERED UNION (RANK): June 20, 1863 (35)

MOTTO: *Montani semper liberi.* (Mountaineers are always free.)

TREE: Sugar maple

FLOWER: Rhododendron

BIRD: Cardinal

NICKNAME: Mountain State

FAMOUS WEST VIRGINIAN: Brad Paisley, musician

Guess what? *West Virginia has a thriving marble industry. Playing marbles was a popular pastime in West Virginia during the mining boom of the early 20th century, and marble factories are still in business there today. The Marble King factory, in Paden City, West Virginia, manufactures more than 1 million marbles every day.*

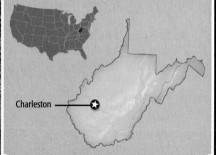

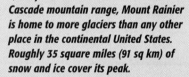

Charleston

United States

Virginia

WISCONSIN

CAPITAL: Madison

LARGEST CITY: Milwaukee

POSTAL CODE: WI

LAND AREA: 54,314 square miles (140,673 sq km)

POPULATION (2011): 5,711,767

ENTERED UNION (RANK): May 29, 1848 (30)

MOTTO: Forward

TREE: Sugar maple

FLOWER: Wood violet

BIRD: American robin

NICKNAMES: Badger State, Dairy State

FAMOUS WISCONSINITE: Frank Lloyd Wright, architect

Guess what? *The first kindergarten in the United States was founded in Watertown, Wisconsin, in 1856, by German immigrant Margarethe Meyer Schurz.*

Milwaukee

Madison

WYOMING

CAPITAL: Cheyenne

LARGEST CITY: Cheyenne

POSTAL CODE: WY

LAND AREA: 97,105 square miles (251,502 sq km)

POPULATION (2011): 568,158

ENTERED UNION (RANK): July 10, 1890 (44)

MOTTO: Equal rights

TREE: Plains cottonwood

FLOWER: Indian paintbrush

BIRD: Meadowlark

NICKNAMES: Big Wyoming, Equality State, Cowboy State

FAMOUS WYOMINGITE: Jackson Pollock, artist

Guess what? *Independence Rock, Wyoming, is sometimes referred to as "the register of the desert." Located along the route of the Oregon, Mormon, California, and Pony Express Trails, the rock is covered with names and messages from thousands of pioneers who used the trails.*

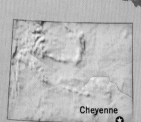

Cheyenne

WASHINGTON, D.C.

The District of Columbia, which covers the same area as the city of Washington, is the capital of the United States. The seat of the U.S. government was transferred from Philadelphia, Pennsylvania, to Washington, D.C., on December 1, 1800.

LAND AREA:
68.25 square miles (177 sq km)

POPULATION (2011): 617,996

MOTTO: *Justitia omnibus* (Justice for all)

TREE: Scarlet oak

FLOWER: American beauty rose

BIRD: Wood thrush

FAMOUS WASHINGTONIAN:
John Philip Sousa, composer

U.S. TERRITORIES

In addition to the 50 states and the District of Columbia, the United States government administers some tiny, mostly uninhabited islands around the world, including Kingman Reef, Palmyra Atoll, and Howland Island. The major U.S. territories are Puerto Rico, American Samoa, Guam, the U.S. Virgin Islands, and the Northern Mariana Islands.

PUERTO RICO is in the Caribbean Sea, about 1,000 miles (1,609 km) southeast of Miami, Florida. A U.S. possession since 1898, it consists of the island of Puerto Rico plus the adjacent islets of Vieques, Culebra, and Mona. Both Spanish and English are spoken there. Its capital is San Juan. Puerto Rico has a population of approximately 3,998,908.

AMERICAN SAMOA, a group of islands in the South Pacific Ocean, is situated about halfway between Hawaii and New Zealand. It has a land area of 76 square miles (199 sq km) and a population of approximately 68,061.

GUAM, in the North Pacific Ocean, was given to the United States by Spain in 1898. It has a land area of 209 square miles (541 sq km) and a population of approximately 185,674.

U.S. VIRGIN ISLANDS, which include Saint Croix, Saint Thomas, Saint John, and many other islands, are located in the Caribbean Sea, east of Puerto Rico. Together, they have a land area of 136 square miles (351 sq km) and a population of approximately 109,574.

THE NORTHERN MARIANA ISLANDS are located in the North Pacific Ocean. They have a land area of 179 square miles (464 sq km) and a population of approximately 44,582.

United States

NATIONAL TREASURES

There are 397 national park areas in the United States. These parks, monuments, preserves, forests, and historic places help to preserve and showcase the country's nature and history.

The General Sherman tree in **Sequoia National Park,** California, is the largest tree in the world.

The Grand Canyon, in **Grand Canyon National Park,** Arizona, was formed by the Colorado River.

The highest point in North America is Mount McKinley. It stands 20,320 feet (6,194 m) tall in **Denali National Park and Preserve,** Alaska.

Visitors can check out 150-million-year-old dinosaur fossils at Dinosaur National Monument in Colorado and Utah.

The lowest point in the Western Hemisphere is in Death Valley National Park, California.

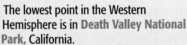

The greatest number of geothermal features (like geysers and hot springs) in the world are found in Yellowstone National Park, in Wyoming, Montana, and Idaho.

The longest cave system in the world, with more than 390 miles (628 km) of mapped caves, is in **Mammoth Cave National Park,** Kentucky.

Amazingly well preserved 1,000-year-old cliff dwellings are found at Montezuma Castle National Monument, Arizona. This five-story dwelling has 20 rooms.

Yosemite Falls is the highest waterfall in North America. It is in Yosemite National Park, California.

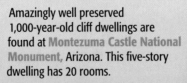

At 1,593 feet (486 m) deep, the deepest limestone cave in the United States is in **Carlsbad Caverns National Park,** New Mexico.

The deepest lake in the United States is in **Crater Lake National Park,** Oregon. It is 1,943 feet (592 m) deep.

The Edgar Allan Poe National Historic Site in Pennsylvania honors a great American writer.

The only place in the world where alligators and crocodiles live side by side is Everglades National Park, Florida.

Two of the world's most active volcanoes are in **Volcano National Park,** Hawaii.

Parts of the first English colony in North America are preserved at the Fort Raleigh National Historic Site on Roanoke Island, North Carolina.

A famous federal prison—**Alcatraz**—is preserved off the coast of California. It is part of the Golden Gate National Recreation Area.

The Antietam National Battlefield in Maryland commemorates the bloodiest single-day battle of the U.S. Civil War.

OT FOR THEMSELVES BUT 'OR THEIR COUNTRY

EPTEMBER 17. 1862

United States

THE UNITED STATES

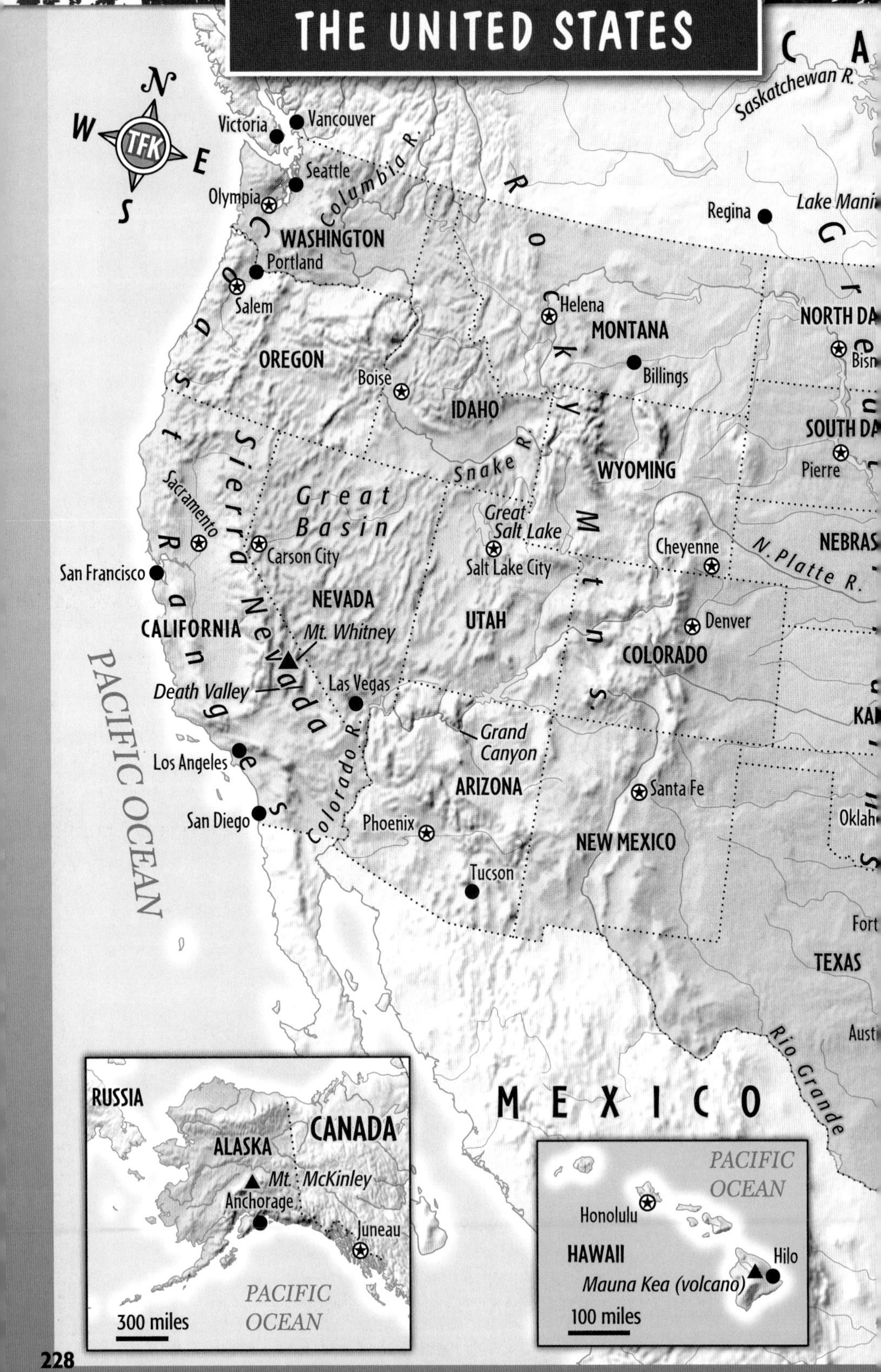

N W E S TFK

CANADA

Saskatchewan R.

Victoria
Vancouver
Seattle
Olympia
WASHINGTON
Portland
Salem

Columbia R.

Regina
Lake Mani

Helena
MONTANA
Billings

OREGON

Boise

IDAHO

Snake R.

WYOMING

Cheyenne

N. Platte R.

NORTH DA

Bisn

SOUTH DA
Pierre

NEBRAS

Sacramento

*G r e a t
B a s i n*

*Great
Salt Lake*
Salt Lake City

San Francisco

Carson City

NEVADA

UTAH

Denver

COLORADO

KA

CALIFORNIA

Mt. Whitney

Death Valley

Las Vegas

*Grand
Canyon*

S i e r r a   N e v a d a

C o a s t   R a n g e s

Los Angeles

San Diego

Colorado R.

ARIZONA

Phoenix

Tucson

Santa Fe

NEW MEXICO

Oklah

Fort

TEXAS

Austi

PACIFIC OCEAN

R o c k y   M t n s.

M E X I C O

Rio Grande

Inset: Alaska

RUSSIA

CANADA

ALASKA

Mt. McKinley
Anchorage

Juneau

*PACIFIC
OCEAN*

300 miles

Inset: Hawaii

*PACIFIC
OCEAN*

Honolulu

HAWAII

Hilo

Mauna Kea (volcano)

100 miles

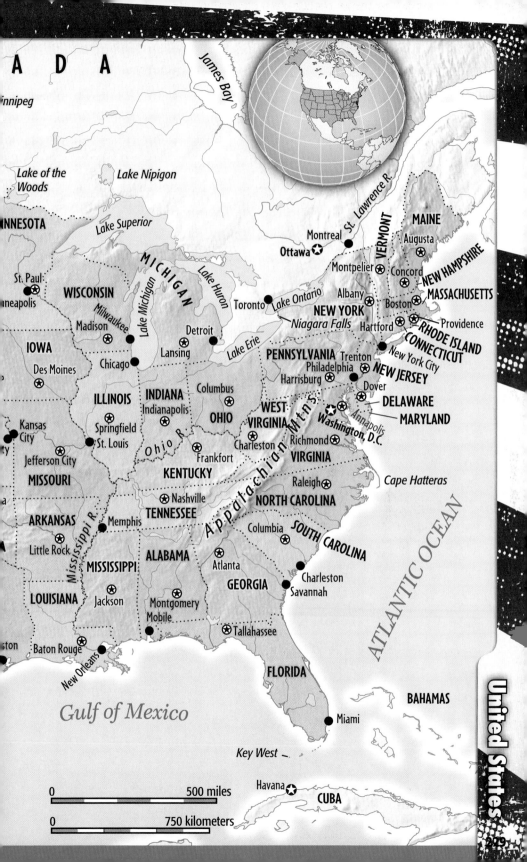

CA**N**A**D**A

nnipeg

James Bay

St. Lawrence R.

Lake of the Woods

Lake Nipigon

MI**N**NESOTA

Lake Superior

St. Paul ✪

neapolis

WISCONSIN

M I C H I G A N

Lake Huron

Montreal

Ottawa ✪

VERMONT

MAINE

Augusta

Montpelier ✪

Concord

NEW HAMPSHIRE

Milwaukee

Madison

Lake Michigan

Toronto

Lake Ontario

Albany ✪

Boston ✪

MASSACHUSETTS

IOWA

Detroit

Niagara Falls

NEW YORK

Hartford ✪

Providence

RHODE ISLAND

Des Moines ✪

Lansing

Lake Erie

PENNSYLVANIA

CONNECTICUT

Chicago

Trenton

New York City

ILLINOIS

INDIANA

Columbus

Philadelphia ✪

NEW JERSEY

Springfield ✪

Indianapolis ✪

OHIO ✪

Harrisburg ✪

Dover ✪

DELAWARE

Kansas City

St. Louis ✪

Ohio R.

WEST VIRGINIA

Annapolis ✪

MARYLAND

Jefferson City ✪

y

Frankfort ✪

Charleston ✪

Washington, D.C. ✪

MISSOURI

KENTUCKY

Richmond ✪

VIRGINIA

a

ARKANSAS

Nashville ✪

TENNESSEE

Raleigh ✪

Cape Hatteras

Mississippi R.

Little Rock ✪

Memphis

A p p a l a c h i a n   M t n s.

NORTH CAROLINA

Columbia ✪

SOUTH CAROLINA

ALABAMA

MISSISSIPPI

Jackson ✪

Atlanta ✪

GEORGIA

Charleston

A T L A N T I C   O C E A N

LOUISIANA

Montgomery ✪

Mobile

Savannah

ston

Baton Rouge ✪

Tallahassee ✪

New Orleans

FLORIDA

BAHAMAS

ton

Gulf of Mexico

Miami

Key West

0   500 miles

0   750 kilometers

Havana ✪

CUBA

The Power of We

By TFK Kid Reporter Sahil Abbi

On September 27, 2011, about 18,000 enthusiastic kids filled the Air Canada Center, in Toronto, Canada. They came to celebrate We Day, which is an annual event organized by the charity Free The Children, the world's largest network of children helping children through education. The goal of the event was to raise awareness of global issues, including poverty, and to empower youth to lend a helping hand. Each participant earned tickets by volunteering or helping out with Free The Children's projects.

> **Free The Children founder Craig Kielburger wants to get out a very important message: "We're recruiting!"**

"We based Free The Children on what we dreamed of doing to help others when we were young," says Craig Kielburger, who founded the charity at age 12.

STAR-STUDDED SUPPORT

Many celebrities attended We Day to show their support. There was a long list of performers, including Nelly Furtado and the Kenyan Boys Choir, who sang "In the Jungle." Joe Jonas sang "See No More."

After her performance, Furtado revealed her donation of $1 million to Free The Children. She said she was inspired to make the donation after a trip to Kenya. Furtado was rewarded with a surprise visit from Susan, a Kenyan girl she met on that trip.

"Free The Children doesn't invite celebrities for the day," Kielburger told TFK. "We want them to go overseas, work on a project, and then come back and spread the message."

FOR KIDS, BY KIDS

All of Free The Children's projects are "for the kids, by the kids," says Kielburger. Halloween for Hunger asks kids to trick-or-treat for nonperishable goods for food banks. Vow of Silence is a day without any form of communication, to recognize children without a voice.

"It's impossible to go to We Day and not be inspired," says 12-year-old Kyle Santia. Kyle has helped organize fund-raisers and is starting an Adopt a Village program as well. Adopt a Village is a Free The Children program that has provided clean water, health care, and schools to 1 million people around the world. "The fact that these young people are doing such creative and empowering things is amazing," Jonas told TFK. "They are an inspiration to me."

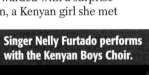

Singer Nelly Furtado performs with the Kenyan Boys Choir.

KIDS SHARE THEIR TIME

According to a report by The Volunteer Family and Harris Interactive, about 73% of people between the ages of 12 and 18 do some kind of volunteering. Kids spend about 1.3 billion hours of their time doing community service every year. Here are some favorite volunteer activities for kids between 8 and 18 years old.

- Helping children in need (29%)
- Advocating for the environment (27%)
- Assisting the elderly, sick, or disabled (21%)
- Helping animals in need (18%)
- Supporting the homeless (14%)

RAISE MONEY FOR A CAUSE

Often the best way you can help people or charitable organizations is by sending money. Here are some ways to raise funds for good causes. Make sure to tell everyone involved which cause you've chosen to support.

Plan a car wash. Gather your friends (during the warmer weather, of course) and hold a weekend car wash. Design colorful flyers and hang them up in local stores and restaurants.

Put on a show. Prove that America really does have talent! Hold a student talent show and charge admission. Create posters to get the word out and ask your parents to help you call your local newspaper to advertise the event.

Arrange a fund-raising event. Plan a walk-a-thon, read-a-thon, dance-a-thon, or jump-rope-a-thon. Collect pledges from friends, family, and others for each mile you walk, book you read, hour you dance, or minute you jump rope!

Host a bake sale. There's a simple reason why bake sales work: Nearly everybody loves treats! Make sure you get a lot of volunteers to bake and work the tables. Offer a wide variety of food items and label all of the treats carefully.

Sell your crafty creations. Selling handmade objects can be fun and can raise a lot of money. Find a craft you enjoy—pottery, jewelry making, crocheting, for example—and create some useful objects. If you're really ambitious, ask your friends to join you and put together a whole array of crafts to sell at a crafts fair or on a website.

MICROLOANS

Sometimes, just a little bit of money can make a huge difference in someone's life. For example, a donation of $10 to Heifer International (*heifer.org*) will buy a tree seedling that will grow into a tree that can provide nuts for food and trade, offer shade, and make soil healthier. A donation of $2 to Just a Drop (*justadrop.org*) will buy a 10-year supply of safe drinking water for a child.

Microloans are another way that small amounts of money can be used to improve a person's life. Microloans are small loans that allow people with very little money to buy the supplies they need to start up a business. An organization called Kiva helps match borrowers from all over the world with people who are able to make small loans. You can loan just $25 toward helping someone's dream of owning a business come true. Find more information at *kiva.org*.

Kokou Dzide, from Togo, used his microloan to buy a new sewing machine for his tailoring business.

Volunteering

231

PICK A CAUSE, LEND A HAND

Whether you want to share your talents, learn more about a topic, or just meet other people, you can't go wrong with volunteering. Before setting out to be a volunteer, think about the cause that you would like to help most. You will get more from the experience if you choose an issue you care about. Here are a few causes that might interest you and some ideas for how you can work for them in your community.

Animals

Many animal shelters and rescue groups rely on volunteers to help keep their facilities clean or to foster pets that are up for adoption. Volunteers may also feed, brush, or walk abandoned or abused animals. Call your local animal shelter or rescue group for more information, or look for action tips at *aspca.org*.

Homelessness and Hunger

There are many ways to help. You could help serve lunch at a local soup kitchen or organize a schoolwide canned-food or warm-clothing drive. If you are looking for a bigger commitment, you might consider helping Habitat for Humanity build a house for a needy family. Have your parents log on to *habitat.org*.

Music

If you enjoy singing or playing an instrument, look for a choir or another group that performs for nursing homes, hospitals, or community centers.

Elderly People

Spend time at a nursing home, playing cards, doing crafts, or just talking with the residents.

Disaster Relief

When man-made or natural disasters (such as hurricanes, earthquakes, tornadoes, floods, or fires) strike, people need help quickly. Read, watch, or listen to the news to find the names of reputable organizations that are collecting cash donations, canned food, clothing, blankets, and other supplies.

Sports

Participate in a race for a cause you think is important. If you don't want to race, you can distribute water and cheer on others. Special Olympics International, a program that provides sports training and competition for adults and children with disabilities, relies on volunteers. Visit *specialolympics.org*.

VOLUNTEER

DONATION BOX

Kids and Adults with Illnesses

Many hospitals and clinics have opportunities for volunteers. You may help serve meals, make beds, and deliver gifts to patients. Or you might lift a sick person's spirits by playing board games or reading stories aloud. Call a health-care center nearby and ask about volunteering opportunities for kids your age.

The Environment

Volunteer at a nearby state or national park, or organize a tree-planting day at your school for Arbor Day or Earth Day. Participate in a stream, pond, or beach cleanup day to help keep our waterways free of trash and pollution. Become part of the Green Squad (visit *nrdc.org/greensquad*) and learn how to make your school a healthier and greener place.

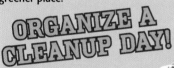

ORGANIZE A CLEANUP DAY!

WE RECYCLE

YOUNG PEOPLE HELPING OTHERS

It's never too early to make a difference in the world. Here is a trio of inspiring efforts by big-hearted kids.

When Sydney Martin was 10, she was diagnosed with a rare blood disorder called histiocytosis. By the time she was 13, she'd raised more than $127,000 for research by selling homemade beach-rock necklaces on her website, *sydrocks.com*.

Animal lover Kira Neilson plans to be a vet one day. At 10, she raised more than $1,000 for the recovery of Patriot, an injured bald eagle. The bird was found hurt near Kira's hometown of Bend, Oregon.

In 2007, 12-year-old Rujul Zaparde visited the village of Paras, India. The people there had to walk several miles to get to a water source. Even worse, the water wasn't clean. When he got back home to Plainsboro, New Jersey, Rujul helped start the nonprofit Drinking Water for India to raise money to build wells. So far, the organization has built 47 wells.

MYSTERY PERSON

I was a chemist who was born in Sweden in 1833. I was especially interested in explosives. In 1867, I invented dynamite. It was used to create canals, blast tunnels, and make railroads. Before I died, I asked that most of my money be used for international awards to honor advances in science and culture. The prizes are named for me.

WHO AM I? _____

Answer on page 243.

Volunteering

A Talk with a Hurricane Expert

Eric Blake is a hurricane specialist with the National Oceanic and Atmospheric Association's (NOAA) National Hurricane Center. He helped track Hurricane Irene, a powerful storm that struck the Carribbean and the eastern coasts of the United States and Canada in August 2011, leaving widespread damage and flooding. He says a combination of factors contributed to a rise in storms in 2011.

Hurricane specialist Eric Blake tracks Hurricane Irene on August 24, 2011, at the National Hurricane Center, in Miami, Florida.

TIME: When is the hurricane season, and what does an average season look like?

ERIC BLAKE: August through October is the busiest time, and September is the peak month. But we can still see damaging landfalls in October, and it is not out of the question to have a hurricane into November. An average season has about 12 storms.

TIME: What factors lead to an active season forecast?

BLAKE: There are a variety of factors. One of the things is, how warm is the Atlantic Ocean? How warm is it compared to an average year? The other factor is the status of El Niño (el *neen*-nyo).

TIME: Has the Atlantic Ocean been unseasonably warm?

BLAKE: Year after year over the longer term of 20 to 30 years, we have seen the Atlantic warmer than average, mostly due to sea-surface temperatures.

TIME: Do you gauge the power of a season on quantity or intensity of storms?

BLAKE: Actually, both. The strength and duration of the storms is the formula we use, and we combine them into accumulated cyclone energy. If you get 10 short-lived storms, a couple of big ones count a lot more.

El Niño is a natural shift in the way winds and ocean currents cross the Pacific Ocean. It happens every few years, affecting the weather. Some countries that usually receive a lot of rain may suffer from droughts, while heavy rains and flooding often surprise other areas.

A farm in Florida after Hurricane Irene

HURRICANE NAMES

The National Hurricane Center uses six lists of names for storms. These lists repeat in cycles. However, if a storm is very damaging like Katrina, its name is retired. Here are the names for 2013.

ATLANTIC		EASTERN NORTH PACIFIC	
Andrea	Lorenzo	Alvin	Manuel
Barry	Melissa	Barbara	Narda
Chantal	Nestor	Cosme	Octave
Dorian	Olga	Dalila	Priscilla
Erin	Pablo	Erick	Raymond
Fernand	Rebekah	Flossie	Sonia
Gabrielle	Sebastien	Gil	Tico
Humberto	Tanya	Henriette	Velma
Ingrid	Van	Ivo	Wallis
Jerry	Wendy	Juliette	Xina
Karen		Kiko	York
		Lorena	Zelda

WHERE DOES WIND COME FROM?

Winds are caused by the sun's heat falling on different parts of Earth at different times of the day and year. The temperatures over water and land change at different rates during the day and night. In addition, warm air rises and cool air sinks. These fluctuations cause the movement of air in different patterns, called winds.

Scientists measure wind with a device called an **anemometer.** The most common type of anemometer, the cup anemometer, has three cups extending from a central point. Wind is measured by how fast the cups spin. Most cup anemometers also have weathervanes that tell the direction of the wind.

Weathervane

Cups

Guess what? When someone says she's in the doldrums, it means she is feeling sad or listless. That word is also used for a region of calm, light, shifting winds. Ships in the Doldrums can't catch enough wind to get moving quickly.

WHAT'S A FRONT?

We hear weather forecasters talk about fronts all the time—warm fronts, cold fronts, high fronts, low fronts. A front is the boundary between two masses of air with different temperatures, wind speeds, and amounts of moisture. In a cold front, cooler air is advancing and displacing the warm air ahead of it. In a warm front, warm air pushes into the cold air in front of it. Cold air is heavier than warm air. When a front is warm, the warmer air generally rises above the cool air. As the warm air is pushed upward, it cools quickly. If there is moisture in the air, it will probably rain.

Fronts can move quickly or slowly depending on the difference in temperature between them. Sometimes, fronts take a long time to move. These are called stationary fronts.

THUNDER AND LIGHTNING

The spectacular bolts of lightning that light up the sky are caused by ice crystals and water droplets that bump together and move apart to create electricity.

You need cold air and warm air to make lightning. The warm air rises and makes thunderstorm clouds full of water droplets. The cold air holds ice crystals. During a thunderstorm, the droplets and crystals rub against each other, creating static electricity (just like sparks are sometimes created when you shuffle along the carpet in your socks). Clouds have positive (plus) and negative (minus) sides, like batteries. The positive charges are on top, and the negative charges are on the bottom. When the negative charges are strong enough, they let off energy. This energy jumps through the air until it finds a place with the opposite charge. Sometimes it goes from one cloud to another and then back up to the original cloud. And that's when it makes a bolt of lightning. The flash heats up the air, which makes the air spread quickly—and that movement makes the sound we hear as thunder.

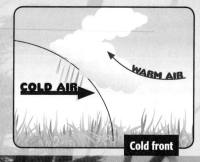

Cold front

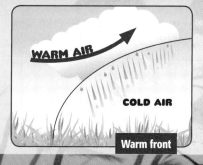

Warm front

Weather

WILD WEATHER

Good weather is a balance between cold and hot, wet and dry, and calm and wild. When the weather hits extremes in temperature, precipitation, or wind speeds, land is damaged and people suffer. Some extreme weather conditions, like droughts, occur slowly. Others, like tornadoes, form rapidly without much warning and generally last just a few minutes or hours.

DROUGHTS

A drought is an unusually long period of insufficient rain or snowfall. Droughts can last for years, though most last only a few weeks or months. In the 1930s, vast areas of the Great Plains, from Texas to Canada, suffered from drought, creating huge "dust bowls" of swirling, dry dirt. Thousands of farmers abandoned their homes and headed to other parts of the country, looking for new lands to settle. Many emigrated to California, leading to a huge growth in population in that state. In 2011, Texas suffered a terrible drought that harmed crops and caused trees to dry up and topple over. The state received less than 10% of its average rainfall.

HURRICANES, TYPHOONS, AND CYCLONES

These are tropical storms with winds stronger than 75 miles per hour (120 km/h). They're called hurricanes when they form in the northern Atlantic Ocean and the northeastern or southern Pacific Ocean, typhoons when they form over the northwestern Pacific, and cyclones when they form over the Indian Ocean. These dangerous storms form when tropical winds gather moisture as they pass over water that is at least 80°F (27°C). The winds of a hurricane rotate around an eye, or center of the storm. Hurricanes are strongest when they're over water, but they can remain fierce after reaching land, which is where they do the most damage. They are measured in categories, ranging from Category 1, which have winds from 74 to 95 mph (119 to 153 km/h) to Category 5, which have winds greater than 155 mph (250 km/h).

Within the eye of a hurricane, the weather is calm. It can even be sunny. Outside the eye, the warm ocean waters give energy to the storm, causing swirling wind and pounding rain.

FLOODS

Floods are usually caused by rivers or lakes overflowing their banks or by surges of ocean water during hurricanes and tropical storms. The Galveston Flood of 1900 in Texas was caused by a hurricane surge and took the lives of more than 5,000 people. As Hurricane Irene traveled up the East Coast of the United States in 2011, it left areas in upstate New York and Vermont underwater.

RECORD BREAKER The biggest hailstone recorded fell in Vivian, South Dakota, on July 23, 2010. It was 8 inches (20.3 cm) in diameter and weighed 1.93 pounds (0.88 kg).

SNOW

Water droplets form in clouds. When they get too heavy for the clouds to hold them, rain falls. But when the temperature of the air in the clouds is lower than freezing, the moisture turns into snowflakes.

Sometimes, snowflakes change as they pass through the clouds. When a snowflake passes between warmer and colder layers of air in the cloud, it can take on more moisture and end up as a hailstone. Some hailstones are as large as tennis balls. Under other conditions, snowflakes can turn into freezing rain, sleet, or ice. It all depends on the temperature in the clouds and on the ground.

Almost every area of the continental United States, including southern Florida, has had snow. Snowstorms can be deadly, causing traffic accidents, power failures, and 20-foot-tall (6.1 m) drifts that can bury cars and people. A blizzard is a snowstorm that has winds of more than 35 mph (56 km/h) for at least three hours. During the Great Blizzard of 1888, most of New England was blanketed with 40 to 50 inches (1 to 1.25 m) of snow. More than 400 people died.

guess what?

Every year, an average of 105 snowstorms occur in the United States.

TORNADOES

Tornadoes are funnel-shaped clouds made of fast-spinning winds that can reach 300 mph (483 km/h). They generally form out of giant storms that occur when warm, moist air on the ground rushes upward and smacks into cooler, drier air. This colder air causes the warm air to cool down. As the warm air cools, the moisture in it condenses and forms huge thunderclouds. The thunderclouds pull up warm air from the ground, which causes air to swirl around. It is this process that creates the distinct funnel shape of a tornado.

Some tornadoes measure only a few feet in diameter. Others are much wider—up to a mile (1.6 km) in diameter. Some build up quickly and disappear. Others move across the land at 30 to 70 mph (48 to 113 km/h) sometimes for hundreds of miles. The winds that make up a tornado can be strong enough to pick up homes, cars, trees, and anything else in their path. While wind causes most of a tornado's destruction, hail formed in the thunderclouds can also do a lot of damage.

Most large tornadoes form in the central and southern United States, in an area known as Tornado Alley. Though tornadoes do occur in other countries, by far the most occur in the United States; roughly 1,000 a year.

Weather

What's Next?

$1,200

IBM'S NEW CHIP

Researchers at IBM have developed a new generation of computer chip. A chip is a small piece of material that is embedded with circuits that run the processor and memory of a computer. This new chip is designed to work like a human brain to recognize, understand, and use the data it gathers. It will analyze a lot of information and learn from its experiences. For example, a computer using the new chip could monitor the world's water and analyze its temperature, pressure, waves, sounds, and tides. It would be able to issue a tsunami warning when it decides one is needed.

> IBM also created Watson, a computer system capable of processing and answering questions asked by people in natural language. Watson beat two of *Jeopardy!'s* biggest winners.

INFINITY AND BEYOND

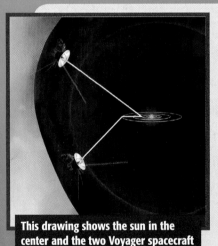

This drawing shows the sun in the center and the two Voyager spacecraft nearing the edge of our solar system.

Voyagers 1 and 2 are spacecraft that have been traveling through space for 34 years. After exploring Jupiter and Saturn (their primary mission), the Voyagers went deeper into space. Soon, they will pass from the outermost boundary of the solar system into uncharted regions of interstellar space.

There's no way of knowing the exact point at which the solar system ends, but it is about 12 billion miles (19.3 billion km) from the sun. In late 2011, Voyager 1 was about 11 billion miles (17.7 billion km) away from the sun, and Voyager 2 was about 9 billion miles (14.5 billion km) away. Voyager project scientist Ed Stone says the spacecraft can travel a billion miles (1.6 billion km) in about three years, so NASA expects them to reach uncharted areas pretty soon. No one knows what they will find. "Interstellar space is filled with material ejected by explosions of nearby stars," Stone said. "Voyager 1 will be the first human-made object to cross into it." And space buffs are eagerly looking forward to the new information that will be sent back to Earth.

guess what? To keep the Voyager spacecraft going for so long, there are tiny nuclear power plants on board. Power is expected to last until 2025.

HEALTH AND ENVIRONMENT

Malaria is carried by mosquitoes.

PROGRESS IN FIGHTING A TERRIBLE DISEASE

Malaria is a disease that kills nearly 800,000 people every year and makes many more sick. In 2010, there were approximately 216 million cases of malaria around the world. Found mostly in warm climates, such as sub-Saharan Africa and South Asia, malaria causes people to have chills, fever, and other flulike symptoms. Left untreated, it can be deadly. After many years of trying, researchers may have developed a vaccine to prevent people from getting the disease. If this vaccine continues to perform well in trials, it may be ready to save lives on a large scale by 2015.

FARMS OF THE FUTURE

Getting fresh food from local farms can be difficult in big cities. There is a possible solution: Farm up. Some architects and scientists are urging people to build vertical farms in multistory buildings. "Sky farms" are ideal for cities because they use a fraction of the land of traditional farms. Because they are indoors, these farms aren't harmed by hurricanes, droughts, and floods. Several vertical farms are already in operation in places like South Korea, Japan, and the Netherlands. Vertical farms are also being built in Wisconsin and Wyoming. Dickson Despommier, a professor at Columbia University, says "Agriculture in tall buildings will soon revolutionize the way we eat, and live, in cities."

Plantagon International broke ground on a vertical farm in Sweden on February 9, 2012.

An earth-friendly billboard in the Philippines

A HEALTHY BILLBOARD

Many companies are looking for ways to help clean up the environment. In the Philippines, the environmental group World Wide Fund for Nature (WWF) and Coca-Cola have found a creative way to ease pollution and make the air healthier for people to breathe. They built a 60-foot-tall (18 m) billboard that is covered with a special variety of Fukien tea plant. Each plant can absorb up to 13 pounds (6 kg) of carbon dioxide. About 3,600 pots (all made from recycled products) were used. The billboard can absorb about 46,800 pounds (21,228 kg) of carbon dioxide from the atmosphere in its lifetime.

What's Next?

SCREENS, BIG AND SMALL

TERRIFIC TOUCH SCREENS

Appliance makers, retailers, and restaurateurs are finding new uses for interactive digital displays. At Barney's, a department store in New York City, touch screens are embedded into café tables. Customers can scroll through merchandise and place orders as they eat. An interactive

Draqie

device called the Draqie will debut soon as well. It's a glass surface that looks like a table, but does a whole lot more. Patrons can use Draqie to review a menu, place an order, or summon a waiter. The device responds only to deliberate finger touches, so you won't accidentally order tons of food every time you put your wrists on the table. Expect to see other new and creative uses for touch screen technology in the future.

ALL THE RIGHT MOVES

Imagine being able to change the channel on your television without touching a single button. Soon you'll be able to use gestures to activate all your electronic devices. "What we want to do is bring (our technology) into all consumer devices," said Tal Dagan of PrimeSense, the company that developed Kinect for Xbox360. This sort of technology is currently being used for games, but in the near future, computers, TVs, phones, GPS devices, and other electronics (perhaps even robots!) will be able to respond to simple hand gestures and voice commands. There are even medical applications. With the simple movement of a hand, people with disabilities could perform tasks they were not able to do before.

3D Game Experience

Gesture recognition, for gaming or other uses, is made possible by motion sensors and cameras.

Guess what? Some electronics companies are working on creating televisions controlled by your brain waves. In the future, you may be able to turn up the volume by simply thinking about it!

ON-SCREEN TEXTURES

Tiny dots called pixels make up the pictures you see on computer and phone screens. A Finnish company called Senseg has developed Tixels, or tactile pixels, that allow users to feel pictures in addition to seeing them. The new system uses vibrations and electrical fields to make a touch screen feel smooth like glass, bumpy like gravel, rough like sandpaper, and other textures. At some point in the future, you may be able to feel lots of different textures on tablets, TVs, phones, and more.

In a trial for the Senseg technology, users got to feel the marbles they could see on the screen.

COMING SOON TO A THEATER NEAR YOU

The Amazing Spider-Man 2
The Croods
Despicable Me 2
Frankenweenie
Frozen
The Hobbit: An Unexpected Journey
The Hobbit: There and Back Again
How to Train Your Dragon 2
Iron Man 3
The Little Mermaid 3D
Man of Steel
Me and My Shadow
Monsters University
Oz: The Great and Powerful
Percy Jackson and the Olympians: The Sea of Monsters
Phineas and Ferb
Rise of the Guardians 3D
The Seventh Son
The Smurfs 2
Star Trek 2
Thor 2
Turbo
Walking with Dinosaurs 3D

LIVE-ACTION CGI

For many years, effects artists have been creating characters with CGI (computer-generated imagery) software. Now, they will be able to change the shape and size of live actors. Using a program called MovieReShape, which was produced by programmers at Germany's Max Planck Institute, filmmakers will be able to quickly make a character appear thinner, paler, or more muscular—or even change their clothing—digitally.

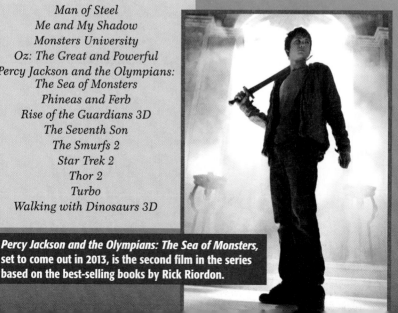

Percy Jackson and the Olympians: The Sea of Monsters, set to come out in 2013, is the second film in the series based on the best-selling books by Rick Riordon.

Answers

PAGE 25:
WILD ANIMAL MATCHUP
1. Africa–zebra
2. Australia–koala
3. North America–bald eagle
4. South America–piranha
5. Antarctica–emperor penguin
6. Europe–Alpine ibex
7. Asia–panda

PAGE 27:
MYSTERY PERSON: Louis Pasteur

PAGE 29:
IDENTIFY YOUR INSIDES
1. Liver
2. Stomach
3. Heart
4. Brain
5. Kidney
6. Lungs

PAGE 33:
A FRESH START
1. Red
2. Oranges
3. Noodles
4. Flowers

PAGE 35:
MYSTERY PERSON: Abraham Lincoln

PAGE 41:
READ THE SIGNS
The answer is TWITTER.
This kind of puzzle is called a rebus. In a rebus, words or syllables are represented in letters, pictures, and symbols. If you decode the rebus, you'll find the name of something familiar. This is how it works.

PAGE 80:
MYSTERY PERSON: William Shakespeare

PAGE 81:
WHO DOES WHAT?
CONDUCTOR–a leader of an orchestra
CHOREOGRAPHER–a person who creates steps for dances
COMPOSER–someone who writes music
PLAYWRIGHT–someone who writes scripts for plays

PAGE 96:
MYSTERY PERSON: George Washington Carver

PAGE 97:
AROUND-THE-WORLD DISHES

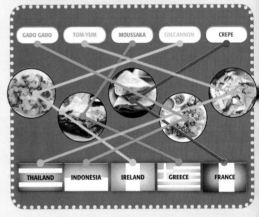

PAGE 103:
MYSTERY PERSON: Ferdinand Magellan

PAGE 115:
GEOGRAPHIC JUMBLE
South America
Asia
Pacific
Atlantic
Australia
Arctic
North America
Europe
Africa
Antarctica
Southern
Indian

SPECIAL PHRASE: Maps are fun!

PAGE 131:
MYSTERY PERSON: William the Conquerer

PAGE 135:
MYSTERY PERSON: Clara Barton

PAGE 139:
MYSTERY PERSON: Alexander Graham Bell

PAGE 145:
MYSTERY PERSON: Dr. Seuss (Theodor Seuss Geisel)

PAGE 147:
MYSTERY PERSON: Sir Isaac Newton

PAGE 153:
MYSTERY PERSON: J.K. Rowling

PAGE 156:
MYSTERY PERSON: Billie Holiday

PAGE 159:
MUSICAL WORD SEARCH

PAGE 175:
MICROSCOPIC MATCHUP
1. Football
2. Walnut
3. Butterfly wing
4. Orange
5. Sunflower
6. Cactus

PAGE 179:
MYSTERY PERSON: Yuri Gagarin

PAGE 195:
LOST LOCKER!

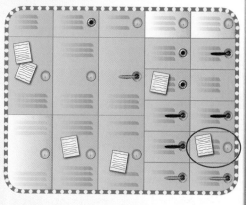

MYSTERY PERSON: Jesse Owens

PAGE 199:
MYSTERY PERSON: Chuck Yeager

PAGE 233:
MYSTERY PERSON: Alfred Nobel

NO CHEATING!

Photo Credits

FRONT COVER: ilolab/Shutterstock.com (background); NASA Module by Michael Carbajal (Apollo); Johan Larson/Shutterstock.com (frog); AP Photo/Charlie Riedel (Cruz) or AP Images/Bill Kostroun (Lin); S. John/Shutterstock.com (molecule); PeterMooij/Shutterstock.com (plant); Christian Musat/Shutterstock.com (penguin); AP Photo/Katy Winn (Hemsworth, Lawrence, Hutcherson); Fedor Selivanov/Shutterstock.com (Leaning Tower); C Flanigan/FilmMagic/Getty Images (Gomez).

CONTENTS: All photos repeated in the interior. *See individual pages.*

WHAT'S IN THE NEWS: 8–15: Igorsky/Shutterstock.com (border). 8: AP Photo (bin Laden); AP Photo (protest); AP Photo/David Guttenfelder (Kim Jong Un). 9: AP Photo/Manoocher Deghati (Facebook); AP Photo/Hugo Burnand, Clarence House (wedding); AP Photo/Hassan Ammar (Saudi women). 10: Photo by Tim Burkitt (Irene); AP Photo/David Karp (99%). 11: Mesut Dogan/Shutterstock.com (MLK); AP Photo/Erich Schlegel (soldier); Official White House Photo by Pete Souza (debt meeting). 12: NASA/Ames/JPL-Caltech (Kepler-22b); sianc/Shutterstock.com (lunch); AP Photo/Richard Drew (e-reader). 13: AP Photo/Christopher Quock, San Francisco State University (bee); AP Photo/Hasbro, Ray Stubblebine (game); AP Photo/National Science Foundation (dinosaurs). 14: AP Photo/John Amis (Falcons); AP Photo/Frank Franklin II (Lin); AP Photo/Marcio Jose Sanchez (soccer). 15: AP Photo/Arthur Mola (Gomez); AP Photo/Peter Kramer, NBC (Adele); AP Photo/Katy Winn (Hemsworth, Lawrence, Hutcherson).

ANIMALS: 16–25: stockpix4u/Shutterstock.com (border). 16: Rob McKay/Shutterstock.com (owl in flight); Barry Maas/Shutterstock.com (male owl); Stephaniellen/Shutterstock.com (dog); Dr. Morley Read/Shutterstock.com (snake). 17: hainaultphoto/Shutterstock.com (camel); Arto Hakola/Shutterstock.com (jackrabbit); Christian Musat/Shutterstock.com (fennec fox); Dmytro Pylypenko/Shutterstock.com (seal); visceralimage/Shutterstock.com (Arctic fox); Antoine Beyeler/Shutterstock.com (walruses). 18: tillydesign/Shutterstock.com (backbone); Mircea BEZERGHEANU/Shutterstock.com (owl); Johan Larson/Shutterstock.com (frog); Alivepix/Shutterstock.com (crocodile); Aleynikov Pavel/Shutterstock.com (fish); Kjersti Joergensen/Shutterstock.com (otter). 19: watthanachai/Shutterstock.com (beetles); Silvia Iordache/Shutterstock.com (sponges); Vittorio Bruno/Shutterstock.com (octopus); Little Miss Clever Trousers/Shutterstock.com (worm); Egor Arkhipov/Shutterstock.com (sea star); Zeamonkey Images/Shutterstock.com (coral). 20: cynoclub/Shutterstock.com (Labrador retriever); Eric Isselée/Shutterstock.com (Yorkie, beagle, molly); Nikolai Tsvetkov/Shutterstock.com (dachshund); Hugo Silveirinha Felix/Shutterstock.com (German shepherd); WilleeCole/Shutterstock.com (shih tzu); bluehand/Shutterstock.com (goldfish); SOMMAI/Shutterstock.com (betta); Johannes Kornelius/Shutterstock.com (tetra, swordtail, guppies, plants); Dariush M./Shutterstock.com (cichlid). 21: Dudarev Mikhail/Shutterstock.com (Persian); vlad_star/Shutterstock.com (exotic); Vasiliy Koval/Shutterstock.com (Siamese); Eric Isselée/Shutterstock.com (Maine coon, sphinx); Kirill Vorobyev/Shutterstock.com (Abyssinian); Yuliya Koldovska/Shutterstock.com (leaves); Atovot/Shutterstock.com (rabbit); Andrea Booher/FEMA (search dog); U.S. Navy photo by Mass Communication Specialist 2nd Class Rafael Martie (dolphin). 22: Chagares/Shutterstock.com (bears); Riaan van den Berg/Shutterstock.com (lions); Achim Baque/Shutterstock.com (albatrosses); Ian Scott/Shutterstock.com (shark). 23: pix2go/Shutterstock.com (birds); Jean-Edouard Rozey/Shutterstock.com (butterflies); Image Focus/Shutterstock.com (wildebeests); JIANG HONGYAN/Shutterstock.com (crab); ArtTomCat/Shutterstock.com (bat); Rich Carey/Shutterstock.com (turtle); irin-k/Shutterstock.com (ladybug). 24: AP Photo/Rob Griffith (Irwins); Photo by U.S. Fish and Wildlife Service (entomologist). 25: JP Chretien/Shutterstock.com (bee); Dr. Morley Read/Shutterstock.com (spider); Pan Xunbin/Shutterstock.com (millipede); p.studio66/Shutterstock.com (fried grasshopper); FloridaStock/Shutterstock.com (eagle); Johan_R/Shutterstock.com (piranha); prapass/Shutterstock.com (zebra); Eric Isselée/Shutterstock.com (koala, panda); Anna Kucherova/Shutterstock.com (penguin); Marco Barone/Shutterstock.com (Alpine ibex).

BODY AND HEALTH: 26–29: Creations/Shutterstock.com (border); jscreations/Shutterstock.com (background). 26: SergiyN/Shutterstock.com (boy); cabania/Shutterstock.com (running); Kruchankova Maya/Shutterstock.com (cooking); caimacanul/Shutterstock.com (hands). 27: maska/Shutterstock.com (basketball girl); Library of Congress, Prints and Photographs Division (Pasteur); Patrick Hermans/Shutterstock.com (bike); ©Dana Bartekoske/123RF.COM (sunscreen); JuTi/Shutterstock.com

com (sleeping); Rob Byron/Shutterstock.com (eating); Paman Aheri–Malaysia Event/Shutterstock.com (biker); ©iStockPhoto.com/Patrick Heagney Photography (laughing). 28: alxhar/Shutterstock.com (all). 29: Spectral-Design/Shutterstock.com (bacteria); Guido Vrola/Shutterstock.com (brain); suprun/Shutterstock.com (heart); Nataliia Natykach (kidney, stomach); Oleksii Natykach/Shutterstock.com (liver); mitya73/Shutterstock.com (lungs).

CALENDARS AND HOLIDAYS: 30–35: Morgar/Shutterstock.com (background); Molodec/Shutterstock.com (border). 31: Zhabska Tetyana/Shutterstock.com (orbit). 32: UltraViolet/Shutterstock.com (Washington); ppart/Shutterstock.com (mask); Stephen Coburn/Shutterstock.com (Easter basket); Jaimie Duplass/Shutterstock.com (sign); Chas/Shutterstock.com (turkey); Fotoline/Shutterstock.com (chocolates); Cheryl Casey/Shutterstock.com (Mardi Gras girl); 1xpert/Shutterstock.com (Earth); My Lit'l Eye/Shutterstock.com (pumpkins); Brad Thompson/Shutterstock.com (girl with flag). 33: Illustration for TIME For Kids by Barbara Pollak. 34: AP Photo/Chiaki Tsukumo (Bean Throwing Day); Jeroen van den Broek/Shutterstock.com (Buddha); Library of Congress, Prints and Photographs Division (Native American). 35: Dirk Ercken/Shutterstock.com (rhino); AP Photo/Fernando Bustamante (Tomatina); Picsfive/Shutterstock.com (tomato); tipograffias/Shutterstock.com (skeleton); Library of Congress, Prints and Photographs Division (Lincoln).

COMPUTERS AND COMMUNICATION: 36–41: Tischenko Irina/Shutterstock.com (background); alexptv/Shutterstock.com (border). 36: AP Photo/*Milwaukee Journal Sentinel*, Jeff Sainlar. 37: NASA Module by Michael Carbajal (Apollo 11); Photo by U.S. Army (ENIAC); U.S. Naval Historical Center Photograph (bug). 38: AP Photo/Paramount Pictures (*Puss in Boots*); worldswildlifewonders/Shutterstock.com (Bieber); Martin Allinger/Shutterstock.com (team). 39: Ilyashenko Oleksiy/Shutterstock.com (GPS); Picsfive/Shutterstock.com (pacemaker); Nickelodeon (Monkey Quest). 40: Tara Flake/Shutterstock.com (girl); Image by PopCap Games/Electronic Arts (Bookworm); Elena Elisseeva/Shutterstock.com (eye); Image by NimbleBit, LLC (Pocket Frogs). 41: Sidney Paige and Bruce F. Molnia, Glacier Photograph Collection, National Snow and Ice Data Center/World Data Center for Glaciology, NASA (glacier); Architect of the Capitol (*capitol.gov*); National Geographic (National Geographic Kids); Gelpi/Shutterstock.com (twins); Aprilphoto/Shutterstock.com (beet); Peter Waters/Shutterstock.com (bee); AISPIX/Shutterstock.com (batter); Kirsanov/Shutterstock.com (bat).

COUNTRIES: 42–77: EastVillage Images/Shutterstock.com (border). 42: Steve Broer/Shutterstock.com (UN); UN Photo/Albert Gonzalez Farran (Darfur). 43: MarcelClemens/Shutterstock.com. 44: AP photos/Wong Maye-E. 45: Jan Krcmar/Shutterstock.com (mud volcano); pandapaw/Shutterstock.com (flamingo); Dr. Morley Read/Shutterstock.com (frog); AP Photo/Hasan Jamali (voting). 46: Beth Schroeder/Shutterstock.com (Altun Ha); trevor kittelly/Shutterstock.com (Ganvie); Solnechnaja/Shutterstock.com (Bosna). 47: Johan Swanepoel/Shutterstock.com (elephant); Eric Isselée/Shutterstock.com (monkeys); Juri/Shutterstock.com (gold). 48: AP Photo/Al Behrman (bongo antelopes); LittleMiss/Shutterstock.com (poutine); ©Bidouze Stephane/Dreamstime.com (ouri). 49: Fedor Selivanov/Shutterstock.com (moai); Dropu/Shutterstock.com (kite); ultimathule/Shutterstock.com (orchid). 50: Picsfive/Shutterstock.com. 51: Kosarev Alexander/Shutterstock.com (cat). 52: totophotos/Shutterstock.com (coffee). 53: worldswildlifewonders/Shutterstock.com (quetzal); Benny Trapp (frog). 55: 3dmentor/Shutterstock.com (royal palm); Mikhail Markovskiy/Shutterstock.com (Danube). 56: Scott Norsworthy/Shutterstock.com. 57: Fedor Selivanov/Shutterstock.com (Pisa); Blacqbook/Shutterstock.com (ackee); Fukuoka Irina/Shutterstock.com (Fuji); Linn Currie/Shutterstock.com (Arabian oryx); ©Savenkov/Dreamstime.com (vanilla). 58: Photo by Korea Institute of Industrial Technology (EveR-1); Dave Long/Photos.com (Pristina). 59: Eric Isselée/Shutterstock.com (red panda); AJE/Shutterstock.com (Riga Castle); Olga Miltsova/Shutterstock.com (pygmy hippo). 60: Vaida/Shutterstock.com (Trakai Castle); Dejan Gileski/Shutterstock.com (Kuklica); Subbotina Anna/Shutterstock.com (vanilla). 61: Anthony Worsdell/Shutterstock.com. 62: Khoroshunova Olga/Shutterstock.com (coral); Press Association via AP Images (race). 63: wongweiyee/Shutterstock.com (cashews); ©iStockPhoto.com/Patrick Hadyniak (bell); Eric Isselée/Shutterstock.com (cheetah). 64: THP/Tim Hester Photography/Shutterstock.com. 65: Vladimir Melnik/Shutterstock.com. 66: Norman Chan/Shutterstock.com (soybeans); barbaradudzinska

Shutterstock.com (pierogi); Abraham Badenhorst/Shutterstock.com (Dias); Ronald Sumners/Shutterstock.com (ball). 67: AP Photo/Eugen Enachescu. 68: Abel Tumik/Shutterstock.com. 69: Nuno Miguel Duarte Rodrigues Lopes/Shutterstock.com (bulbul); ffolas/Shutterstock.com (carp); AP Photo/Franka Bruns (horse); Eldred Lim/Shutterstock.com (orchid). 70: sbarabu/Shutterstock.com (paella); Nattika/Shutterstock.com (cinnamon). 71: ©iStockPhoto.com/Anne Kreutzer-Eichhorn (alpenhorn); AP Photo/Pressens Bild Fredrik Funck (Ice Hotel). 72: enote/Shutterstock.com (Kilimanjaro); Inga Spence/Visuals Unlimited/Getty Images (candlenuts); Glenda M. Powers/Shutterstock.com (limbo). 73: ra-design/Shutterstock.com (Carthage); Elena Blokhina/Shutterstock.com (borscht). 74: yykkaa/Shutterstock.com (Burj Khalifa); Eduard Kyslynskyy/Shutterstock.com (pig). 75: gary yim/Shutterstock.com (Angel Falls); Stasis Photo/Shutterstock.com (pho). 76–77: ©iStockPhoto.com/essxboy. 76: Modestlife/Shutterstock.com (Sagrada Família); Lisa S./Shutterstock.com (Statue of Liberty); somchaij/Shutterstock.com (Golden Gate); Gretalorenz/Shutterstock.com (Teotihuacán); Eduardo Rivero/Shutterstock.com (Machu Picchu); gary yim/Shutterstock.com (Iguazú Falls); Styve Reineck/Shutterstock.com (Leptis Magna). 77: Maksym Gorpenyuk/Shutterstock.com (pyramid); Grgs/Shutterstock.com (Uluru); Mehdi Farahmandfar/Photos.com (Petronas Twin Towers); Faraways/Shutterstock.com (Blue Mosque); Ollirg/Shutterstock.com (Temple of Apollo); Dimon/Shutterstock.com (St. Basil's).
DANCE AND DRAMA: 78–81: 06photo/Shutterstock.com (border). 78: AP Photo/Mark J. Terrill (P.S. 22); ©iStockPhoto.com/Sarah Bossert (girl); AP Photo/Mary Altaffer (kids). 79: Vaskevich Anna/Shutterstock.com (ballet); R. Gino Santa Maria/Shutterstock.com (hip-hop); Kuzmin Andrey/Shutterstock.com (ballroom); AP Photo/Livingston County Daily Press & Argus, Gillis Benedict (Irish); AP Photo/York Daily Record/Sunday News, Jason Plotkin (step); AYakovlev/Shutterstock.com (jazz); Paul Matthew Photography/Shutterstock.com (tap). 80: William A. Hough High School (Our Town); AP Photo/The Imperial Valley Press, Cuauhtemoc Beltran (Beauty and the Beast); AP Photo/Jennifer Graylock (Grint); c./Shutterstock.com (statue). 81: AVAVA/Shutterstock.com (sewing); ©iStockphoto.com/Nuno Silva (practicing); Mark Herreid/Shutterstock.com (painting); argus/Shutterstock.com (ticket).
ENERGY AND THE ENVIRONMENT: 82–91: rangizzz/Shutterstock.com (border). 82: Uryadnikov Sergey/Shutterstock.com. 83: AND Inc./Shutterstock.com (Amazonia); Lockenes/Shutterstock.com (Serengeti); Roberto Tetsuo Okamura/Shutterstock.com (Chaco); javarman/Shutterstock.com (Patagonia); kkaplin/Shutterstock.com (Kimberley); trekandshoot/Shutterstock.com (Mojave); Uryadnikov Sergey/Shutterstock.com (Congo); AP Photo/Pavel Rahman (Sundarbans); Keith Levit/Shutterstock.com (Arctic); Randy Olson/National Geographic/Getty Images (Sudd). 84: Imaginechina via AP Images (smog); Collection of Doug Helton, NOAA/NOS/ORR (oil). 85: Guryanov Andrey Vladimirovich/Shutterstock.com (smoke); Goodluz/Shutterstock.com (scientist); N. Frey Photography/Shutterstock.com (glaciers). 86: Roberto castillo/Shutterstock.com (coal); Krasowit/Shutterstock.com (petroleum); David Gaylor/Shutterstock.com (natural gas); Martin Muránsky/Shutterstock.com (nuclear); AP Photo/Mike Groll (fracking). 87: Agricultural Research Service (ARS) photo by Brett Hampton (biomass); J van der Wolf/Shutterstock.com (geothermal); AP Photo/Don Heupel (hydrogen); mrfotos/Shutterstock.com (wind); Andy Z./Shutterstock.com (dam); elxeneize/Shutterstock.com (solar panel). 88: BlueOrange Studio/Shutterstock.com (background); ©DennisSabo/Dreamstime.com (tuna); studiogi/Shutterstock.com (mussels). 89: Offscreen/Shutterstock.com (shower); R. MACKAY PHOTOGRAPHY, LLC/Shutterstock.com (bulb); Natalou/Shutterstock.com (fridge); trekandshoot/Shutterstock.com (laundry); Lipsky/Shutterstock.com (computer); Mike Flippo/Shutterstock.com (power strip); Matthew Benoit/Shutterstock.com (boy). 90–91: argus/Shutterstock.com (background). 90: National Oceanic and Atmospheric Administration (NOAA), Earth System Research Laboratory (ESRL) (weather balloon); J van der Wolf/Shutterstock.com (car); Eric Isselée/Shutterstock.com (bear); Chris Humphries/Shutterstock.com (eagle). 91: AP Photo/Judi Bottoni (Edible Schoolyard); yalayama/Shutterstock.com (recycle); Kenneth Sponsler/Shutterstock.com

(river); ZanyZeus/Shutterstock.com (girl with bag).
FOOD AND NUTRITION: 92–97: Andi Berger/Shutterstock.com (border); Loskutnikov/Shutterstock.com (background). 92: AP Photo/Susan Walsh (Obama); U.S. Department of Agriculture (MyPlate). 93: Mircea BEZERGHEANU/Shutterstock.com (fruit); Elena Elisseeva/Shutterstock.com (girl); Maksim Shmeljov/Shutterstock.com (veggies); Valentyn Volkov/Shutterstock.com (pomegranate); My Lit'l Eye/Shutterstock.com (quinoa); Photofollies/Shutterstock.com (couscous); MarcoBagnoli Elflaco/Fotolia.com (farro); Le Do/Shutterstock.com (ugli); rj lerich/Shutterstock.com (pluot); Bizroug/Shutterstock.com (ground cherry); rodho/Shutterstock.com (edamame); Serhiy Shullye/Shutterstock.com (Romanesco broccoli). 94: Shah Rohani/Shutterstock.com (milk, beans, eggs, cheese); Joe Gough/Shutterstock.com (steak); Valentyn Volkov/Shutterstock.com (proteins); photokup/Shutterstock.com (pretzels); Norman Chan/Shutterstock.com (rice); Nattika/Shutterstock.com (potatoes); Bryan Solomon/Shutterstock.com (pasta); Brenda Carson/Shutterstock.com (bagels); AGorohov/Shutterstock.com (oil); Santje09/Shutterstock.com (avocado); Multiart/Shutterstock.com (butter). 95: wavebreakmedia ltd/Shutterstock.com (family); Madlen/Shutterstock.com (carrots); Anna Kucherova/Shutterstock.com (citrus); Shah Rohani/Shutterstock.com (yogurt); Yasonya/Shutterstock.com (spinach); Elena Elisseeva/Shutterstock.com (greens); valda/Shutterstock.com (herbs); littleny/Shutterstock.com (girl). 96: Dudarev Mikhail/Shutterstock.com (frozen); luchschen/Shutterstock.com (pizza); atoss/Shutterstock.com (banana); Chas/Shutterstock.com (sandwich); oksana2010/Shutterstock.com (chips); L Barnwell/Shutterstock.com (popsicle); Fotoline/Shutterstock.com (candy cane); Library of Congress, Prints and Photographs Division (Carver). 97: Iakov Filimonov/Shutterstock.com (girl); Elena Aliaga/Shutterstock.com (grocery); ©Andrea Skjold/Dreamstime.com (colannon); jabiru/Shutterstock.com (moussaka); Liv friis-larsen/Shutterstock.com (crepes); erwinova/Shutterstock.com (gado gado); sutsaiy/Shutterstock.com (tom-yum).
GEOGRAPHY: 98–115: FreeSoulProduction/Shutterstock.com (border). 98: Ralph Loesche/Shutterstock.com (background); Sam DCruz/Shutterstock.com (rift); Daniel Wiedemann/Shutterstock.com (Andes). 99: Tihis/Shutterstock.com (clocks); Ooi Sze Erh/Shutterstock.com (map); Manamana/Shutterstock.com (ocean). 100: Thomas Nord/Shutterstock.com (archipelago); R McIntyre/Shutterstock.com (Faafu); LiliGraphie/Shutterstock.com (bay); Galyna Andrushko/Shutterstock.com (butte); Nickolay Stanev/Shutterstock.com (canyon). 101: Loskutnikov/Shutterstock.com (Earth); David P. Lewis/Shutterstock.com (plateau); Anton Podrezov/Shutterstock.com (isthmus); tr3gin/Shutterstock.com (oasis). 102: Chris P./Shutterstock.com (map); Konstantin L/Shutterstock.com (Lake Superior); Galyna Andrushko/Shutterstock.com (Everest); Dr. Morley Read/Shutterstock.com (Amazon); ssguy/Shutterstock.com (Shanghai); George Nazmi Bebawi/Shutterstock.com (Nile). 103: Galyna Andrushko/Shutterstock.com (Goreme); trevor kittelty/Shutterstock.com (Ganvie); Mi.Ti./Shutterstock.com (Matera); djcodrin/Shutterstock.com (Venice); Library of Congress, Prints and Photographs Division (Magellan). 104–115: Maps by Joe Lemonnier and Joe Lertola. 115: maraga/Shutterstock.com (boy).
GOVERNMENT AND LAW: 116–123: MaxyM/Shutterstock.com (background); Jerric Ramos/Shutterstock.com (border). 116: AP Photo/Korea Central News Agency via Korea News Service (Kim Jong Il); AP Photo/Alastair Grant (Elizabeth); Dave Newman/Shutterstock.com (Supreme Court). 117: Rich Koele/Shutterstock.com (Constitution); Library of Congress, Prints and Photographs Division (Madison, convention). 118: SFC/Shutterstock.com. 119: AP Photo/Senate Television (vote); Official White House Photo by Pete Souza (Obama). 120: Official White House Photo by Pete Souza (Obama); Official White House Photo by Lawrence Jackson (ambassador); Official White House Photo by David Lienemann (Biden). 121: Official White House Photo by Pete Souza (all). 122: AFP/Getty Images (Justices); Library of Congress, Prints and Photographs Division (classroom, Scott). 123: bikeriderlondon/Shutterstock.com (couple); Lisa F. Young/Shutterstock.com (driver); shock/Shutterstock.com (classroom); Andy Dean Photography/Shutterstock.com (sign).

Library of Congress, Prints and Photographs Division (Gagarin). **SPORTS:** 180–195: Darren J. Bradley/Shutterstock.com (border). 180: AP Photo/*The Salt Lake Tribune*, Francisco Kjolseth (White); AP Photo/*Sun Journal*, Russ Dillingham (Diggins). 181: AP Photo/Misha Japaridze (Chan, Ando); AP Photo/Jeff Chiu (Davis and White). 182: Heinz Kluetmeier/Sports Illustrated (Manningham); Robert Beck/Sports Illustrated (Manning); Al Tielemans/Sports Illustrated (Brady); Bill Frakes/Sports Illustrated (Birk); Damian Strohmeyer/Sports Illustrated (Rodgers). 183: Bill Frakes/Sports Illustrated (Norwood); Greg Nelson/Sports Illustrated (Griffin); John Biever/Sports Illustrated (Game 1). 184: Al Tielemans/Sports Illustrated (Game 1); Chuck Solomon/Sports Illustrated (Reyes). 185: AP Photo/Tom E. Puskar (both Little League images); Kohjiro Kinno/Sports Illustrated (Kimbrel); Bob Rosato/Sports Illustrated (Verlander). 186: Greg Nelson/Sports Illustrated (Nowitzki, Durant); John W. McDonough/Sports Illustrated (James, Love); Heinz Kluetmeier/Sports Illustrated (Nash). 187: AP Photo/Elaine Thompson (Taurasi); AP Photo/Tom Olmscheid (Whalen); AP Photo/Jessica Hill (Charles); AP Photo/David Goldman (Augustus). 188: David E. Klutho/Sports Illustrated (Thomas); Carlos M. Saavedra/Sports Illustrated (Donovan). 189: AP Photo/AJ Mast (Indy 500); AP Photo/Steve Sheppard (Martinsville); AP Photo/Nigel Kinrade (Stewart, Edwards). 190: Jessica Kluetmeier/Sports Illustrated (Li Na); Simon Bruty/Sports Illustrated (Djokavic); AP Photo/Jeff Chiu (Slater). 191: AP Photo/Christophe Ena/AP/dapd (Evans); Simon Bruty/Sports Illustrated (McIlroy); Carlos M. Saavedra/Sports Illustrated (Tseng). 192: AP Photo/Koji Sasahara (Wieber, Uchimura); AP Photo/Tony Dejak (Stack-Eaton); AP Photo/*Anchorage Daily News*, Bob Hallinen (Iditarod). 193: Gerald Bernard/Shutterstock.com (girl); Bill Frakes/Sports Illustrated (Ruler on Ice). 194: AP Photo/Jae C. Hong (Adams); AP Photo/Bret Hartman (Huston); AP Photo/*Denver Post*, Kristin Wright (Wise); Doug Pensinger/Getty Images (Maltais). 195: Alhovik/Shutterstock.com (lock); Liusa/Shutterstock.com (handle); Nicemonkey/Shutterstock.com (locker); Davi Sales Batista/Shutterstock.com (boy); AP Photo (Owens); AP Photo/*The Canadian Press*, Adrian Wyld (2008 Olympics).
TRANSPORTATION: 196–199: Patrycja Mueller/Shutterstock.com (border). 196: Keattikorn/Shutterstock.com (grass); alexan55/Shutterstock.com (Ford); Dikiiy/Shutterstock.com (Model T). 197: pking4th/Shutterstock.com (plane); AISPIX/Shutterstock.com (girl); Vibrant Image Studio/Shutterstock.com (clouds); Maksim Toome/Shutterstock.com (car). 198–199: Keattikorn/Shutterstock.com (grass); AntoMale/Shutterstock.com (pavement). 198: Bildarchiv Preussucher Kulturbesitz, Berlin (balloon); Library of Congress, Prints and Photographs Division (steamboat, streetcar, plane). 199: Photo by NASA (*Columbia*); Imaginechina via AP Images (Airbus A380); Juan Camilo Bernal/Shutterstock.com (car); Library of Congress, Prints and Photographs Division (Yeager); Rob Wilson/Shutterstock.com (bus).
UNITED STATES: 200–229: Christophe BOISSON/Shutterstock.com (border). 200–201: Scott Prokop/Shutterstock.com (AZ). 200: Library of Congress, Prints and Photographs Division (Ivy Green); Lone Wolf Photos/Shutterstock.com (volcano). 201: Robert27/Shutterstock.com (bridge); Konstantin_S/Shutterstock.com (apple blossom). 202–203: John Hoffman/Shutterstock.com (CO). 202: Caitlin Mirra/Shutterstock.com (tar pit); Tam C. Nguyen/Newscom (butterfly). 203: John W. McDonough/Sports Illustrated (Camby); Sipa via AP Images (Phillippe). 204–205: XAOC/Shutterstock.com (HI). 204: U.S. Fish and Wildlife Services (pelican); ©~intangible~/Dreamstime.com (Cherokee rose). 205: Alex Staroseltsev/Shutterstock.com (pineapple); Photo by Vincentdenno (Balanced Rock). 206–207: MaxyM/Shutterstock.com (IL). 206: Henryk Sadura/Shutterstock.com (Adler); Melinda Fawver/Shutterstock.com (peony). 207: Telegraph Herald/ASSOCIATED PRESS (RAGBRAI); Martha Marks/Shutterstock.com (meadowlark). 208–209: Romchew/Shutterstock.com (MD). 208: Bryan Busovicki/Shutterstock.com (bridge); Natalia Bratslavsky/Shutterstock.com (Vieux Carré). 209: Richard Semik/Shutterstock.com (Acadia); Mark Herrald/Shutterstock.com (black-eyed Susan). 210–211: Romchew/Shutterstock.com (MA). 210: Eric Broder Van Dyke/Shutterstock.com (Fenway Park); Library of Congress, Prints and Photographs Division (Model T). 211: Bettmann/Corbis/AP Images (Fitzgerald); Henryk Sadura/Shutterstock.com (lighthouse). 212–213: Steve Bower/Shutterstock.com (MT). 212: Planet5D LLC/Shutterstock.com (Gateway Arch); Katherine Welles/Shutterstock.com (Clark). 213: Chad Bontrager/Shutterstock.com (Carhenge); Simon Bruty/Sports Illustrated (Agassi). 214–215: Alberto Loyo/Shutterstock.com (NM). 214: Evgenia Bolyukh/Shutterstock.com (Tupperware); Slowfish/Shutterstock.com (Lucy). 215: Songquan/Shutterstock.com (USS Intrepid); Photo by NPS (White Sands). 216: Dave Allen Photography/Shutterstock.com (NC). 216: Patrick Johnson/Shutterstock.com (lighthouse); Mboe/Shutterstock.com (Peace Garden). 217: Bryan Busovicki/Shutterstock.com (cardinal); Fribus Ekaterina/Shutterstock.com (mistletoe). 218–219: Tusharkoley/Shutterstock.com (OR). 218: Photography by George Vetter (sand castle); Al Parker Photography/Shutterstock.com (ruffed grouse). 219: Library of Congress, Prints and Photographs Division (Stuart); ©Crystalseye-Fotolia.com (flowers). 220–221: Steve Schlaeger/Shutterstock.com (TX). 220: Sukharevskyy Dmytro/Shutterstock.com (pasqueflower); ©Mesquite53/Dreamstime.com (mockingbird). 221: AP Photo/Eric Gay (bat); Sheri Hagwood @ USDA-NRCS PLANTS Database (sego lily). 222–223: Mary Terriberry/Shutterstock.com (VA). 222: Daniel W. Slocum/Shutterstock.com (bridge); Wendy Farrington/Shutterstock.com (ponies). 223: Neelsky/Shutterstock.com (Rainier); Olaru Radian-Alexandru/shutterstock.com (marbles). 224: Stephanie Coffman/Shutterstock.com (WY); Sebastian Knight/Shutterstock.com (robin); Caitlin Mirra/Shutterstock.com (Independence Rock). 225: SergiyN/Shutterstock.com. 226–227: Library of Congress, Prints and Photographs Division (background). 226: Rebecca Connolly/Shutterstock.com (sequoia); John Glade/Shutterstock.com (Grand Canyon); 375Ultramag/shutterstock.com (Mount McKinley); Photo by NPS (dinosaur); Sharon Eisenzopf/Shutterstock.com (Death Valley); Christopher Kolaczan/Shutterstock.com (Yellowstone); Plamen/Shutterstock.com (Mammoth Cave); Caitlin Mirra/Shutterstock.com (Montezuma); fototehnik/Shutterstock.com (Yosemite). 227: Mariusz S. Jurgielewicz/Shutterstock.com (Carlsbad Caverns); zschnepf/Shutterstock.com (Crater Lake); Daniel M. Silva/Shutterstock.com (Poe); Vlad Ghiea/Shutterstock.com (Everglades); U.S. Department of the Interior, U.S. Geological Survey (volcano); Photo by NPS (Fort Raleigh); topseller/Shutterstock.com (Alcatraz). 228–229: Joe Lemonnier.
VOLUNTEERING: 230–233: Keo/Shutterstock.com (background); milka-kotka/Shutterstock.com (border). 230: AP Photo/Arthur Mola (Kielburger); George Pimentel/WireImage/Getty Images (Furtado). 231: ©iStockPhoto.com/Gchutka (car wash); Konstantin Sutyagin/Shutterstock.com (dance); ©Luchschen/Dreamstime.com (cookies); holbox/Shutterstock.com (pottery); Kiva/Abby Gray (Dzide). 232: olly/Shutterstock.com (musician); Lee Morris/Shutterstock.com (owl); sima/Shutterstock.com (elderly); mangostock/Shutterstock.com (donation box); Laura Stone/Shutterstock.com (running). 233: Morgan Lane Photography/Shutterstock.com (recycling); Photo by DrinkingWaterForIndia (well); Photos.com/Photos.com (Nobel).
WEATHER: 234–237: Carolina K. Smith, M.D./Shutterstock.com (border). 234–235: B747/Shutterstock.com (background). 234: Joe Raedle/Getty Images News (Blake); FEMA News Photo/G. Mathieson (cows). 235: National Weather Service Forcast Office (anemometer); Jhaz Photography/Shutterstock.com (lightning); My Portfolio/Shutterstock.com and Our Hero Productions (fronts). 236–237: dmitriyGo/Shutterstock.com (background). 236: Galyna Andrushko/Shutterstock.com (drought); Photo by Dave Gatley/FEMA News Photo (floods); Vladislav Gurfinkel/Shutterstock.com (eye). 237: Rafal Olechowski/Shutterstock.com (snow); lafoto/Shutterstock.com (tornado background); sdecoret/Shutterstock.com (tornado).
WHAT'S NEXT?: 238–241: Santiago Cornejo/Shutterstock.com (border). 238: IBM Image Gallery (Watson); NASA/JPL-Caltech (Voyager). 239: Dmitrijs Bindemanis/Shutterstock.com (mosquito); WWF Philippines/Lory Tan (billboard); Image by Plantagon/Sweco (vertical farm). 240: Draqie/Milan Kazarka (Draqie); AP Photo/Julie Jacobson (gesture). 241: AP Photo/Julie Jacobson (marbles); FOX 2000 PICTURES/The Kobal Collection/Art Resources, NY (*Percy Jackson*). **BACK COVER:** ilolab/Shutterstock.com (background); martiin ||fluidworkshop/Shutterstock.com (Saturn); Rich Carey/Shutterstock.com (turtle); Image by Curventa and Siemens (Bloodhound SSC); AP Photo/Fernando Bustamante (Tomatina); AP Photo/Chris Pizzello (Swift); Anthony Worsdell/Shutterstock.com (boats).